Postcolonial Con-texts

Literature, Culture and Identity

Series Editor: Bruce King

This series is concerned with the ways in which literature and cultures are influenced by the complexities and complications of identity. It looks at the ways in which identities are explored, mapped, defined and challenged in the arts where boundaries are often overlapping, contested and re-mapped. It considers how differences, conflicts and change are felt and expressed. It investigates how such categories as race, class, gender, sexuality, ethnicity, nation, exile, diaspora and multiculturalism have come about. It discusses how these categories co-exist and their relationship to the individual, particular situations, the artist and the arts.

Published titles:

1492: The Poetics of Diaspora, John Docker
Imagining Insiders: Africa and the Question of Belonging, Mineke Schipper
The Intimate Empire: Reading Women's Autobiography, Gillian Whitlock
Yesterday, Tomorrow: Voices from the Somali Diaspora, Nuruddin Farah

Postcolonial Con-texts

Writing back to the Canon

JOHN THIEME

continuum
LONDON • NEW YORK

Continuum
The Tower Building, 11 York Road, London SE1 7NX
370 Lexington Avenue, New York, NY 10017–6503

First published 2001

British Library Cataloguing-in-Publication Data
A catalogue record for this book is available from the British Library.

ISBN 0–8264–5465–8 (hardback)
     0–8264–5466–6 (paperback)

Library of Congress Cataloging-in-Publication Data
Thieme, John.
     Postcolonial con-texts: writing back to the canon/John Thieme.
       p. cm.
     Includes bibliographical references and index.
     ISBN 0-8264-5465-8 — ISBN 0-8264-5466-6 (pbk.)
     1. Commonwealth literature (English)—History and criticism. 2. English
literature—Appreciation—Commonwealth countries. 3. Commonwealth literature
(English)—English influences. 4. Postcolonialism—Commonwealth countries.
5. Commonwealth countries—In literature. 6. Decolonization in literature. 7. Canon
(Literature). 8. Intertextuality.   I. Title.

PR9080.5 .T48 2001
820.9'9171241–dc21   2001028180

Typeset by BookEns Ltd, Royston, Herts
Printed and bound in Great Britain by CPD Printers, Ebbw Vale

Contents

Acknowledgements

Though this book was written recently, it has been a long time in the making and my interest in Caribbean responses to the Brontës and Defoe goes back over two decades. So, as always, I know that I have more debts to pay than I can even remember. These include thanks to students I have taught at the Universities of Guyana, North London and Hull and at South Bank University. I suspect that my indebtedness to colleagues at the University of Hull, particularly to Owen Knowles's work on Conrad and Patsy Stoneman's on Brontëan derivatives, is more extensive than my references to their publications indicate. I am grateful to Robert Clark for a stimulating conversation about *Heart of Darkness* and to Donald Hawes for information on Dickens. Much earlier, Louis James and Denis Judd pointed me in the right direction with regard to particular aspects of *Wide Sargasso Sea*. Robert Kroetsch kindly confirmed his indebtedness to Conrad in *Badlands*. M. J. Kidnie introduced me to *Harlem Duet* and shared some of her insights into Sears's play. Bruce Bennett, Bernard Hickey and Geraldine and Ray Stoneham were all quick to respond to queries on aspects of Australian culture. Many years ago, Trevor R. Griffiths kindly provided me with a copy of his essay ' "This Island's Mine": Caliban and Colonialism'. Sarah Lawson Welsh generously supplied me with a copy of her paper 'Imposing Narratives: European Incursions and Intertexts in Pauline Melville's *The Ventriloquist's Tale* (1997), prior to its publication in the Proceedings of the EACLALS/ASNEL 'Colonies, Missions, Cultures' Conference, Tübingen, 1999; and Cecile Sandten has been equally kind in allowing me to read her essay 'Violent Racial Memory: Strategies of "Writing Back" in George Lamming's Novel *Water with Berries*' in manuscript. Suzanne Scafe helped me to locate Lamming's novel's violence in its period context. Bill Leahy and Alan Bower lent me invaluable source material.

South Bank University and Jeffrey Weeks provided financial and moral support that made it possible to complete aspects of the library research needed for this book; and I am also grateful to library staff at the University of Hull and the University of London Library at Senate House.

Part of Chapter 4 has been adapted from my article ' "Apparitions of Disaster": Brontëan Parallels in Jean Rhys's *Wide Sargasso Sea* and V. S. Naipaul's *Guerrillas*', *Journal of Commonwealth Literature*, 14 (1) (1979), pp. 116–33. Material on Amitav Ghosh in the same chapter and on A. D. Hope and J. M. Coetzee in Chapter 3 has been reworked from my essay 'Passages to England', originally published in *Liminal Postmodernisms: The Postmodern, the (Post-)Colonial and the (Post-)Feminist (Postmodern Studies 8)*, eds Theo d'Haen and Hans Bertens, Amsterdam: Rodopi, 1994, pp. 55–78. In both cases I am grateful for permission to recycle material, albeit while making numerous changes.

Finally, I am grateful to Bruce King and Janet Joyce of Continuum, without whom the book would not have been possible.

For Barbara

1

Introduction: parents, bastards and orphans

Death of the Father would deprive literature of many of its pleasures. If there is no longer a Father, why tell stories? Doesn't every story lead back to Oedipus? Isn't storytelling a way of searching for one's origin?

(Roland Barthes 47)

'Oh for chrissake. Why don't you stop fussing so much about that bloody little bastard,' her son shouted.

Laura heard no more for after one long moment when her heart somersaulted once there was no time for hearing anything else for her feet of their own volition had set off at a run down the road and by the time she got to the school gates she had made herself an orphan and there were no more clouds.

(Olive Senior 53)

I

'Writing back', 'counter-discourse', 'oppositional literature', 'con-texts': these are some of the terms that have been used to identify a body of postcolonial works that take a classic English text as a departure point, supposedly as a strategy for contesting the authority of the canon of English literature. In Helen Tiffin's words, such texts are not 'simply "writing back" to an English canonical text, but to the whole of the discursive field within which such a text operated and continues to operate in post-colonial worlds' (23). It is a subject that has attracted considerable attention over the last two decades, particularly when postcolonial con-texts have been seen as engaging in the kind of combative relationship with the canon that Tiffin describes, and this study attempts to survey some of the distinctive characteristics of such writing, albeit through an approach that is at best only representative. I began it with an

awareness that it would be futile to attempt comprehensive coverage and that
it was unlikely that one would be able to arrive at an overarching thesis to
distinguish the counter-discursive method of texts drawn from a heterogeneous range of societies that had experienced very different forms of
colonialism. It seemed likely, for example, that there would be major disparities
between the ways in which Caribbean and Canadian works that engaged with
the canon 'wrote back' and I decided to make this a particular focus for my
chapters on responses to the Brontës and *The Tempest*. Additionally,
postcolonial societies have been, and are, the ever-changing syncretist
outcomes of varied cultural formations and their writers of multiple ethnic,
gender, communal and other backgrounds. Nevertheless I felt reasonably
sanguine about the possibility of identifying some *commonalities* in the counter-
discursive practice of the various texts to be considered.

Along the way, I became less confident still about the possibility of
sustaining broad general conclusions. This was not only because of the cultural
heterogeneity of the con-texts. It also became increasingly apparent that the
canon to which they were writing back was far from unitary and that the texts
to which they were responding were unstable objects that were, in effect,
being constructed anew by each postcolonial writer's gaze in a kind of parodic
reversal of the process by which postcolonial subjects had been constructed as
'other' during the heyday of imperialism, an optic that has continued into the
era of multinational capitalism. In the case of responses to the two Shakespeare
pre-texts that are examined in this book, *The Tempest* and *Othello*, this was
perhaps only to be expected: plays are, after all, reinvented each time they are
performed. More generally, reader-response theory has taught us that books
read people, even as people read books. Nevertheless, given that texts engage
in an interactive rather than a passive relationship with their intertexts, the
extent to which postcolonial responses to the canon were moving their
originals onto a world of shifting sands seemed to offer a heightened example
of this literary equivalent of Heisenberg's uncertainty principle. Whether or
not they set out to be combative, the postcolonial con-texts invariably seemed
to induce a reconsideration of the supposedly hegemonic status of their
canonical departure points, opening up fissures in their supposedly solid
foundations that undermined the simplism involved in seeing the relationship
between 'source' and con-text in terms of an oppositional model of influence.
Attractive though binary paradigms have been to some postcolonial theorists,
the evidence invariably suggested a discursive dialectic operating along a
continuum, in which the influence of the 'original' could seldom be seen as
simply adversarial – or, at the opposite extreme, complicitous.

Since the relationship between postcolonial con-text and canonical pre-text
is invariably a complex and ambivalent one, this study uses the terms 'counter-

discourse' and 'writing back', rather than 'oppositional', to cover the varied range of interpretive strategies adopted by the con-texts: they are counter-discourses that write back to the canon in a multiplicity of ways and simply to label their stances 'oppositional' is invariably reductive. Salman Rushdie popularized the term 'writing back' in the early 1980s, when, playing on the title of the *Star Wars* sequel, *The Empire Strikes Back* (1980), he entitled a newspaper article on British racism, 'The Empire Writes Back with a Vengeance'. It subsequently became fairly generally associated with the project of dismantling Eurocentric literary hegemonies, particularly when Bill Ashcroft, Gareth Griffiths and Helen Tiffin adopted it as the title of an influential 1989 study of 'theory and practice in post-colonial literatures'. 'Counter-discourse' has a not dissimilar provenance, since it was introduced into postcolonial studies in the late 1980s by Tiffin, who adopted it from Richard Terdiman's *Discourse/Counter-Discourse: The Theory and Practice of Symbolic Resistance in Nineteenth-Century France* (1985), a study that offers a nuanced and theorized investigation of the problematics of putative adversarial discourse.

Terdiman argues that, while dominant discourses may be challenged by counter-discursive practices, counter-discourse cannot ultimately offer 'genuine revolution' (Terdiman 15–16; quoted by Tiffin 33). He examines the ambivalent nature of the struggle of nineteenth-century French writers to achieve 'separation' from the dominant discourse of the middle-class world (12), taking his departure point from a phrase used by Flaubert in his *Dictionnaire des idées reçues*:

> 'Tonnerre contre' – 'Thunder against' (Denounce, as we might translate
> it, vituperate, condemn). This sardonic motto stigmatizes the intolerance
> of an increasingly dominant bourgeoisie, whose opinions the *Dictionnaire*
> seeks to represent in all their smug vulgarity. (11)

He goes on to point out the 'double-edged' quality of the phrase, 'Tonnerre contre'. Although it sets out to identify a characteristically middle-class attitude of discursive combat, its engagement with this attitude involves it in the very 'combat which is its subject' (11). So the strategy of satirizing the attitude by giving it voice implicates the writer in a complicitous relationship with the very rhetoric that is under attack. Consequently the tactic becomes 'labyrinthine' and the writer finds the effort to achieve separation from the dominant discourse 'constantly elusive' (12). Terdiman sees the nineteenth-century French writers who are his subject – Flaubert, Balzac, Daumier, Baudelaire, Mallarmé and, revealingly, Marx – as linked in their struggle against the 'dominant depiction of the world' (12). He argues that the hegemonic discourse is 'totalitarian by implication', because 'it functions to exclude the heterogeneous from the realm of utterance' (14), but he follows Foucault in contending that although 'all discourses are impositions, still the range and penetration of their hegemonies varies considerably' and is quick to concede that 'the "dominant" itself, like any social discourse, was internally fragmented' (18). Nevertheless, for Terdiman, the notion of a dominant discourse still operates, in much the same way as Saussure's notion of *langue*, as a system which 'naturalizes our blindness concerning the alternative discourses which would contest the stability of its stabilizing norms' (15). Such 'stabilizing norms' exist, then, as a shared social fiction, at least in the perception of their adversaries.

Tiffin's appropriation of the term for a postcolonial practice clearly proposes an analogy between the nineteenth-century French authors' attempt to *épater les bourgeois* and postcolonial writers' need to engage in a similar contestation of the hegemony of a colonially constructed canon of literary texts, with particular instances of writing back to an English canonical text being viewed as metonyms for engaging with 'the whole of the discursive field within which such a text operated and continues to operate in postcolonial worlds'. The difficulties inherent in such an approach are numerous. They include the problem identified by Terdiman – the danger of the adversarial discourse becoming locked in a complicitous relationship with the discourse under fire – the lack of uniformity in the object of attack and the heterogeneous positions of the putative combatants. While the latter are frequently linked by a sense of exclusion from power, occasioned by having been constructed by 'the other's interference' (Lamming, *Castle* 214), the West's attempts to define itself in terms of contradistinction from alterity[1] has generated a broad and varied range of stereotypes, including those of Africa as the Dark Continent, Asia as the exotic Orient and Australia as a 'down under' hell. Some of these stereotypes are addressed in detail in this study – the myth of African savagery in the chapter on reactions to *Heart of Darkness*; European myths about Australia in the chapter on responses to *Great Expectations* – and, to avoid the trap of essentializing the 'postcolonial', I have commented, not only on the variety of the hegemonic discourses against which the particular con-texts are being written, but also, in most instances, on the reception of the pre-texts concerned, particularly, but not exclusively, in postcolonial societies.

My use of the terms 'con-text', to indicate postcolonial texts that engage in direct, if ambivalent, dialogue with the canon by virtue of responding to a classic English text, and 'pre-text', to refer to the canonical texts to which they respond, is not simply a convenient shorthand. It is also intended to suggest the need to locate the postcolonial works in broader *contexts* than those offered by the apparently determinant *pretexts* for writing provided by their English 'parents'. So, although 'con-texts' is a term that may initially suggest oppositionality, it is used here to refer also to the full range of discursive situations (contexts), many of which have little or nothing to do with the canon, from which the counter-discursive works emerge. Often the English pre-texts are only invoked as a launching pad (pretext) for a consideration of broader concerns. The aim, then, is two-fold: to examine ways in which postcolonial counter-discourse *does* write back to the canon and to suggest the limitations inherent in a view that only locates such writing in relation to its English 'originals', when they are frequently disputing the very ground on which any such encounter might take place. Moreover, while some of the texts discussed very obviously foreground cultural agendas, others only do so obliquely and demonstrate little or no obvious interest in engaging the canon in battle.

Looking at ways in which particular con-texts engage with the canon frequently necessitated locating them in relation to obvious material determinants of their production (race, class, gender, nation, etc.), but this approach threatened to leave other, more individual influences unexplained. George Lamming's novel *Water with Berries* (1971) offers an example. The title, which alludes to a speech by Caliban in Act I, scene 2 of *The Tempest*, clearly locates the text in relation to Shakespeare's most obvious allegory of colonialism and also inserts it into a body of twentieth-century writing that identifies Prospero and Caliban as racially opposed types of colonizer and colonized.[2] In contrast, naming one of the novel's main characters Roger Capildeo offers the average reader no such immediate reference point. However, Roger's surname contains a veiled allusion to V. S. Naipaul, a writer with whom Lamming had crossed swords in print more than once.[3] Naipaul's mother's maiden name was Capildeo and through this allusion Lamming seems to be identifying his fictional character's attitudes with beliefs supposedly held by Naipaul. The two contexts are, of course, not exclusive, since Lamming's character is the embodiment of a certain type of Caribbean artist, but their difference in origin and point of departure – the one alluding to Shakespeare and a discourse on colonialism that was already in broad circulation; the other cryptically private and concerned with Caribbean specifics rather than writing back to the canon – confirms the need to be attentive to a broad spectrum of pretexts, including individualistic identifications that cannot easily be located within obvious identity categories. So, although I employ a materialist approach, I have cast the net wide and where appropriate discussed what at least superficially may appear to be more personal shaping forces, in the belief that, since much of the theory that has constructed notions of what determines identity has been Marxist-led, an approach that restricted itself to the obvious labels was likely to impose a Eurocentric filter.

This said, many subject positions *can* be located within a complex of the obvious categories and Homi Bhabha's enumeration of the positions that inhabit identity – in a passage that stresses the importance of the enunciative moment and the need to avoid originary accounts of subjectivity – provides a useful checklist of some of the most obvious determinants:

> The move away from the singularities of 'class' or 'gender' as primary conceptual and organizational categories, has resulted in an awareness of the subject positions – of race, gender, generation, institutional location, geopolitical locale, sexual orientation – that inhabit any claim to identity in the modern world. What is theoretically innovative, and politically crucial, is the need to think beyond narratives of originary and initial subjectivities and to focus on those moments or processes that are produced in the articulation of cultural differences.
>
> (Bhabha 1)

To this inventory, one needs to add the type of colonization involved (as something more specific than 'geopolitical locale'?), particular factors that contribute to the uniqueness of writing situations and authors' individual characteristics and eccentricities that frustrate attempts at neat categorization.

In recent years, the term 'postcolonial', which initially promised liberation from some of the hegemonic assumptions of the Western academy, has itself threatened to become a straitjacket, shackling or occluding the differences that exist amid the particular creative energies of the many peoples, places and agendas it has subsumed into its project. I have employed it here mainly because my concern *is* with Anglophone writing from societies that have experienced some form of colonialism in recent centuries and it is now the term by which such writing has generally become known. At the same time I have decided against including what during the 1990s and at the beginning of the new millennium has been more or less de rigueur for studies such as this, namely a discussion of postcolonialism's 'discontents' that agonizes over and interrogates the use of the term. Additionally, there is, of course, the issue of *how* the term is to be applied and again my usage puts the primary emphasis on writing produced in the wake of colonization, rather than adopting an exclusive approach which emphasizes 'race' and the multiplicity of overlapping discourses that constitute the field of 'ethnic studies'. These are, of course, inextricably intertwined with the 'postcolonial', but so too are the experiences of the settler communities of Canada, South Africa and Australasia and since any analysis of counter-discourse inevitably engages with an abundance of colonialisms, I have wanted to range as widely as possible. Expressing this in terms of the archetypes from *The Tempest* (discussed in Chapter 6) that have been widely used as a shorthand for the subject positions initiated by colonial encounters, I have attempted to discuss not only Caliban's rejoinders to Prospero, but also the metamorphoses of Prospero and the roles assigned to Miranda, Ariel and even a figure such as Gonzalo, in counter-discursive con-texts. The endeavour is to keep the emphasis on the specificity of the circumstances in which particular texts have been produced, while trying to discover what consanguinities link con-texts produced in different parts of the world, in societies that have had very different histories of colonialism and, last but not least, are written by writers whose subject positions differ enormously in ways such as Bhabha's helpful inventory suggests – and in ways that are not covered by his list. Responses to *The Tempest* produced by the descendants of Loyalist Canadians, who supported the British colonial mission in North America, may be very different from those emanating from the descendants of the Afro-Caribbean slaves of the Middle Passage, but the complex and hybrid origins of all those who inhabit postcolonial societies quickly erode any attempt to separate settler colonies from societies that have suffered at the sharp edge of colonialism. So, in Canadian con-texts, Native, feminist, regional and multicultural agendas are among the determinants that produce writing that is decidedly uncomfortable with Prospero's hegemony; and ultimately even in texts, such as Robertson Davies's *Tempest-Tost*, where one might expect complicity with the English metanarrative, the ex-centric situation of the writer frustrates any attempt to construct linear genealogies.

II

The extent to which postcolonial con-texts are indebted to their English pre-texts varies considerably and the relationship is virtually always complicated by the introduction of other intertexts that unsettle the supposedly direct line of descent form the canonical 'original'. Thus, to borrow Edward Said's terminology, filiative relationships are replaced by affiliative identifications (*World* 174), straightforward lines of descent, such as one, at least supposedly, finds in canonical English literature, are replaced by literary genealogies that reject colonial parent figures, or at least only allow such figures to exist as members of an extended, and usually hybrid, ancestral family. Said traces his use of the 'family metaphor of filial engenderment' (*World* 117) back to Vico, referring to Vico's account of how social institutions such as marriage and community complicate the 'father's place' of 'unassailable eminence' (118) by competing with genealogy for authority. Said is not, in this instance, concerned with imperialism or postcolonial societies, but he is using the family metaphor as a trope for discussing literary genealogies and it provides a particularly useful prism through which to view postcolonial literary relationships with the canon. Problematic parentage becomes a major trope in postcolonial con-texts, where the genealogical bloodlines of transmission are frequently delegitimized by multiple ancestral legacies, usually but not always initiated by imperialism. Orphans and bastards abound in postcolonial texts and the engagement with issues of parentage is often as intense as in, say, a Fielding novel where the social order can be reaffirmed by the revelation that the picaresque hero of uncertain birth is really a gentleman. The difference is, of course, that postcolonial texts seldom, if ever, offer such comfortable resolutions. Illegitimacy preponderates, a metonym for both social plurality and the severing of the bloodlines from the supposed colonial father. Postcolonial texts such as Salman Rushdie's *Midnight's Children* (1981) and Olive Senior's short story, 'Bright Thursdays', which appeared in her collection, *Summer Lightning* (1986), attest to the positive potential latent in the roles of bastard and orphan.

In *Midnight's Children*, the protagonist Saleem Sinai assumes the right, in the absence of his biological father and mother, to give birth to an 'endless series of parents' (258). From the very beginning of the text it is clear that Saleem, born at the exact moment of Indian Independence, as the clock strikes midnight on 15 August 1947, is 'handcuffed to history' (9); and later he receives a telegram from Nehru telling him: 'You are the newest bearer of that ancient face of India.... We shall be watching over your life with the closest attention; it will be, in a sense the mirror of our own' (122). The novel sustains this comic analogy between Saleem's micro-history and the macro-history of post-independent India throughout Saleem's picaresque travels, both actual and, through the magical powers he possesses as a child of midnight, telepathic to the four corners of the nation. So, in a striking personification of Fredric Jameson's argument that third-world cultural production can be distinguished by its concern with national allegory (68),[4] Saleem *is* India and in the latter part of the novel, set during the 'Emergency' of the 1970s, he imagines himself vying with Indira Gandhi to assert the centrality of his version of the nation's cultural identity:

> Was my lifelong belief in the equation between the State and myself transmuted in 'the Madam's' mind, into that in-those-days famous phrase: *India is Indira and Indira is India?* Were we competitors for centrality — was she gripped by a lust for meaning as profound as my own ...? (420)

It is a version that insists on multiplicity and with Saleem, as narrator, telling us that he is crumbling into six hundred and thirty million particles (a number approximately equivalent to India's population in the mid-1970s) in the present, one interpretation is that there are as many Indias as there are Indians. Saleem's own claim to multiple parentage localizes this through affiliative identification with an encyclopaedic range of cultural and communal strands. His biological father, Methwold, is an Englishman, whose departure from India at the moment of Independence, is accompanied by the revelation that he is bald and has been wearing a wig, an epiphany that provides an Emperor's New Clothes-like exposure of the superficiality of the Raj's power. Although the filial relationship that Saleem is never able to have with this absent father is supplanted by the multiple surrogate fathers that he claims for himself, Methwold's legacy — he sells his estate on the condition that the new owners change nothing for six months and he *is*, after all, Saleem's father genetically — suggests the continuing influence of English culture in post-Independence India, particularly among the upper middle class. It is, however, only one element. Saleem is illegitimate, though this is not apparent in the early sections of the novel, and his biological mother, who dies in giving birth to him, is a Hindu. As a result of an exchange of name tags with the baby of the couple who become his 'real' parents, he is brought up in a secular Muslim family and also lays claim to no less than six other fathers (127–8, 426), who represent various aspects of India's hybrid society. Similarly, although his real mother is a Hindu, his other mothers include the Goan Catholic nurse, who changes the babies' name-tags, his aunt and, of course, the mother who brings him up as her son. Beyond this, the text poses the further question of Saleem's right to claim centrality for himself as the representative protagonist of the promise of post-Independence India, since the changeling swap means that he has usurped the privileges of his alter ego, Shiva, a figure who is particularly associated with Indira Gandhi and the second, much more sinister midnight hour of the Emergency.

Saleem's claim to be able to invent new parents whenever he chooses also has a metafictive dimension: it relates directly to the text's practice of constructing its own literary genealogy from a multiplicity of sources. On one level *Midnight's Children* asks what constitutes an appropriate fictional practice for an Indian novel and it answers this question by drawing on a diverse array of intertexts, among them the *Ramayana*, *Mahabharata* and *Panchatantra*, *The Thousand and One Nights* and the *Quran*, Laurence Sterne's *Tristram Shandy* and Günter Grass's *The Tin Drum*, Gabriel García Márquez's *One Hundred Years of Solitude* and Thomas Pynchon's *Gravity's Rainbow*. This very partial listing of the novel's intertexts suggests both the extent to which Rushdie is anxious to promote an anti-essentialist view of Indian culture (Muslim and Hindu intertexts rub shoulders with a range of other communal discourses in this Bombay talkie of a novel) and how incidental his response to the English canon is. Taking *Tristram Shandy* as his main 'English' reference point involves an identification, not only with one of the most eccentric novels to be accorded a place in the English canon, but also with a self-referential text that can be read as a parody of the 'realist' fictional autobiography, of which *Robinson Crusoe* is the first great example. Beyond this, however, there is another conclusion to be drawn. What initially looks to be a paradigm text for Jameson's assertion that third-world cultural production privileges national allegory reveals itself, through its concern with constructing a hybrid literary genealogy, to be a striking instance of a globalized text that refuses to be located in national terms, even if Saleem is India and even if his telepathic powers only operate within the nation's borders. This may or may not be a case of Rushdie having his cake and eating it, but either way it is a very clear instance of affiliative identifications, which comfortably include a diverse range of Western intertexts, supplanting a filiative relationship. Saleem mentions that Methwold is his biological father, but looks elsewhere to invent a version of his 'origins'.

In Olive Senior's short story, 'Bright Thursdays', from which the passage quoted as the second epigraph to this chapter is taken, the protagonist, Laura, adopts a different strategy, but again it is one that involves a choice that interrogates notions of legitimacy and uncomplicated genealogical descent. Laura is the child of an extramarital liaison between a dark-skinned country-woman and 'a young man of high estate' (Senior 38), who, since her birth, has been shipped off to the United States. At the point where the story begins, she has been sent by her mother to live in the household of her middle-class paternal grandparents with the instruction to 'let them know you have broughtupcy' (36). This movement between households is a recurrent pattern in *Summer Lightning* and Senior has said that it replicates the experience of her own youth,[5] which made her socially, as well as racially, 'a child of mixed worlds, socialized unwittingly and simultaneously into both' (Rowell 481). At the same time, the predicament of the relocated child who undergoes a double socialization provides a medium for representing and commenting on schisms that operated in Jamaican society more generally during the period in question, the late colonial period of the 1940s and 1950s,[6] as the child attempts 'to create self-identity out of chaotic personal and social history' (Rowell 482). Focusing on the socialization of the 'child of mixed worlds' not only provides a basis for extremely effective naturalistic narrative; it also opens up windows on issues of class, race, religion, education, gender, sexuality, language and migration.

Any division between the personal and the social in Senior's stories is, then, extremely porous and Laura's particular situation, like that of most of the child protagonists in *Summer Lightning*, offers an index of the extent to which Jamaicans of the late colonial period found themselves caught between discrepant social and discursive codes, operating along a creolized continuum that had the official colonial culture at one hypothetical extreme and the Afro-

Caribbean folk culture at the other. Laura soon learns that any 'broughtupcy' she does have still leaves her a misfit in her new middle-class environment and imagines her father as a rescuer figure, whose return will release her from her sense of insecurity. However, when he does return to Jamaica with his white America wife, she is swiftly disillusioned. She overhears him refer to her as a 'bloody little bastard' and immediately resolves to make herself 'an orphan' (53). In so doing she liberates herself both from romantic expectations of deliverance through her paternal ancestry and from the middle-class social aspirations inculcated in her by her mother. Still a child, she is hardly aware of the import of her decision, but like Rushdie's Saleem Sinai she is effectively rejecting filiative relationships for affiliative identifications, even if (unlike some of the other children in *Summer Lightning*) she has yet to find an adult legacy with which she can identify.

The situations staged by Rushdie and Senior open up the possibility of a different approach to genealogy, whether personal, social or literary, from those predicated by most Western critics. Models of literary transmission, such as those advanced by Harold Bloom and most Freudian and post-Freudian critics, have foregrounded the Oedipal encounter, while feminist critics, such as Gilbert and Gubar have argued against privileging paternal genealogies (3–92). In postcolonial contexts, where 'parentage' is less certain, or lacking in legitimacy, further factors come into play. Narratives of mother-loving and father-killing tend to obscure the complex discursive networks produced by displaced and multiple ancestries; maternal genealogies may offer preferable alternatives, especially if the colonizer has been constructed as masculine and, as is often the case, the colony as inert female space, but this model also tends to simplify. In 'Bright Thursdays' Laura feels that 'Life had played her tricks, and there was, after all, no space allotted for her' (37). If the postcolonial subject is to claim a space for herself, she needs to do so through affiliative impulse rather than filiative acceptance. Parentage becomes a major trope for the movement between these two positions in postcolonial counter-discourse and it is no coincidence that writers as different from one another as Rushdie and Senior, Margaret Laurence, Keri Hulme, J. M. Coetzee and Peter Carey thematize issues of cultural identity through a focus on the parentage, biological or surrogate, of their characters.

III

The derivatives of each of the English pre-texts, on which I have chosen to focus, merit a book-length study in their own right. Some of them have already elicited such books, for example Martin Green's *The Robinson Crusoe Story*

(1990), Lieve Spass and Brian Stimpson's *Robinson Crusoe: Myths and Metamorphoses* (1996) and Patsy Stoneman's *Brontë Transformations* (1996), though these have been mainly been concerned with the general, rather than the specifically postcolonial, dissemination of the texts concerned. So, as mentioned above, my aim is representative, rather than comprehensive. Said insists that culture and imperialism are inextricably linked (*Culture and Imperialism*) and following his example I have chosen to discuss responses to texts that very obviously engage with colonialism (*The Tempest, Robinson Crusoe* and *Heart of Darkness*) and racial alterity (these three texts and *Othello*), along with texts where the relationship is, at least superficially, slightly more tenuous (*Great Expectations*,[7] *Jane Eyre* and *Wuthering Heights*). If one accepts Said's premise, the division is questionable, but nevertheless it seems reasonable to draw a distinction between works that can be read as blueprints of imperialism and those where its presence is more latent. To have focused exclusively on responses to overtly imperialist texts would itself have been a strategy that privileged colonial discourse. In choosing to range more broadly, part of my aim has been to examine the broader impact of cultural imperialism, but again it needs to be emphasized that canonical texts are slippery, mongrel-like creatures in the hands of postcolonial writers. Readers invariably refashion what they read to fit their local situations and individual proclivities, but because of the ruptures endemic in cross-cultural reading, the variants tend to multiply when works are borne across cultures. As Rushdie reminds us, 'The word "translation" comes, etymologically, from bearing across' (*Imaginary Homelands* 17) and translation and adaptation are central to cross-cultural reading practices.[8] Thus, in different situations *Robinson Crusoe* has been read as: an allegory of imperialism or of economic man more generally; as a novel about being Adam, the first man in the world; as a forerunner of the do-it-yourself manual, a text that in an age of increasing specialization of occupations offered its contemporary readers an insight into *how to* perform such practical tasks as baking bread (Watt 73–5); as a 'spiritual autobiography' (Starr); as an allegory of inter-racial relationships; as a realist classic establishing the codes of verisimilitude that were to dominate the eighteenth- and nineteenth-century English novel; and simply as an adventure story. Although the first of these readings has predictably been paramount in postcolonial contexts, it nevertheless represents just one of the ways in which con-texts have engaged with Defoe's pre-text.

Despite the desire to say something about the reception of the various pre-texts under consideration, when I first set out on this study I had no intention of attempting any kind of critique of these texts themselves. Not only was this not part of my agenda; it would also clearly be impossible within the compass of a book such as this to do more than add the smallest of footnotes to the vast critical literature that exists on authors such as Dickens, the Brontës and Conrad or to dip a toe into the waters of the burgeoning field of postcolonial Shakespeare studies. My purpose was, and is, simply to illustrate and analyse ways in which postcolonial writers have responded to the canonical texts in question. However, as mentioned above, I repeatedly found that the postcolonial con-texts refracted back on the pre-texts in question, opening up possibilities of variant readings, by undermining the notion of the stable text. In some cases the postcolonial writers concerned have commented very explicitly, in essays or interviews, on the texts to which they are supposedly writing back. Thus Chinua Achebe takes issue with the 'racism' of *Heart of Darkness*; V. S. Naipaul and Ngugi wa Thiong'o find Conrad a kindred spirit. Wilson Harris takes issue with Achebe, seeing Conrad's novella as a 'threshold' text, poised on the edge of dismantling European monolithic biases. Robert Kroetsch takes a not dissimilar view in seeing Conrad as constructing a set of irreconcilable binary oppositions.

Interesting though these critical pronouncements by fictional practitioners are, they are finally less illuminating than their responses to Conrad in their own novels. Conrad's fiction, and particularly *Heart of Darkness*, provokes a set of responses which in turn direct one back to the original novella and open up the possibility of reading it as incipiently 'postcolonial', at least in the sense that it exposes tensions at the heart, not of African darkness, but of the imperial project. Its own discourse interrogates both the language and assumptions of colonialism, in an obvious sense by reflecting widespread unease about Belgian colonialism in the Congo, but also by staging the disquiet about imperialism more generally in the figure of Marlow, the outsider who not only finds himself unable to sustain the complex, cross-cultural ethical code he has evolved during his years at sea, but more seriously, as both character in the tale he tells and as narrator of the story, struggles unsuccessfully to arrive at a language that will liberate himself from inscription within the colonial project. Putting this simply, then, I began with the assumption that I would assess postcolonial con-texts against canonical pre-texts in an attempt to arrive at conclusions, however piecemeal and tentative, about the extent to which they adopted an adversarial or complicitous stance in relation to their English 'parents'. I ended convinced that the evidence suggested a model of affiliation predicated upon postcolonial texts' frequently embracing illegitimacy and choosing multiple parents or orphaning themselves. At one point it began to seem that the parent–child paradigm, which after all in its original filiative form infantilizes the postcolonial subject, was simply being discarded, but ultimately there seemed to be more instances that suggested that, once the biological bloodlines between pre-text and con-text had been sundered, the relationship might be retained with the erstwhile children beginning to adopt, or even engender, ageing and wayward former parents as part of a process of affiliative reconstruction. As Rushdie's Saleem Sinai puts it, 'I have had more mothers than most mothers have children; giving birth to parents has been one of my stranger talents — a form of reverse fertility ...' (*Midnight's Children* 243).

Notes

1. See, e.g., Said: 'For there is no doubt that imaginative geography and history help the mind to intensify its own sense of itself by dramatizing the distance between what is close to it and what is far away' (*Orientalism* 55).
2. See the discussion in Chapter 6 below.
3. Naipaul had written a scathing review of Lamming's novel, *Of Age and Innocence*, in the *New Statesman*, 6 December 1958, p. 826, and may have had Lamming in mind in the character Blackwhite, in the title novella of *A Flag on the Island*, a Caribbean author whose latest work includes a passage on the 'tremendousness' of being Caliban (154). Lamming had previously attacked Naipaul's satirical stance in *The Pleasures of Exile* (30 and 224–5).
4. Jameson has, of course, been attacked for the totalizing tendency implicit in such thinking by Aijaz Ahmad (95–122) and others.
5. Unpublished talk, University of North London, 8 May 1990.
6. One story in *Summer Lightning*, 'Country of the One-Eye God', is set in a later period, the 1970s, and suggests that the divisions within Jamaican society, e.g. between rural and urban, persist, albeit in changing forms.
7. Briefly discussed by Said, *Culture and Imperialism* xv-xvii.
8. See, e.g. Mukherjee and Bassnett and Trivedi (eds), on postcolonial translation theory and practice.

2

Conrad's 'hopeless' binaries: *Heart of Darkness* and postcolonial interior journeys

I keep rereading *Heart of Darkness*, ... one of the things that intrigues me is the number of embedded stories in it that are themselves fragments which Conrad's trying to deal with. And then there is that beautiful binary of Marlow and Kurtz which is so hopeless that it is never going to become a completion. ... The mystery of the feminine is there for me – the two women, again, paired, women.

(Robert Kroetsch in Neuman and Wilson 12)

It was unearthly, and the men were – No, they were not inhuman. Well, you know, that was the worst of it – this suspicion of their not being inhuman. It would come slowly to one. They howled and leaped, and spun, and made horrid faces; but what thrilled you was just the thought of their humanity – like yours – the thought of your remote kinship with this wild and passionate uproar.

(Joseph Conrad, *Heart* 51)

I

This chapter considers a range of postcolonial responses to Conrad's *Heart of Darkness* (1902) with two particular focal points. It investigates the charge that the novella is racist in its dehumanization of Africans as the savage alterity against which 'civilized' European subjectivity can be measured;[1] and it discusses novels that have followed *Heart of Darkness* in using the journey into a physical interior as a correlative for a journey into a psychological heartland. The charge of racism is explored with particular reference to a polemical essay by Chinua Achebe, which sparked a continuing controversy by arguing that the text's representation of Africa and Africans was offensive, and to the reaction to Conrad implicit in Achebe's own novel, *Arrow of God* (1964;

revised 1974). It also examines the views of V. S. Naipaul and Ngugi wa
Thiong'o, whose response to Conrad has been more positive, and a number of
postcolonial novels that follow *Heart of Darkness* in using the journey into a
physical interior as a correlative for a parallel psychic quest, which usually has
national (or regional), ethnic and gender implications. Novels from this sub-
genre include Patrick White's *Voss* (1957) and *A Fringe of Leaves* (1976) and
Margaret Atwood's *Surfacing* (1972), which are briefly considered here; Wilson
Harris's *Palace of the Peacock* (1960) and Robert Kroetsch's *Badlands* (1975)
receive rather more detailed attention.

Heart of Darkness has long been something of a litmus test for debates about
European constructions of 'otherness', as well as issues relating to colonialism
more generally. While some postcolonial writers have reacted to Conrad in a
straightforwardly hostile manner, others have seen him as an important
precursor, either identifying with the relativism of his fictional technique or his
dialogic investigation of non-Western societies. This chapter endeavours to
illustrate the diversity of responses to *Heart of Darkness*, and to a lesser extent
Conrad's work in general, in an attempt to explain why it has aroused such
animosity among some postcolonial writers and commentators, while serving
as a model with which others have readily identified. Arguably, this divergence
arises from variant responses to Conrad's distinctively individual form of
modernist irony, a mode that reflects the ambivalence of his position within
English letters at the turn of the twentieth century.

Although Conrad is often regarded as a canonical English novelist,[2] he was
of course an émigré whose early years as a Pole growing up in the Russian-
dominated Ukraine and subsequent career as a merchant sailor travelling to all
the world's continents had given him first-hand experience of many forms of
imperialism, as well as an acquaintanceship with non-European cultures rare
among his literary contemporaries. He became a naturalized British subject at
the age of twenty-nine and came to adopt many of the ethical codes of the
English middle classes, but the first half of his life left his consciousness
indelibly imprinted with a sense of the relativism of beliefs that Europe had
naturalized as aspects of the human condition. *Heart of Darkness* reflects the
complexities of his socialization and is a text that occupies a particularly
ambiguous place within the English canon: while it challenged many of the
preconceptions of the late Victorian reading public,[3] it has subsequently had its
own cultural politics called into question. As Edward Said, an admirer of many
aspects of Conrad's work, and others have argued, culture and imperialism
cannot be separated and genres such as the novel 'were immensely important
in the *formation* of imperial attitudes, references, and experiences' (*Culture and
Imperialism* xii; my italics). Yet mainstream English culture often occluded its
implication in the imperial project. Said's not entirely original discussion of

Jane Austen's *Mansfield Park* (1814) makes this point forcefully by demonstrating how emphasis on the conservative stability associated with Austen's quintessentially English literary site of the country house sublimates the material reality on which it is based: an Antiguan sugar plantation. Disruption occurs when the patriarch, Sir Thomas Bertram, has to go to the Caribbean to sort out problems that could destabilize the basis of this economy; and misrule, in the form of potentially carnivalesque theatricals, enters the house, threatening to unsettle its status as a bastion of the status quo. The emergence of unseemly behaviour within the house is clearly linked to the absence of the father – an absentee in two senses, since he is not only physically absent from Mansfield during the course of the novel's action, but more generally an absentee Caribbean plantation owner (James, S. 41) – who is busy sorting out another form of deviant action. At the same time, the situation of the heroine, Fanny Price, the poor relative within the household, provides an interesting instance of an English outsider's attempts to accommodate herself in the upper-middle-class social world that represents stability in the Condition of England.[4] The colonial motif in *Mansfield Park* is, however, obscured to the point where it appears to many readers to be little more than an excuse for removing Sir Thomas from the scene of the main action. As such it provides an apt metonym for the exclusions of middle-class English culture and its tendency not only to mask the economic basis of much of post-Renaissance Britain's wealth, but also to conceal its umbilical relationship with the colonial world it has created. Said perhaps overstates the extent to which *Mansfield Park* 'synchronizes domestic with international authority' (*Culture and Imperialism* 104): Austen contrasts the rural security of Mansfield Park with turmoil in the urban worlds of London and Portsmouth, while Antigua is an absence that at most only serves to define Mansfield through implied contradistinction. Nevertheless his assertion that 'Jane Austen sees the legitimacy of Sir Thomas Bertram's overseas properties as a natural extension of the calm, the order, the beauties of Mansfield Park, one central estate validating the economically supportive role of the peripheral other' (94) clearly does pinpoint the *underlying* spatial dynamic of the text.[5]

Said is, of course, at pains not only to foreground the implication of culture in the imperial project, but also to argue against 'unitary or monolithic or autonomous' (15) constructions of cultures; and, while imperialism may have been a hidden metanarrative in much Western cultural production until comparatively recently, 'English literature' has nonetheless produced its fair share of texts that are very explicitly about the colonial enterprise. These range from the adventure novels of writers such as Captain Marryat, an important early influence on Conrad, Rider Haggard and G. A. Henty to a triptych of works occupying a more central place in the canon, which provide paradigmatic accounts of imperialism: *The Tempest, Robinson Crusoe* and *Heart of Darkness*. All three offer blueprints of colonial practices, at particular historical moments, and like Conrad's novella, *The Tempest* and *Robinson Crusoe* have also elicited a range of varied, but often hostile, responses from postcolonial writers and critics. Of the three, though, *Heart of Darkness* is the text that most obviously sets out to criticize the economic exploitation inherent in the colonial 'idea'. An oft-quoted passage[6] indicts the 'conquest of the earth' as mostly meaning 'the taking it away from those who have a different complexion or slightly flatter noses than ourselves', saying it 'is not a pretty thing when you look into it too much' (*Heart* 10). Nevertheless, it has frequently been read as a racist work, as in the following comments by Achebe in an essay entitled 'An Image of Africa: Racism in Conrad's *Heart of Darkness*':

> *Heart of Darkness* projects the image of Africa as 'the other world', the antithesis of Europe and therefore of civilization, a place where man's vaunted intelligence and refinement are finally mocked by triumphant bestiality. ...
>
> Students of *Heart of Darkness* will often tell you that Conrad is concerned not so much with Africa as with the deterioration of one human mind caused by solitude and sickness. They will point out to you that Conrad is, if anything, less charitable to the Europeans in the story than he is to the natives, that the point of the story is to ridicule Europe's civilizing mission in Africa. A Conrad student informed me in Scotland that Africa is merely a setting for the disintegration of the mind of Mr Kurtz.
>
> Which is partly the point. Africa as setting and backdrop which eliminates the African as human factor. Africa as a metaphysical battlefield devoid of all recognizable humanity, into which the wandering European enters at his peril. Can nobody see the preposterousness and perverse arrogance in thus reducing Africa to the role of props for the break-up of one petty European mind? But that is not even the point. The real question is the dehumanization of Africa and Africans which this age-long attitude has fostered and continues to foster in the world.
>
> (Achebe, *Hopes* 2, 8)

Achebe's view of Conrad's representation of Africa as the Dark Continent clearly informs his 'village' novels *Things Fall Apart* (1958) and *Arrow of God*, revisionist fictional histories which attempt to recuperate Africa from negative Eurocentric construction and to invest his Ibo people's past with a dignity previously denied it in anglophone writing about West Africa. In a well-known comment in his essay 'The Novelist as Teacher', originally published in 1965,

Achebe said he would be content if his novels 'did no more than teach my readers that their past — with all its imperfections — was not one long night of savagery from which the first Europeans acting on God's behalf delivered them' (*Hopes* 30). Consequently, he says in the same essay, it may be necessary for the time being 'to counter racism with ... an anti-racist racism' (30). Such a comment, along with the didacticism affirmed in the title of the essay, suggests that his writing of this period belongs to the negritudinist phase of African writing. The Negritude movement opposed essentialist European construc-tions of African identity by promoting a view of the distinctiveness and dignity of the African personality that ran the risk of promulgating an alternative essentialism, in which African subjects remained locked into European agendas by virtue of seeking to combat their stereotyping practices without changing the grounds of debate. This raises a crucial question for African counter-discourse: given that European racism has played a major role in the definition of African subjectivities, economies and discourses, at least since the moment of the late nineteenth-century scramble for Africa onwards, how can African writers create a space in which to redefine themselves outside Western discursive pre-texts? In one sense, this is the problem that Terdiman identifies in his study of nineteenth-century French writers' attempts to separate themselves from the bourgeois culture that they are contesting, but the imperatives become more urgent in an African situation founded upon blatant economic exploitation and racist stereotyping.

   Achebe's response to Conrad is an object lesson in how to achieve such redefinition. The method he employs to counter what he sees as racism in Conrad is the construction of an alternative historiography of the period in which European colonial society was establishing itself in West Africa and his fiction replaces the Eurocentric point of view with those of local focalizers. The two village novels are written from within Ibo society, often employing registers that suggest an English that is transcribing local idioms. *Things Fall Apart* makes extensive use of Ibo proverbs and its third-person narrator could well be a local villager. It is set in much the same chronological period as *Heart of Darkness*, the late nineteenth century, and deals with the first incursions of European colonialism into the tribal society of Iboland, here represented by the microcosm of the nine villages of Umuofia. Its readers are immediately taken into the intricacies of Ibo society and the novel offers a particularly complex reconstruction of its codes of manhood, undergoing interrogation at a time of social transition. European intervention is part of its subject — and is one of the main causes of the communal fragmentation suggested in the novel's Yeatsian title[7] — but it is *only* part and the text's Europeans are as much bit players in the drama, as Conrad's Africans, though they are less dehumanized. *Arrow of God* is set rather later, in the 1920s, a period when Britain was trying to introduce a system of indirect rule into Iboland. However, despite being further removed from *Heart of Darkness* in fictional time, at one point it echoes Conrad more directly. This occurs in a passage that temporarily deserts the vividly realized warts-and-all picture of Ibo social life (the 'past – with all its imperfections'), to provide a glimpse into the European mind. Although Achebe's Europeans lack the complexity of his Ibo characters, they are never as shadowy as Conrad's Africans. Their most developed representative in *Arrow of God* is the figure of Captain Winterbottom, a colonial administrator, who is a firm believer in 'the value of the British mission in Africa' (30). At one point Winterbottom's view of Africa clearly echoes Marlow's in *Heart of Darkness*. Marlow's sense of alienation is expressed in passages such as the following:

> We penetrated deeper and deeper into the heart of darkness. It was very quiet there. At night sometimes the roll of drums behind the curtain of trees would run up the river and remain sustained faintly, as if hovering in the air high above our heads, till the first break of day. Whether it meant war, peace, or prayer we could not tell. The dawns were heralded by the descent of a chill stillness; the wood-cutters slept, their fires burned low; the snapping of a twig would make you start. We were wanderers on prehistoric earth, on an earth that wore the aspect of an unknown planet. We could have fancied ourselves the first of men taking possession of an accursed inheritance, to be subdued at the cost of profound anguish and of excessive toil. ...
> ... Ugly. Yes, it was ugly enough; but if you were man enough you would admit to yourself that there was in you just the faintest trace of a response to the terrible frankness of that noise, a dim suspicion of there being a meaning in it which you – you so remote from the night of first ages – could comprehend. And why not? The mind of man is capable of anything – because everything is in it.
>
> (*Heart* 50–2)

The following passage in *Arrow of God* fairly obviously responds to this, not only in its use of similar language and imagery, but also in the way it suggests the extent to which physical dislocation induces a corollary sense of mental alienation:

> Captain Winterbottom had not known real sleep since the dry, cool harmattan wind stopped abruptly in December; and it was now mid-February. He had grown pale and thin, and in spite of the heat his feet often felt cold. ... At night he had to imprison himself inside a mosquito-net which shut out whatever air movement there was outside. His

bedclothes were sodden and his head formed a waterlogged basin on the pillow. After the first stretch of unrestful sleep he would lie awake, tossing about until he was caught in the distant throb of drums. He would wonder what unspeakable rites went on in the forest at night, or was it the heart-beat of the African darkness? Then one night he was terrified when it suddenly occurred to him that no matter where he lay awake at night in Nigeria the beating of the drums came with the same constancy and from the same elusive distance. Could it be that the throbbing came from his own heat-stricken brain? He attempted to smile it off but the skin on his face felt too tight. This dear old land of waking nightmares!

(Arrow 29–30)

Towards the end of *Heart of Darkness*, there is an even more obvious intertext for this *Arrow of God* passage, as Marlow remembers how, at Kurtz's station, he listened to the sound of a drumbeat in the night and 'confounded the beat of the drum with the beating of my heart' (93). In both novels it is fairly clear that the real heart of darkness is to be located within the European mind, and in Conrad's case the mind of *Marlow*, the experiencing consciousness of the novel, is more central than that of Kurtz.

Marlow's fear of alterity can be related to the various ideologies that had unsettled traditional belief-systems in the late Victorian period: among them, Darwinism, the higher criticism of the Bible and the nexus of philosophical writings redefining humanity's role in the universe that had issued from the Hegelian dialectic. In this sense, at least, Achebe's understandable protest at the notion that Africa is reduced to the 'role of props for the break-up of one petty European mind' partly misses the point, since it refers to Kurtz, while the challenge offered by the alterity of the silent continent is developed in a fuller and more complex manner in relation to the main protagonist, Marlow. What exactly Marlow represents has, of course, proved a happy hunting-ground for critical speculation, but on one level he can be seen to epitomize a pragmatic sensibility that enables him to survive the existential testing-ground that destroys Kurtz's obsessive, ultimately demonic, idealism. Achebe is alert to the possibility of distance between author and narrator, pointing out that Marlow's narrative is itself framed by a 'second, shadowy person', but he nevertheless takes the view that Conrad fails 'to draw a cordon sanitaire between himself and the moral and psychological *malaise* of his narrator ... because he neglects to hint, clearly and adequately, at an alternative frame of reference by which we may judge the actions and opinions of his characters' (*Hopes* 7; italics in original).

Achebe's emphasis on the extent to which Africa has been rendered a 'metaphysical battleground' rather than allowed to exist in its own right remains unexceptionable, but if one admits that the text's deployment of the trope of the Dark Continent is primarily related to the 'psychological *malaise*' of Marlow and that the view of Kurtz as the demented bringer of light is refracted through his consciousness, it becomes clear that it is more than a backdrop for the mental breakdown of a single European. Contrasted though Kurtz and Marlow are, their symbiotic pairing seems to represent two variations on the notion of 'the European mind'. It remains true that no viable alternative is put forward, but nevertheless the text not only indicts the economic exploitation of Africa by Europe, but also hovers on the edge of exposing the racism that was integral to many forms of late nineteenth-century European socialization. At the risk of promoting an essentialist view of European society at this time, it seems reasonable to suggest that *Heart of Darkness* depicts the 'Dark Continent' as a European discourse that cuts across national and gender boundaries; and it is the contemplative traveller Marlow who comes close to grasping its dehumanizing consequences.

Achebe's response in *Arrow of God* is to allow the Conradian view just enough space for its limitations to be apparent. Winterbottom's view of Africa as a 'dear old land of waking nightmares' gets little more than a passing mention in a novel that depicts the complexity of Ibo social life through an accretion of circumstantial detail, which both fulfils the educative purpose that Achebe outlines in his 'Novelist as Teacher' essay and explores moral and psychological difficulties that result from trying to adhere to traditional social codes in a changing environment. The novel's main protagonist is Ezeulu, the Chief Priest of the cult of Ulu, a man torn between strict observance of his role as a custodian of his people's culture, and a view that allows him to exercise authority in his own right by adapting the traditional culture to shifting social situations – in this case occasioned by the intervention of English colonizers into the collective of the six villages of Umuaro. In the first few sentences Achebe not only brings Ezeulu alive as a complex character in the grip of a dilemma, but also makes it clear that he is the product of an evolving culture, which is passing into a new phase at the moment at which the text begins. The opening provides a very different vision of the African night from Marlow's in *Heart of Darkness* – or Winterbottom's nightmare vision which will come later in the text – and establishes Ezeulu's role as an interpreter of the cosmos:

This was the third nightfall since he began to look for signs of the new moon. He knew it would come today but he always began his watch three days early because he must not take a risk. In this season of the year his task was not too difficult; he did not have to peer and search the sky as he might do when the rains came. Then the new moon sometimes hid itself for days behind rain clouds so that when it finally came out it was

already halfgrown. And while it played its game the Chief Priest sat up
every evening waiting.

(*Arrow* 1)

From the outset, then, it is clear that the 'signs' need to be read. Despite
Achebe's understandable rejection of Conrad, his emphasis on the need to
understand natural phenomena as indices of symbolic meaning has much in
common with Conrad's hermeneutic approach to the meaning of 'Africa'.
Although in one sense Achebe completely reverses Conrad's perspective, he
shares his scepticism about the impossibility of definitive readings; and, as the
events of *Arrow of God* unfold, they stage a complex debate about the relative
merits of a steadfast adherence to the traditional way of life and the desirability
of adaptation to changing social situations, in which Ezeulu emerges as a tragic
scapegoat figure, sacrificed at the intersection of two cultures.

II

Other postcolonial writers, such as V. S. Naipaul and Ngugi wa Thiong'o, have
taken a very different view of Conrad to Achebe. In a 1974 essay entitled
'Conrad's Darkness', Naipaul talks about how, after having initially been far
more influenced by the social comedy of novelists such as Dickens and Wells,
he eventually came 'round to Conrad' (*Return* 207). As he gradually forsook his
early 'fantasy' of England as a 'purely literary region, where, untrammelled by
the accidents of history or background, I could make a romantic career for
myself as a writer' (216), he found a kindred spirit in Conrad, another non-
British-born writer whose absorption into the English tradition had done little
to dispel his sense of cultural dislocation. Such dislocation exhibits itself in the
work of both novelists on the levels of both form and theme. Formally,
Conrad's frequent use of a first-person narrator whose point of view is partial,
in the sense both of being limited and of being partisan, and a disjointed
narrative technique, have the effect of creating a relativistic atmosphere far
removed from the certitudes of most earlier English novels, and Naipaul's
fiction from *The Mimic Men* (1967) onwards has demonstrated a similar sense
of cultural relativism, while frequently representing third-world societies in a
negative light. Naipaul also speaks of having begun to feel a strong sense of
affinity for Conrad's subjects and, in 'Conrad's Darkness', he describes how he
came to regard him as his most significant literary predecessor, because his lack
of a sense of social belonging made him an acute commentator on the social
and psychological turbulence of the modern world:

It came to me that the great novelists wrote about highly organized societies. I had no such society; I couldn't share the assumptions of these writers; I didn't see my world reflected in theirs .... .

... The new politics, the curious reliance of men on institutions they were yet working to undermine, the simplicity of beliefs and the hideous simplicity of actions, the corruption of causes, half-made societies that seemed doomed to remain half-made: these were the things that began to preoccupy me. ... And I found that Conrad ... had been everywhere before me. Not as a man with a cause, but a man offering, as in *Nostromo*, a vision of the world's half-made societies as places which continually made and unmade themselves and where always 'something inherent in the necessities of successful action ... carried with it the moral degradation of the idea'.

(Return 213, 216)

Despite the disparaging view of the non-European world as 'half-made', these remarks are perceptive in identifying Conrad's interest in colonial fragmentation. From the point of view of more recent – and more fashionable – hybridization theory, they locate both Conrad and Naipaul as analysts of the cultural fault lines and fusions produced by European colonialisms. However, Naipaul mainly foregrounds the negative consequences of such contacts and several of his characters look back nostalgically to a time of racial purity. Ralph Singh, the narrator/protagonist of *The Mimic Men*, dreams of a pure Aryan past, while in *A Bend in the River* (1979) the narrator, Salim, is shocked to find a Virgilian motto twisted to sanction miscegenation (69).

A Bend in the River is set in a central African republic, based on Zaire, and with the title evoking Marlow's reference to 'a mighty big river ... resembling an immense snake uncoiled' (*Heart* 12), Naipaul is clearly revisiting the geographical terrain of *Heart of Darkness*. Similarly, in the title novella of *In a Free State* (1971), where two British expatriates journey by road through a newly independent East African country at a time of crisis, Conrad's 'book' (170) is an explicit intertext. His influence is omnipresent in Naipaul's later fiction, but it is in *The Mimic Men*, where the debt is most overt. The novel contains two overt references to Conrad (165, 180) and the name of the fictional Caribbean island, Isabella, where much of the action is set, appears to echo that of 'The Isabels', the three offshore islands of Conrad's *Nostromo*. Such references are, however, only the tip of an iceberg. More generally, *The Mimic Men* is Conradian in its use of a fragmentary and unchronological narrative structure, a form used by Conrad in such novels as *Lord Jim* and *Nostromo*, and in its employment of a centre of consciousness through whom events are filtered to the reader and whose reliability is open to question. Ralph Singh, is an effete and often aloof narrator, who increasingly distances himself from his birthplace, Isabella, where he has been a populist political leader. His often disdainful aloofness may suggest ironic distance on Naipaul's part, but he shares certain characteristics with his creator: among them an education at his country's leading secondary school,[8] a father who becomes known as 'Gurudeva' (the name of the eponymous hero of a collection of short stories Naipaul's father, Seepersad, published in 1944),[9] a period working as a clerk in a government department after leaving school and a sense of disillusionment with London.[10] Consequently, the issue of how his character is to be read has divided critics, with interpretations varying between viewing him as an alter ego for Naipaul (e.g. Nazareth 139), arguing that there is a distinction to be made between the 'supercilious' Ralph of the story, who is 'a poseur and a libertine', and the 'recluse' Ralph who narrates it (Ramraj 134), and suggesting that it is at least possible that Naipaul may be exposing the persona of the narrator as well as this former self (e.g. Thieme, *Web* 115, 137). Whatever conclusion one comes to, Singh clearly shares the view of the world's 'half-made' societies that Naipaul writes about in the Conrad essay and he has hoped to communicate this in a Gibbonesque history of Empire which will 'give expression to the restlessness, the deep disorder, which the great explorations, the overthrow in three continents of established social organizations, the unnatural bringing together of peoples who could achieve fulfilment only within the security of their own societies and the landscapes hymned by their ancestors, ... has brought about' (38). Ostensibly this history has not been written; it has been supplanted by the much more personal memoir that Singh is writing. However, the memoir encompasses the theme of the projected history in miniature, particularly since it suggests relationships between the socio-political and the psychological consequences of imperialism. In short, *The Mimic Men* can be read as a jaundiced latter-day equivalent of *Nostromo*, embodying Naipaul's view of Conrad as a writer who provided an incisive 'vision of the world's half-made societies' and 'the corruption of causes', with ' "the moral degradation of the idea" ' finding clear parallels in Singh's abortive quest for an ideal order, which all too easily gives way to vapid sexual encounters and political cynicism.

Since Naipaul has frequently been seen as a writer who has turned his back on societies such as the colonial Trinidadian world in which he grew up, it is perhaps hardly surprising that he not only differs from Achebe's view of Conrad, but actually identifies with him. His sympathetic response to Conrad is, however, far from unique among postcolonial writers and an African novelist whom one might expect to be closer to Achebe in outlook, Ngugi wa Thiong'o,[11] has expressed similar sentiments. In interviews given in the year when his first novel, *Weep Not Child* (1964), was published, Ngugi spoke of his

admiration for Conrad and of being impressed, like Naipaul, both by Conrad's
ability to immerse himself in an initially alien language:

> ... I understand he knew his first word of English at nineteen; that may
> be an exaggeration but I think what is interesting about Conrad is this
> very factor: that he was able to beat a language which was not his own
> into various shapes to give ... well ... meaning to the physical and moral
> world around him.
>
> (Duerden and Pieterse 126)

and by his moral relativism:

> I'm impressed by the way he questions things .... He questions what I
> would call 'the morality of action'. What is 'success', for instance, what is
> 'action'? Is failure to make a decision a moral action or not?
>
> (Duerden and Pieterse 124)[12]

The parallels with his own situation are fairly obvious. As a writer who first
began to learn English when he was about twelve, he has shared Conrad's
situation of having to express himself in a language which, at least initially,
was not his own, though unlike Conrad he has become increasingly uneasy
about the appropriateness of African writers using English and turned to
Gikuyu and the East African lingua franca of Kiswahili.[13] At the same time, his
comments on Conrad's questioning 'the morality of action' are close to
Naipaul's later remarks on 'the moral degradation of the idea' and in novels
such as A Grain of Wheat (1967; revised edition 1986) and Petals of Blood
(1977), he turned to a Conradian technique[14] that employed a multiplicity of
focalizers and time shifts to suggest the problems of arriving at a definitive
version of historical events.[15] The events concerned are recent and relate to the
moral and psychological consequences of the Mau Mau freedom struggle
against British rule in Kenya. On one level, the project of these novels is
analogous to Achebe's, in that their politics are concerned with contesting
colonial authority,[16] the local perspective is instated as central – in A Grain of
Wheat the third-person narrative voice is identified with that of a local villager
on several occasions (155,156, 162, 177, 187ff.) – and expatriate characters are
relegated to the margins of the text. At the same time, however, a novel such
as A Grain of Wheat is distinctly Conradian in its interrogation of heroism.
Thus, the character to whom readers are first introduced and with whom most
will sympathize, Mugo, is gradually revealed as the Judas of the text, the man
who has betrayed the war hero, Kihika. As such he is a study in lost honour
who can be compared with Conrad's Lord Jim, and, despite the novel's anti-

colonial stance, issues relating to the 'morality of action' among the local population are its main focus. For most readers, Mugo remains altogether more sympathetic than the character hitherto presumed to be Kihika's betrayer, Karanja, who has colluded with white authority in the suppression of his people, but it *is* Mugo who has been responsible for the central act of betrayal. At the same time, all of the other major protagonists are held up to similar scrutiny and all are seen to be morally compromised in one way or another. In short, although, as in Achebe, the anti-colonial stance is a *donnée*, *A Grain of Wheat* is an interrogative text which not only suggests that no culture has a monopoly of virtue, but also demonstrates the thin line that separates heroes from betrayers in popular constructions of history, forcing its readers to ask Conradian questions about 'the morality of action' and the hegemonic exercise of *author*-ity, whether it be by colonial rulers or postcolonial writers.

III

There have, of course, been numerous other readings of Conrad by third-world writers and critics, who remain alert to the racism endemic not only in the colonial past, but also the postcolonial present. Wilson Harris, for example, speaks of his 'sympathy' for Achebe's view resting on 'an appreciation of his uneasiness in the face of biases that continue to reinforce themselves in post-Imperial Western establishments', but nevertheless concludes that Achebe's charge of racism is 'a profoundly mistaken one'. He goes on to argue for the 'capacity of the intuitive self to breach the historical ego' (*Explorations* 134), a position which reflects his own reluctance to subscribe to any form of historical determinism and which is particularly interesting since his own first novel, *Palace of the Peacock* (1960), follows in Conrad's footsteps by taking its protagonists, a mixed crew representative of the various ancestral strands of the Guyanese population,[17] or more generally of the crew of mankind, on a journey upriver into the country's continental heartland.[18] The crew appears to be following in the wake of a much earlier crew, which was engaged on a mission of colonial conquest. The previous crew has perished in the rapids of an interior stretch of the river, but increasingly the two journeys begin to merge into one, as temporal and other distinctions between what would usually be regarded as discrete experiences are eroded. While the journey in *Palace of the Peacock* has clear national, and cross-cultural, implications, as in Conrad it is also a journey into the psyche.

Numerous other postcolonial writers have used the motif of the Conradian interior journey for similar purposes, albeit to arrive at very different conclusions. Harris's fiction apart, novels employing this pattern include the works by Patrick White, Margaret Atwood and Robert Kroetsch mentioned above. Ostensibly each of these novels has more in common with *Heart of Darkness* than *Palace of the Peacock* does, since they use the interior journey as a structure for investigating the relationship between 'settler' society and native space. As in Conrad, the focus is on how 'civilized' humans behave when removed from the support systems of Western society. In each case, albeit in very different ways, the protagonists are unsettled by their journey into an ab-original world where their previously held cultural values and epistemo-logical assumptions appear to have little relevance. White's *Voss* and Kroetsch's *Badlands* (like *Palace of the Peacock*, discussed in more detail below) deal with expeditions into 'prehistoric' territory, in which Western values are measured against an indigene way of life (Australian Aboriginal culture in *Voss* and Blackfoot, as well as Chinese, codes in *Badlands*) and found wanting. White's *A Fringe of Leaves* shipwrecks a nineteenth-century Englishwoman[19] amid a group of Aborigines and again interrogates the most basic of notions of what is normally considered 'human', with the protagonist engaging in the 'unspeakable rite' of cannibalism.[20] Atwood's nameless protagonist in *Surfacing* is a contemporary commercial artist who has repressed painful aspects of her past life, but is forced to confront them when she journeys into the northern Québec bush to look for her father who has gone missing. It quickly becomes clear that the quest on which she is engaged is as much a quest for self as for her absent father and the central epiphany of the novel occurs when she dives into a lake at a spot sacred to the Native inhabitants of the region. At the same time, all four novels interrogate gender assumptions that seem to be umbilically linked with the male colonial vision, whether it be nineteenth-century German, as in the case of *Voss*, a character whose belief in the power of the Individual Will appears to derive from White's reading of Schopenhauer and is reminiscent of Kurtz's megalomania,[21] or twentieth-century American, as in *Surfacing*.

Palace of the Peacock appears to be written from the other side of the settler/indigene divide: Harris's crew comprises several of the various ethnic strands that make up Guyanese society: Afro-Caribbean, Amerindian, Portuguese and European among them.[22] In fact, it is at pains to dismantle the settler/indigene binary and its complex, dream-like structure, in which what appeared to be fossilized experience is metamorphosed as 'past' events recur in new forms and 'dead' characters in new incarnations, can be read as a strategy for offering emancipation from the colonial vision. In one sense, then, the interior journey of *Palace of the Peacock* retraces that of *Heart of Darkness* and there are clear Conradian echoes, for example when the Kurtz-like protagonist Donne remembers a house he has built 'with the closeness and intimacy of a horror and a hell, that horror and that hell he had himself elaborately constructed from which to rule his earth' (130). Yet its technique enacts the impossibility of sustaining partitionist views of human experience, such as the civilization/ savagery dichotomy that appears to lie at the heart of 'Conrad's darkness'. The novel is partly located within the settler consciousness of Donne but he is a composite two-sided figure, and his double nature both epitomizes and challenges the settler view that native space is a site for conquest. Similarly, the other members of the text's crew represent a complex set of overlapping identities that subvert essentialist notions of personality.

Postcolonial con-texts frequently uncover meanings in their English pre-texts that may not be apparent when the latter are read in isolation, or with the assumption that they are constitutive parts of the English canon, and this is the case when *Heart of Darkness* is re-read in the light of the aesthetic developed in *Palace of the Peacock* – to an even greater extent than when the novella is read through the prism of Naipaul's or Ngugi's approach to Conrad. Simply to read Conrad's novella as structuring Marlow's encounter with alterity in terms of a binary opposition between civilization and savagery is to miss the subtle way in which Conrad erodes such shadow lines.[23] Although the 'racist' reading of Conrad suggests that his vision constructs binary oppositions between European civilization and African savagery, this reading overlooks a crucial aspect of the novella. Given that it would, as Achebe says, be 'perverse arrogance' to reduce Africa to 'the role of props for the break-up of one petty European mind', this mental collapse itself erodes the apparent binary oppositions of the text. Breakdown takes on a different meaning, if one perceives Kurtz, the demented bringer of light as the ultimate savage of the text and as such a metonym for the collapse of the colonial project. Conrad is unsparing in his censure of the exploitation of what he had witnessed in the Congo during the six months he spent there in 1890 and many critics have very reasonably taken the view that this suggests a specific attack on Belgian King Leopold II's policies in the 'Congo Free State' (Knowles and Moore 67–8, 71–2). However, the text's deliberate occlusion of national specifics points towards a more general indictment of colonialism and, along with it, the putative liberalism that becomes complicit in its economic exploitation of subject peoples. Marlow's role in this debate is central, since he, after all, is the focalizer who *apparently* demonizes Africans, by mainly consigning them to the role of flitting shadows glimpsed in the prehistoric forest. However, at the very moment when his alienation from what he presents as a primeval world appears to be at its most extreme, his consciousness suggests that the borderline between savagery and civilization is altogether more porous than the European mind recognizes. A section omitted from the lengthy passage quoted above, which is central to the case mounted against Conrad as a racist, makes this explicit:

The earth seemed unearthly. We are accustomed to look upon the
shackled form of a conquered monster, but there — there you could look
at a thing monstrous and free. It was unearthly, and the men were — No,
they were not inhuman. Well, you know, that was the worst of it — this
suspicion of their not being inhuman. It would come slowly to one. They
howled and leaped, and spun, and made horrid faces; but what thrilled
you was just the thought of their humanity — like yours — the thought of
your remote kinship with this wild and passionate uproar. (51)

Disturbingly for the late Victorian mind, he is suggesting the consanguinity of
the 'civilized' and the 'savage' and, if his representation of the extra-cultural
status of the latter suggests racist stereotyping, the subject is not the collapse
of a single mind, but rather the European mind's problem in grappling with
alterity. Marlow not only lives to tell the tale, but is reassimilated into the
shared social fictions of polite society, as he tells Kurtz's Intended the lie that
masks the fact that he has found a more disturbing darkness in the 'moral
degradation of [Kurtz's] idea' than in the physical terrain of the 'place of
darkness' (12). Kurtz's degeneration is, then, a metonym for the 'horror' he has
found at the heart of the colonial project, which provided the material basis for
the wealth and apparent social stability of so much of nineteenth-century
European society. One way of expressing this might be to point out that the
text's cultural politics are more or less diametrically opposed to those implicit
in *Mansfield Park*, where this material foundation is an uninterrogated *donnée*
and where we never doubt that the paternal Sir Thomas Bertram will return
from the troubled site of Antigua to restore order in the English country house.
In Jane Austen's world there is never, of course, any suggestion that he will be
required to *speak* the kind of social lie that Marlow tells the Intended, but if one
reads the 'horror' of *Heart of Darkness* as a trope for the cover-up of the
symbiotic relationship between colonizer and colonized and the extent to
which polite society is founded on colonial exploitation, the apparent distance
between the two works of fiction rapidly begins to shrink.

The lie crystallizes the central theme of the novella. Throughout his
narrative Marlow is troubled by the inability of European discourse to express
the experience he is undergoing. He has envisaged Kurtz as 'a voice' and is
both captivated by his rhetorical power and aware of its ambivalence:

[O]f all his gifts the one that stood out pre-eminently, that carried with it
a sense of real presence, was his ability to talk, his words — the gift of
expression, the bewildering, the illuminating, the most exalted and the
most contemptible, the pulsating stream of light, or the deceitful flow
from the heart of an impenetrable darkness. (67–8)

It is the collapse of this 'gift' that signals the failure of the European mission in Africa and what Marlow discovers at the Inner Station leaves him doubting not only the efficacy of the kind of language represented by Kurtz's discourse, but also of communication more generally. However, lest this suggests a pre-Derridean reluctance to allow that language can give voice to lived experience, one should hasten to add that *Heart of Darkness* creates its own particular idiolect. F. R. Leavis's famous discussion sees the vocabulary of the novella as characterized by an 'adjectival insistence upon inexpressible and incomprehensible mystery', which detracts from the 'charged concreteness' of the 'essential vibration' of its 'particular incidents' (196–7). This is a view that both identifies a crucial aspect of the lexis of the text and fails to recognize the effect it produces. It is *Marlow*, who is left grappling to find a terminology that will enable him to articulate what is inexpressible within the parameters of late nineteenth-century European discourse. The idiolect of the text discovers its own correlative for this – in the language that Leavis felt was too abstract and insistent – and it seems reasonable to argue that *Heart of Darkness* is ahead of its time in foregrounding the need to fumble towards alternative modes of utterance, if the binaries that Marlow sees as socially constructed fictions ('the thought of their humanity – like yours – the thought of your remote kinship with this wild and passionate uproar') are to be undermined. In short, the novella is *about* racism, but it does more to expose the racist thinking that permeated late nineteenth-century psyches, whether exemplified by Kurtz or Marlow, than to perpetuate it.

So, from this point of view and despite its apparent construction of Africa as 'savage', Conrad's novella is a work that anticipates postcolonial attacks on the colonizer's hegemonic control of language. And such a view lies behind Wilson Harris's response to Achebe's reading. For Harris, *Heart of Darkness* is a 'frontier novel' which stands on the threshold of transforming 'biases grounded in homogeneous premises' (*Explorations* 135, 134). Harris's whole œuvre has been dedicated to the promotion of communal, cultural and psychic heterogeneity and his *Heart of Darkness* essay takes the view that the African tradition 'tends towards homogeneous imperatives' (135). Consequently it can, although Harris does not make this particular point, as happened during the negritudinist phase, provide a mirror image of colonial practices. Or, to put this another way: if counter-discourse takes up an oppositional position, it runs the risk of locking itself into the very codes that it is contesting, because it allows itself to be defined in terms of them, albeit through negation. In South America in contrast, Harris says, 'this is not the case' (135). As we have seen in the central passage quoted above, Conrad, while appearing to construct racist binaries, actually interrogates their prevalence in the late Victorian imperial discourse that was purveyed to the masses – as a linchpin of the culture of 'home' – in everything from the boys' magazines that played a key role in the narrative of Empire-building to the adventure fiction of novelists such as Haggard and Henty. Such novelists not only expounded the colonial ideal through their 'sturdy faith in man's ability to mould nature to his will', but grafted such empirical conviction onto a parallel set of moral or transcendental values, so that 'the imperial idea [became] not an end in itself but a major expression of the problem of self-consciousness' (Sandison viii). Conrad's cosmos inverts this: Kurtz is a failed Nietzschean superman,[24] an embodiment of the insolvency of the colonial enterprise, conceived at a moment when it appeared to be at its apogee, but when even hardened European minds were beginning to be disturbed by rumours about Leopold's Congo Free State. Later Patrick White, whose reading in German philosophy had encompassed Nietzsche (Marr 317) as well as Schopenhauer,[25] personified a very similar condition of bankrupt idealism in the eponymous hero of *Voss*, whose journey into the Australian outback exhibits a comparable megalomania, but Conrad, *pace* Achebe, preceded him by half a century, exposing such hubris at a time when the imperial ideal appeared to be at its height.

Harris, then, finds Conrad a writer who stands on the threshold of questioning 'monolithic codes of behaviour' (*Explorations* 135) and he develops this viewpoint not only in relation to Conrad's 'parody of the proprieties of established order that mask corruption in all societies' (137), which is to be seen in the imagery he uses to expose Kurtz's 'liberal manifesto of imperial good and moral light' (136), but also with reference to his movement beyond the conventions of the novel of manners, a form which he sees as capable of either reinforcing the status quo or protesting against it, but incapable of shifting the ground on which the encounter is taking place. However, for Harris, like Achebe, Conrad's fiction stops short of offering a viable alternative. His work remains locked in a form of parody that unmasks the illusions on which the social order is based, but is unable to offer an alternative vision of consciousness.

His own fiction attempts to provide exactly this. *Palace of the Peacock* employs a phantasmagoric technique in which what has actually happened or is happening is unclear, since the distinction between 'real' and imagined events and between past and present is blurred to the point where they collapse into one another. Tempting though it is to link Harris with other South American novelists and label him a marvellous realist, his technique is uniquely his own. His fictional method synthesizes a multiplicity of intertexts – Amerindian, European, African and Asian – transforming them into a highly individual vision that also owes much to his Guyanese upbringing and early career as a surveyor in the country's interior, which he writes about from the position of an insider/outsider: a Guyanese familiar with the little-known heartland of his country, but nonetheless shaped by his privileged middle-class, late colonial, coastal education. Much of the individuality of his technique lies in its challenge to one of the most basic tenets of post-Cartesian Western thought, the belief in discrete and autonomous selfhood. *Palace of the Peacock* allows the dead to come back to life, collapses the difference between subject and object and between reason and intuition and erodes many of the other binaries that have been seen as central to colonial discursive practices, including the settler/indigene divide.

Initially the story appears to be told by a first-person narrator; during the course of the action he becomes increasingly shadowy as first-person narrative elides into third-person omniscience. However, the 'I' narrator, who appears to dream most of the novel's events, has an alter ego, his brother Donne, the Kurtz figure of the text and a personification of the spiritual impoverishment of the colonial psyche. Donne is named after the seventeenth-century English poet and although this may seem an odd name for an arch-imperialist, it is perhaps a fitting choice if one views John Donne as a psychically divided poet torn between the discourses of secular and sacred love, who in his early life took part in the Earl of Essex's expeditions to Cadiz and the Azores. On one level, the expedition Donne leads into the Guyanese interior represents the original act of European colonization of the Americas. It is characterized by violence and conquest of the indigenous (Amerindian) 'folk' of the region: Donne has abused his Amerindian mistress, Mariella, but her identity remains elusive and shadowy and she is transformed from a person into a place, a mission, possibly suggestive of the reification of personality through another act of colonial violation, the imposition of Christianity. However, as the crew re-enact the voyage of the earlier dead crew, past and present are conflated and psycho-spiritual aspects become dominant. Both crews pursue the 'folk', but the text holds out the promise of a different outcome for the second group of plunderers, even though they begin to perish, one by one, in the rapids of the interior landscape beyond the mission of Mariella. It becomes impossible to distinguish between the two crews. Harris's break with the conventions of the novel of manners ushers his readers into a universe where all actions seem synchronous. Similarly Donne and the 'I' narrator, who represent material and spiritual sides of the same human being (again this helps to make sense of the use of John Donne's name), become indistinguishable and their twin personality merges with the identities of the various other members of the crew, who include a pair of twins and other characters whose pasts are often umbilically linked as the result of past crimes. Conrad's fiction demonstrates a fascination with characters who are doubles of one another, as can be seen particularly in 'The Secret Sharer' and in the doppelganger pairing of Marlow and Kurtz in *Heart of Darkness*. Harris's characterization is, however, more radically unsettling, since while he employs similar strategies in constructing characters who are, usually inverted, doubles of one another, his method, as mentioned above, dismantles the very idea of Cartesian discrete subjectivity in favour of a view of character as malleable process, capable of infinite metamorphoses, as it is continuously reinvented by the exploratory language of the text. Harris commits himself uncompromisingly to an open, dialogic technique, which interrogates the very basis of character construction in the classic European novel, as the dead are resurrected, subject becomes object (Mariella is both woman and place) and belief in the primacy of individual selfhood is quite simply ignored.

So, while Conrad's practice reveals a profound scepticism about binary aesthetics, Harris's technique goes further in reshaping the novel genre to challenge habitual modes of perception. Using his own terms, one might say that *Palace of the Peacock* endeavours to 'unravel' the biases of 'sovereign institutions' that 'have once masqueraded themselves as monolithic absolutes or monolithic codes of behaviour in the Old Worlds from which they emigrated by choice or by force' (*Explorations* 135). For Harris, then, the New World site of the Guyanese interior — both forest and open savannah — is a tabula rasa that offers the possibility of emancipation from the fossilized forms of Old World cultures, whether they be European or African. He crosses the threshold on which he sees *Heart of Darkness* as poised, having started from a response to Conrad that is very different from Achebe's fundamentally hostile reaction. While *Arrow of God* locates itself in very different cultural territory to *Heart of Darkness*, even if its physical terrain has not moved a very great distance, *Palace of the Peacock* uses Conrad's novella as a launching pad for a more radically unsettling epistemological voyage, one which attempts to realize the positive potential of the heartland location and reverse the negative outcome of the initial colonial journey into the Americas.

Palace of the Peacock culminates in a mystical vision in which deaths usher in a resurrection and Christian symbol is fused with Amerindian myth. The surviving members of the crew arrive at the palace of the peacock, situated at 'the highest waterfall they had ever seen' (128)[26] and seek to clamber up the cliffs at its sides. Elsewhere Harris has used waterfall imagery to describe the rupture in the Caribbean and South American experience occasioned by the European 'discovery' of the Americas:

[T]he mainstream of the West Indies in my estimation possesses an enormous escarpment down which it falls, and I am thinking here of the European discovery of the New World and conquest of the ancient American civilizations which were themselves related by earlier and obscure levels of conquest.

(Harris, *Tradition* 30–1)

Despite his use of a metaphor of the fall, Harris does not present pre-Columbian civilization in terms of a prelapsarian wholeness. This passage stresses both the diversity of older American civilizations and their own internecine conflicts. Nevertheless Harris does go on to argue that for convenience one may view the 'divide pre-Columbian/post-Columbian' as the 'main distinction' (31). So one attractive reading of the ending of *Palace of the Peacock* suggests that arrival at the top of the cliff will facilitate a recuperation of the pre-Columbian Amerindian heritage of the Americas. However, this point is never reached, which seems to suggest that perfection is an aspiration not a viable attainment; and the novel stops short of the essentialism that would be involved in identifying its vision of psycho-spiritual integration with any particular cultural group. The harmony towards which it aspires is as available to the guilty colonizer as to the seemingly 'pure' ab-original. The overlapping identity of the characters makes them all equally culpable and equally innocent. All are scarred by past crimes; all can achieve redemption through psychic transformation. The mystical vision of community and integration symbolized by the palace of the peacock at the waterfall remains an aspiration rather than an attainment. The peacock image itself alludes to the final stage of the alchemical process, and, as Michael Gilkes explains, reflects Harris's interest in the *Corpus Hermeticus* and the esoteric side of the alchemical quest,[27] an aspect that had fascinated Jung, who wrote his doctoral thesis on alchemy. From this point of view the alchemical quest is for spiritual and psychological, not material, transformation and its ultimate goal is self-integration (Gilkes 36–7). Harris outlined his view of the alchemical process in a 1970 lecture:

[T]here are three stages, namely first of all the *nigredo* or blackness — sometimes called the *massa confusa* or unknown territory (not to be equated superficially with the colour *black*, but with an undiscovered realm), secondly the *albedo* or whiteness (again not to be equated superficially with the colour *white* since it means an inner perspective or illumination[,] the dawn of a new consciousness), thirdly *cauda pavonis* or the colours of the peacock, which may be equated with all the variable possibilities or colours of fulfilment we can never totally realise.

(Harris, *History* 20)

Elsewhere Harris has referred to 'the *nigredo* of Conrad' ('A Comment' 36) and the river journey in *Palace of the Peacock* begins in similar territory to *Heart of Darkness*, in an 'undiscovered realm' of the psyche. Gradually, though, through 'the dawn of a new consciousness', the crew progresses towards the goal of psychic fulfilment represented by the peacock colours. In aligning its journey

with the *Corpus Hermeticus*, Harris may seem to be following a European model
of influence, but in *Palace of the Peacock*, the alchemical symbolism has a
distinctive South American inflection, since he links the *cauda pavonis* with El
Dorado,[28] the legendary golden city in the Guyanese/Venezuelan interior that
symbolized the duality inherent in many early European constructions of the
'New World'. While the quest for material wealth embodied in the El Dorado
myth was all too real — and was central to the aspirations of adventurers such
as Sir Walter Raleigh — the European imagination also invented El Dorado as a
place of utopian promise, a vision that achieved classic expression in Voltaire's
Candide (1759). History suggests that such an idealistic construction of the
Americas was comparatively short-lived in the Caribbean and South America,
but Harris refuses the legacy of historical determinism, arguing that the
subjective imagination has the power to emancipate itself at any period in
history and from any set of circumstances. His El Dorado is two-sided,
mirroring the duality embodied in Donne and the dreaming 'I' narrator; it is an
'ambivalent creation of man's greed and of his spiritual aspirations' (Maes-
Jelinek, 'True Substance' 158). Harris recreates the Guyanese terrain of the
novel as an open field, in which alternative versions of human identity can be
explored. In such a mode of thinking, oppositional aesthetics become
meaningless and, if colonial pre-texts, such as *Heart of Darkness*, represent
authoritarian 'hegemonic premises', they too need to be reinvested with
significances that will release *their* potential for fulfilment. Just as Raleigh failed
to find El Dorado on his last voyage up the Orinoco and was beheaded in the
Tower of London on his return to England (Harris, *Selected Essays* 55), *Palace of
the Peacock* ends in material failure, with the remaining characters dying, but
simultaneously reborn into potential spiritual fulfilment. So Harris reinvests
one of the first and greatest European myths of the Americas with new
significance. As European conquistadores, Donne and his crew, who die many
deaths, fail to reach El Dorado, but on another level they do arrive at the
legendary golden city, achieving a sense of spiritual and psychic harmony
through a syncretist vision of an Arawak Christ that draws on natural elements
common to both settler and indigene cultures (see Maes-Jelinek, *Naked Design*
46–7; *Wilson Harris* 10). In *Heart of Darkness*, Kurtz, as a would-be bringer of
light to the 'dark continent', appears to stand on the threshold of such a vision,
but his approach remains locked within European biases and, from the
Harrisian point of view, both his ideology and his mental health collapse
because of his failure to engage in cross-cultural dialogue. Expressed in terms
of Harris's use of alchemical symbolism, Kurtz's gold is his obsession with
collecting ivory, a material fixation that can be related to the exoteric side of
the alchemist's quest: he fails to transform base metal into the *spiritual* gold
that is the end-product of the esoteric side of the quest. Reading Harris — both

his critique of Conrad and his own use of the voyage motif in *Palace of the Peacock* — serves, then, to open up new perspectives on Conrad, perspectives that suggest how close he came to transforming 'biases grounded in [the] homogeneous premises' of the colonial vision of his age, even if he finally leaves his readers on the 'threshold' of a new vision of consciousness.

IV

For some readers of Harris's fiction, his dismantling of socially constructed 'biases' remains unsatisfactory in one crucial respect. Despite its open, dialogic technique, *Palace of the Peacock* does little to unsettle the gender stereotypes engrained in classic Western heroic narrative. The novel remains a male quest story in which woman is the passive backcloth against which male adventuring is played out: at best Muse; at worst the object of reification and homogenization.[29] The insubstantial figure of Mariella is first transformed into a place and then conflated with the only other female character of note in the text, an older Arawak woman who accompanies the crew in the first stage of their journey beyond the mission of Mariella. To a certain extent, the novel fits neatly into the archetypal male quest pattern of what Joseph Campbell, in *The Hero with a Thousand Faces* (1949), calls the 'monomyth', which he views as a constant in human experience crossing continents, centuries and cultures. It is the story of the quest for the Grail, the life of the Buddha, Theseus and a 'thousand' other heroic narratives in which the protagonist is a male representative of his community, who absents himself from 'home' to undertake a quest.[30] Within Campbell's Jungian-derived pattern, woman, if present in the story, occupies the role of spectator or object of the quest. Often idealized, she is never allowed to be the prime mover of events.

Clearly such a view of traditional narrative is questionable and Campbell's occlusion of cultural differences glosses over major disparities in both the narratives he comfortably groups together and the cultures that have produced them. If, however, one had to extrapolate a general thesis about gender representation in the group of novels centred on interior journeys listed above, the dominant pattern would seem to be one of gender inversion. *Surfacing*[31] and *A Fringe of Leaves* replace the male protagonist with a female quester and in so doing offer a very direct challenge to the androcentrism of the 'monomyth' pattern. *Voss* and *Badlands* employ a dialectic method, which moves between male and female protagonists. Both novels are concerned with male voyages of exploration — White's novel takes its departure point from the final expedition of the German explorer, Ludwig Leichhardt, who perished in the Australian desert in 1848; Kroetsch writes about a fictional quest for dinosaur bones in the

Alberta Badlands in 1916 — and it would be uncustomary, though obviously not unprecedented historically, to have female members on such expeditions. However, White complements his account of Voss's expedition with the story of a woman, Laura Trevelyan, who stays home in Sydney, but travels with him in her imagination. Though they only meet a few times prior to the start of the expedition, she becomes his spiritual wife, communicating with him telepathically during the final throes of his interior journey and, after his death, functioning as the silent guardian of an alternative version of the meaning of his quest that is very different from the public myth. So she is a major protagonist in her own right. In addition to its third-person account of the 1916 archaeological expedition, *Badlands* employs a contemporary woman narrator, the daughter of William Dawe, the leader of the expedition. She foregrounds the roles accorded to men and women in traditional male quest narrative and indicates her own unsuitability to conform to the usual female stereotypes in an explicit reference to the *Odyssey*:[32]

> Why it was left to me to mediate the story I don't know: women are not supposed to have stories. We are supposed to sit at home, Penelopes to their wars and their sex. As my mother did. As I was doing.
> And yet I was not Penelope because no man wagered his way towards me.
>
> (*Badlands* 3)

In the 1972 'present' of the novel,[33] this narrator, Anna Dawe, abandons her Penelope role and her home on the shore of Georgian Bay, one of the earliest settled regions of Eastern Canada, and goes west to retrace her father's journey, while travelling in the opposite direction to that taken by his expedition. As she tells *her* story, it offers an obvious alternative to what she refers to as 'the western yarn those men were trying to tell each other' (45) and on several occasions her commentary on the expedition suggests the absurdity of male questing.

It is not difficult to relate both *Voss* and *Badlands* to *Heart of Darkness*. In addition to using the pattern of the interior journey, investigating a range of male mentalities and exploring settler/indigene binaries, both novels take their expeditions into mythic landscapes that at certain points are explicitly related to hell and the classical underworld, a trope that looms large in Conrad's novella, which includes hell/underworld intertexts from both Virgil and Dante (see Feder; and Evans). Additionally, as Carolyn Bliss puts it, White shares Conrad's 'radical distrust ... of the self as perceiving instrument and of language as expressive instrument'. After all, it is, she says, the source of 'much of Kurtz's dark power' (184–5).

Kroetsch, the most influential Canadian postmodernist novelist of his generation is, if anything, more sceptical of both the referential dimension of language and its authority in particular discursive situations. Although Canadian con-texts often seem to begin from a complicitous rather than an adversarial position in relation to the texts to which they write back, Kroetsch's fiction is centrally concerned with aspects of the exercise of hegemonic power that involve internal colonization, specifically the marginalization of Canadian regions remote from the centre of power in Ontario and one of the main concerns of *Badlands* is an exploration of the relationship between Canada's West and East. In this sense Anna Dawe's journey westwards is the journey of a 'settler' who, like Atwood's protagonist in *Surfacing*, discovers suppressed aspects of her personality through an encounter with Native Canada. She meets the Blackfoot woman, Anna Yellowbird, who has trailed her father's expedition during most of its river journey fifty-six years before, and this relationship opens up a dimension, not to be found in either Conrad or Harris.

Kroetsch speaks of having repeatedly 're-engaged myself with the influence' of Conrad[34] and his fascination with 'that beautiful binary of Marlow and Kurtz which is so hopeless that it is never going to become a completion' (Neuman and Wilson 19, 12). Unlike Harris he appears to prefer the unresolved opposition in such a binary, choosing to remain on the borderline where dialogue takes place rather than cross the threshold into a resolution of tensions in the harmony of a quasi-mystical fusion. He also discusses another binary pairing, which in Harris's terms suggest that Conrad is also a 'frontier' novelist where gender is concerned:

> Conrad creates a very male kind of world. But I now think of Conrad as having a silent center which is feminine; there's a kind of erotic play around that center. It's curious how silent and alive he can keep it. Of course, when we see it in *Heart of Darkness* it's the sharp contrast of the black woman and the Intended and I think, in my own writing, I kept the mother figures, especially, very silent at the center of the writing ...
>
> (Neuman and Wilson 22)

Stereotyped though Conrad's oppositional representation of the two women is,[35] they represent a duality that interrogates assumptions about what constitutes proper female behaviour, even though the action of the novella obviously reinforces the gender norms of its day.

The Intended is first 'seen' through the portrait of her that Kurtz entrusts to Marlow for safe keeping, a photograph which causes him to reflect: 'She struck me as beautiful − I mean she had a beautiful expression. I know that the sunlight can be made to lie, too, yet one felt that no manipulation of light and pose could have conveyed the delicate shade of truthfulness upon those features' (104). When he meets her, the dominant impression, despite her mourning apparel and dark eyes which seem to be expressive of her 'mature capacity for fidelity, for belief, for suffering', is of a fair, almost pallid, purity, according with the Neoplatonic belief that physical appearance expresses spiritual nature: 'This fair hair, this pale visage, this pure brow, seemed surrounded by an ashy halo from which the dark eyes looked out at me. Their glance was guileless, profound, confident, and trustful' (106). The irony inherent in this is that such fidelity and purity cannot be told the truth and, when Marlow assures her of Kurtz's devotion to her, lying about his dying words as well as what the heart of darkness has revealed about his character more generally, his collusion in the social conventions of his European world exposes inconsistencies in its codes of 'femininity'.

Conrad's construction of gender has been attacked by feminists for its stereotyping of both the Intended and her silent African complementary opposite,[36] but, as with his representation of male Africans, the text supports a reading that locates any such stereotyping within Marlow's consciousness. His narrative demonstrates a distinct scepticism about the contemporary gender socialization of women, even though – as an oral tale told to a group of men, on one of the prime sites of Empire, the river Thames – it remains inscribed within the conventions of male storytelling. Again, comparison with *Mansfield Park* is instructive. Mary Crawford and her brother temporarily destabilize the social order by staging theatricals within the walls of Mansfield Park, while the fundamentally passive Fanny Price remains the repository of moral propriety. However, the comic providence that presides over the novel leaves its readers in little doubt that order will be restored once Sir Thomas returns from Antigua and the Crawfords' carnivalesque transgressions never seriously threaten the status quo. Of course, Austen's gallery of heroines contains figures who are very different from Fanny – Elizabeth Bennet and Emma Woodhouse are both more animated and more proactive – but such protagonists are guilty of indiscretions and misjudgements that have to be remedied before the complications of the plot can be resolved and the social order reaffirmed. Conrad's 'threshold' novella moves in the opposite direction, interrogating rather than reinforcing the conventions of his day in the area of gender as well as the construction of racial alterity. Ostensibly the Intended is the social woman, to whom, despite her purity, the truth cannot be communicated: 'We must help them to stay in that beautiful world of their own, lest ours gets worse', says Marlow (69). However, his saying this opens up alternative possibilities; and Kroetsch questions the nature of the lie she is told, relating this to the text's distrust of 'coherent story' (Neuman and Wilson

12). Seen like this, Conrad is less a modernist novelist, undermining the shared social fictions of the late Victorian period, than an embryonic postmodernist. Kroetsch's comments on the silent feminine centre of Conrad's male world are particularly interesting in relation to both Kurtz's black mistress and the Intended, and the African woman also forms a binary paring with Kurtz himself. Marlow envisages Kurtz as pure voice; the woman is the ultimate silence in the novella, saying less even than the Intended. She is initially described as 'a wild and gorgeous apparition' (87) and the epithets Marlow uses to characterize her suggest a fusion of European discourses of African savagery and darkness and Oriental mystery and exoticism. She is the hole in the centre of the text, whose silence can be seen as a stark contrast not only to Kurtz's volubility, but also to the Intended's need for Marlow's verbal testimony to Kurtz's memory. Achebe's reading of *Heart of Darkness* very reasonably takes the view that its Africans are dehumanized, but this dehumanization needs to be located in two contexts: the text's replication of late Victorian racist stereotypes, which begin to be undermined by the inquiring Marlow's dawning realization of his affinity with what he deems 'savage'; and its refusal to speak for the non-Western 'Other'. Such silencing assumes another dimension if one relates it to more contemporary debates about the legitimacy of appropriating the voice of the 'Other'. Later in this book, this issue is considered in relation to another silent character, the tongueless figure of Friday in J. M. Coetzee's oblique response to *Robinson Crusoe*, *Foe* (1986). At this point, it is perhaps sufficient to recall that Marlow reveals the limitations of European discourse through his exposure of the hollowness that underlies Kurtz's oratorical gift:

> Kurtz discoursed. A voice! A voice! It rang deep to the very last. It survived his strength to hide in the magnificent folds of eloquence the barren darkness of his heart. (98)

and to suggest that, despite the text's Haggard-like sentimentalization of 'savage' African female power, it accords the 'wild and gorgeous apparition' a silent dignity that suggests she is the most knowing character in the text, a personification of the African mystery that challenges the logocentric European codes that have shaped Marlow, bringing him close to breakdown:

> She was savage and superb, wild-eyed and magnificent; there was something ominous and stately in her deliberate progress. And in the hush that had fallen suddenly upon the whole sorrowful land, the immense wilderness, the colossal body of the fecund and mysterious life seemed to look at her, pensive, as though it had been looking at the image of its own tenebrous and passionate soul. (87)

This said, the passage continues to be troubling. However, read as the product of its speaker's inability to establish a dialogue with African alterity and as an expression of his having reached the threshold where he realizes the necessity for such a dialogue, its emphasis on silence can be seen as ahead of its time in foregrounding the problems concerned with articulating subaltern experience.

Achebe emphasizes the 'racism' endemic in such failure to understand alterity and in *Arrow of God* marginalizes his Conrad references by shifting the focus to provide a minutely realized, contingent account of everyday African life during the colonial era. Harris offers reconciliation, albeit through a mystical vision of psychic harmony that pays little attention to gender difference and leaves problems of hegemonic exploitation to be solved by transformations in the subjective imagination. Kroetsch's *Badlands* is arguably more alert to the whole nexus of issues involved. His male crew is made up of an interesting assortment of masculine types, for example the Kurtz figure of the text, the expedition's leader, Dawe, has an interesting foil in the figure of the phallogecentric Westerner, Web, and the doppelgänger element becomes as significant as it is in *Heart of Darkness* or *Palace of the Peacock*, as circumstances bring about an exchange of roles between *these* two complementary opposites. I would, however, like to focus particularly on the representation of women in *Badlands*, since this arguably is the most distinctive aspect of its con-textual response to *Heart of Darkness*.[37]

Most of the third-person male quest story at the centre of *Badlands* is set on board the flatboat on which the men are travelling down Alberta's Red Deer River in their quest for dinosaur bones. However, at one point, in a section reminiscent of the episodes in the towns on the banks of the Mississippi in Twain's *Huckleberry Finn*, the crew go ashore in the town of Drumheller, in 1916 an emerging mining settlement in the heart of the Alberta Badlands.[38] Kroetsch exploits the town's name by following Conrad in explicitly relating its interior setting to hell and the classical underworld. As such it becomes a hell within an underworld: the Badlands are a subterranean landscape, a canyon where the mythical flatness of the prairies gives way to a prehistoric, quasi-subterranean landscape.[39] Anna Dawe comments that when a penitentiary was later built in Drumheller it was 'on the federal premise that hell should be constructed in hell' (76) and the episode involves a series of parallels with the Orpheus myth[40] that are continued in the remainder of the novel. Drumheller in 1916 is described by Anna Dawe as 'a version of civilization', a 'brand-new town', populated by 'displaced citizens from the feudal corners of Europe' (63). It is a frontier location, a town where a society is being forged, where women trying to achieve respectability compete with half a dozen brothels, and the members of the crew clamber ashore to find themselves in the middle of a temperance rally. It transpires that it is the one town in Alberta exempt from the prohibition legislation passed in the province a year before. Prior to their arrival, Web has fantasized about the erotic delights of a final fling in this 'toughest, wildest boom town east of the Great Divide' (60), while Dawe has looked forward to leaving it, and 'civilization' more generally, behind them. However, they no sooner arrive in Drumheller, than Web becomes caught up in the mood of the temperance rally and when a young woman in a long green dress emerges from its centrepiece, a coffin inscribed with the mispunctuated words 'JOHN BARLEYCORN DEAD. AS A DINOSAUR' (64), to deliver a diatribe against the evils of drink, gambling and prostitution, he is instantaneously 'seduced' and converted to her cause by the image of chastity she represents.

In a scene in a bar which follows, Web and Dawe have their fortunes told by a more conventionally seductive blonde woman, named America, whom Anna Dawe's frame narrative simply labels a 'whore':

> Web would divide his women into virgins and whores. And yet it was the virgin who seduced him into his fine mockery of virtue; and I suspect he never went to bed with his whore at all. (76)

The oppositional pairing of the two women, like the binary represented by Dawe and Web, is strongly redolent of Conrad, where 'the sharp contrast of the black woman and the Intended' and the 'hopeless' binary of Marlow and Kurtz both suggest irreconcilable, overlapping identities. As *Badlands* continues, the binary of Web and Dawe collapses further, as an injured Dawe is forced to forgo his megalomaniac obsession to find a perfect dinosaur, while receiving the sexual ministrations of Anna Yellowbird. In so doing, he vicariously fulfils Web's erotic fantasies, while a reluctant Web effectively becomes the leader of the expedition and, against the odds, a hero in the monomyth vein, when he is responsible for finding Dawe's 'perfect *specimen*' (207; italics in original).

This role reversal fairly neatly ironizes 'the western yarn those men were trying to tell each other' and, throughout, the conventions of the monomyth are disturbed by the text's negation of unitary signification, as well as binary thinking. Anna Dawe's comments emphasize the *narrative* aspects of macho behaviour and in the Drumheller episode she associates Web's stereotypical division of women into virgins and whores with male authorship: 'Total and absurd male that he was, he assumed, like a male author, an omniscience that was not ever his, a scheme that was never there' (76). Even as she makes these remarks, she is, of course, appropriating and refashioning the role of such an author, in her own piecemeal and epistemologically altogether more uncertain attempt to make sense of her father's legacy. Most interestingly of all, she undermines the oppositional pairing of the woman in green and America, suggesting not only that Web's binary classification is founded on faulty information, but also that the two women are sisters who have colluded to use the stereotypes for their own ends:

> And if the stories I heard fifty-six years later in Drumheller were true, then the two women were sisters, and the blonde was not really named America — nor for that matter was she blonde — and the dark-haired woman in green had a name I didn't bother to write down and so lost from memory. But they were sisters and made a good deal of money between them and lived together and never married; and when the penitentiary was built ... it was those two sisters who established inside the penitentiary a library and a lounge. (76)

The two women may remain silent, but the text seems to step across the threshold on which *Heart of Darkness* stands, especially since Anna Dawe's comments on the 1916 action and her own 1972 narrative offer the possibility of an 'escape from paternalism on models of influence' (Neuman in Neuman and Wilson 21). The relationship between the two narratives is never clearly fixed, but Anna's later angle of vision allows her to comment on the 1916 action in a way that its undramatized narrator can never emulate. She literally has the last word in the novel and throughout is always in the privileged situation of being able to offer retrospective comment.

The importance of sisterhood in *Badlands* is not confined to the Drumheller episode. Anna Dawe's relationship with Anna Yellowbird in the contemporary action is a more fully developed instance, even if the age gap between the two women initially suggests a mother–daughter relationship. Their coming together erodes the distance between the generations, between the two narratives and between settled East and indigene West. Unlike the 'binary of Marlow and Kurtz which is so hopeless that it is never going to become a completion', there is a genuine rapprochement across cultures, generations and regions — no easy resolution of difference, but a few shared moments of sisterhood in the spirit of the second twentieth-century wave of feminism. Kroetsch has said that his treatment of the quest motif was influenced by feminism, pointing out that this engendered a 're-examination of the very notion of the quest story. We realize most of us aren't on quests; male *literature* said we were on quests' (Neuman and Wilson 34; italics in original). In an obvious sense Anna Dawe *is* a quester: she not only 'mediate[s] the story'; she also deserts her role as a waiting Penelope, to become a travelling Odysseus who enjoys adventures in her own right. Comparing this with *Heart of Darkness*, one might say that she plays Marlow to her father's Kurtz, with her mother occupying the role of the 'silent center' who has stayed home, reading her husband's field notes,[41] the central image of male discourse in the text. Anna's journey west enables her to exorcize the influence that her father's myth – an image of paternal power – has had on her life. When she meets Anna Yellowbird, it is as if the Intended has met the African 'apparition', breaching the barrier between 'civilization' and the mysterious interior world of the 'Other'. This in itself could represent a parodic reworking of the quest motif, but the union of the two Annas becomes more overtly parodic as they appropriate male roles, particularly that of Orpheus, journeying in the opposite direction to the men in the 1916 story, back towards the source of the river. Web has dreamed of reaching this point, even though the expedition has been travelling further and further away from it in its movement *down*river. The women who have been drinking heavily, and in so doing usurping one form of behaviour conventionally ascribed to men in the novel, arrive at the lake at the source of the river in an irreverential mood which prompts them to discard the emblems of male narrative they are carrying with them, literally and metaphorically. Anna Yellowbird has been carrying photographs of the expedition's men; Anna Dawe her father's last book of field notes. Both are now thrown away.

This climax involves a coming together of the two women and an interchange of roles, but it is not a female equivalent of the vision of harmony attained by the resurrected male crew members in *Palace of the Peacock*. Like Harris's waterfall, the lake is itself an ambiguous source, since it is fed by a glacier, implying the impossibility of arriving at an originary moment.[42] Here, though, any resemblance ends, since *Badlands* demonstrates a concern with gender and other forms of socialization that is absent from the more abstract metaphysical discourse of *Palace of the Peacock*. Kroetsch's novel ends with the two women walking away from this end-point of the quest, singing a bawdy song:

> We sang together, that awful song about rolling over in the clover, because that was the only song we both remembered and could sing long enough to see us through. We walked out of there hand in hand, arm in arm, holding each other. We walked all the way out. And we did not once look back, not once ever. (270)

Eurydice appears to have taken over the role of Orpheus, but, with neither woman looking back, their drunken odyssey culminates in a casual disregard of the type of behaviour ascribed to the monomyth pattern. Their rejection of the androcentric metanarratives represented by the photographs and the field notes has been prompted by an image of the futility of male behaviour. They see a grizzly bear that has strayed into tourist campgrounds being carried north by a helicopter, from which it dangles in a nylon net. It is an image of stranded male sexuality that reduces them to uncontrollable laughter:

> But we laughed; we could see now the grizzly's crotch; he was suspended upright by his head and upper limbs in the tangled net; his hind legs swung free in the air, galloped straight at us in the empty air, his sharp claws scratching for the gone earth, his testicles following crazily after.
>
> He was running in the air, straight overhead, so comically human and male that Anna fell backwards, laughing, off the fallen tree; Anna lay fallen, her skirt up, her legs spread, her body shaking with laughter; and I was laughing too, unheard and laughing, against the thudding passage of the yellow machine ...
>
> Anna raised up her photographs .... She flung them up at the bear's balls. (268–9)

What does seem clear — and Anna Dawe's role as narrator has staged this throughout — is that the two characters have emancipated themselves from a paternal model of influence: and in Anna Dawe's case this is achieved through her journey west and her meeting Anna Yellowbird. Fifty-six years earlier Anna Yellowbird has helped William Dawe discover areas of himself he did not know existed. Now she performs the same function for his daughter, while also, it would seem, liberating herself from the shadow that her encounter with the expedition has cast over her life. So the exchange that takes place operates in both directions and Kroetsch avoids a model that simply sees the 'indigene' West educating the 'civilized' East. Nevertheless, the main movement *is* in this direction and it involves collapsing a number of other binary oppositions, among them those of writer and reader and book and storytelling. Elsewhere Kroetsch has spoken of storytelling as male and books as female, with a particular emphasis on the extent to which women occupy the role of passive readers,[43] and to some extent *Badlands* reflects this binary, at least insofar as it represents Web, a walking and talking personification of the popular Alberta tradition of the tall tale, as the main oral storyteller among the characters. However, in its own narrative practice the novel erodes this distinction, too, as Anna, the waiting Penelope, becomes the narrator of a Western story, which moves between mythic seriousness and comic bawdy. Finally, Kroetsch may seem to be engaging in a reversal of one of the most famous mythic accounts of an underworld descent (a story which could be seen as an archaeological layer that lays buried in the text of *Heart of Darkness*), as the two Annas walk away from the source of the river, as Eurydices who could easily assume the role of Orpheus, but eschew this by refusing to 'look back'. The pattern is, however, more complicated than this suggests: Kroetsch's archaeological approach to the issue of influence not only repudiates the notion of an originary moment; it also suggests the impossibility of locating texts in terms of single intertexts. One of the novel's two epigraphs is taken from a Nez Percé Coyote story:

> But suddenly a joyous impulsion seized him: the joy of having his wife again overwhelmed him. He jumped to his feet and rushed over to embrace her. His wife cried out, 'Stop! Stop! Coyote! Do not touch me. Stop!' Her warning had no effect. Coyote rushed over to his wife and just as he touched her body she vanished. She disappeared – returned to the shadowland. ([vi])

The reader who resists the 'joyous impulsion' to try to arrive at the kind of Casaubon-like key to all mythologies that Joseph Campbell's account of heroic narrative proposes is, then, left with at least two provenances for Kroetsch's reworking of the 'don't look back' motif; and somewhere amid these competing discourses lurks the influence of Conrad's use of the classical hero's descent into the underworld as a structure for investigating the ethics of late Victorian European colonialism. Kroetsch's varied repertory of intertexts makes it difficult to view *Badlands* as engaging in either a complicitous or an adversarial reading of influence. The *Western* Canadian cultural agendas that are central to his work operate against the possibility of a filiative relationship with the 'centre', whether it is located in England or Ontario, but he still displays an affiliative identification with canonical authors ranging from Homer to Conrad. In *Badlands* his regional concerns are interlinked with a revisionist approach to Western codes of manhood, but like Conrad he remains a relativist, particularly because his complex use of focalization frustrates interpretations that seek closure. The two stories of *Badlands* never intersect; although Anna Dawe has the last word, her narrative never connects directly with the third-person account of the male expedition and so this, at least in one sense, is left unchallenged, as a viable story in its own right.

Kroetsch's theoretical writing demonstrates a fascination with binary aesthetics and the need to evolve a critical practice and fictional strategies that will initiate movement beyond them. In a discussion of models of Canadian culture, which appeared shortly after *Badlands*, he spoke of the extent to which constructions of the nation's identity had been dominated by binary theorizing:

> The double hook. The total ambiguity that is so essentially Canadian: be it in terms of two solitudes, the bush garden, Jungian opposites, or the raw and the cooked binary structures of Lévi-Strauss. Behind the

multiplying theories of Canadian literature is always the pattern of
equally matched opposites.

Coyote:	God
Self:	Community
Energy:	Stasis

   The balance, whatever the specifics, is always so equal that one
wonders how paradigm can possibly issue into story.[44]

(Kroetsch and Bessai 215)

The text as a whole could be said to involve two solitudes – in its use of the
parallel lines of the 1916 and 1972 narratives that never meet – and yet
through their juxtaposition it offers its *readers* the possibility of making
paradigm issue into story, with possible interpretations including the view that
it is a feminist novel,[45] that the male quest still bulks largest or that the
juxtaposition predicates the possibility of some kind of androgynous fusion
that moves beyond narratives of Western machismo and 'civilized' Eastern
femininity. In any case, Kroetsch's revisiting the wilderness terrain that had
made *Heart of Darkness* such a disturbing novel three-quarters of a century
earlier, offers a site for moving beyond the kind of biases that Wilson Harris
describes and, arguably, he goes considerably further than either Conrad or
Harris in his reinscription of gender. So, like Naipaul and Ngugi, Kroetsch finds
Conrad a precursor, writing from an ambivalent authorial position, who
provides a touchstone for many of the issues he explores in his own fiction. His
response to Conrad is clearly very different to that of Achebe and has more in
common with Harris's view of Conrad as a novelist who stands on the
threshold of transforming 'biases grounded in homogeneous premises', but
unlike Harris he investigates the potential that is implicit, but undeveloped, in
Conrad's binary of the two silent women.
   However, from another point of view, his narrative method in *Badlands*
seems to engage with a set of dualities that are very similar to the binaries for
which Achebe criticizes Conrad. These include dichotomies mentioned in his
list of Canada's 'equally matched opposites' and the oppositions of East and
West, female and male, settlement and wilderness and written and oral
discourse. While these are particularly Canadian dualities, it is not difficult to
relate them to the kind of representation for which Achebe takes Conrad to
task and to see the opposition between civilization and wilderness as central.
Arguably, however, *Badlands* goes beyond the other con-texts discussed in this
chapter in dismantling such shadow lines, particularly in its challenge to the
gender implications of heroic mythologizing. Marlow tells his tale to a
company of men; Kroetsch's two narratives have no obvious interlocutors, but

taken together seem to be promoting the idea of an androgynous reading community. Yet, in varying ways, each of the writers discussed in this chapter offers possibilities for dismantling polarized constructions of alterity; and finally such responses once again bring one back to Conrad and the proposition that *Heart of Darkness* itself opens up the possibility of transcending racial and other binaries. Postcolonial con-texts not only offer different perspectives in themselves, but also for readers who, like Anna Dawe, mediate the story, release new meanings within their supposed pre-texts. So the very notion of the stable text is interrogated and, while this may be a cliché of reader response criticism, it is one which gathers added momentum when supported by the work of creative writers whose response puts flesh on the barebones of such theorizing.

Notes

1. See Knowles and Moore 299–301 for a summary of the critical response to issues of race and racism in Conrad.
2. E.g. Leavis's canonizing him, along with George Eliot and Henry James, as one of the three central figures in his 'great tradition'.
3. Although the novella was first published in book form in *Youth: A Narrative and Two Other Stories*, in 1902, it had previously been serialized in *Blackwood's Magazine* from February to April 1899 and so its first appearance was in the Victorian era. It is based on Conrad's own experiences in the Congo in 1890. See 'The Congo Diary' and 'Up-river Book' (*Congo Diary* 7–16 and 17–38).
4. A term that began to be widely used a little later, in the 1840s, usually in relation to a broader debate about different areas of society in the works of novelists such as Benjamin Disraeli and Elizabeth Gaskell (Lodge 216–17).
5. In a discussion that links Austen's and Jean Rhys's respective treatments of 'the Great House', Selma James refers to Sir Thomas as a 'well-mannered tyrant' who has to deal with two parallel rebellions, that of two of his daughters at home and that of his slaves in Antigua, arguing that Austen may not be making a 'comparison', but is certainly forging a 'connection' (James, S. 41).
6. E.g. Said uses it for the epigraph to *Culture and Imperialism* ([vii]).
7. Taken from 'The Second Coming'.
8. Naipaul attended Queen's Royal College, Port of Spain.
9. Originally published as *Gurudeva and Other Indian Tales*; reissued, with some additional stories added and a Preface by V. S. Naipaul, in 1976 (Naipaul, S.).
10. For a slightly fuller exposition of these correspondences, see my discussion in Thieme, *Web* (110).
11. Ngugi wrote an extended essay on Conrad, while an undergraduate at Makerere University College in Uganda (Williams 6).
12. Ngugi also expresses his admiration for Naipaul in this interview (129), though he does not make an explicit link between Naipaul and Conrad. Cf. his comments on *The Mimic Men* in *Homecoming* (40–1, 90–4).

13. The politics of language usage have loomed large in Ngugi's later work, see particularly *Decolonizing the Mind: The Politics of Language in African Literature* (1986). Since *Devil on the Cross* (1980; English translation 1982) Ngugi has published his novels in Gikuyu, with English translations following.
14. See Robson 125–6; Obumselu; and Sarvan.
15. See Ogude *passim*.
16. James Ogude takes the view that 'While in the earlier novels Ngugi expresses the possibilities of a syncretic culture, in the later novels he displays utter hostility towards anything deemed Western' (13).
17. I have preferred the term 'Guyanese' rather than 'British Guianese', which was current usage at the time of the novel's publication – six years before British Guiana achieved independence in 1966 – since Harris predicates a timeless cosmos and emphasizes future possibilities.
18. Harris subsequently entitled his fifth novel *Heartland* (1964).
19. The novel is generally considered to be based on the experience of Eliza Fraser, who was shipwrecked off the Queensland coast in 1836. Schaffer considers various versions of her story, including *A Fringe of Leaves*, Sidney Nolan's 'Mrs Fraser' series of paintings and the 1976 film *Eliza Fraser*, for which David Williamson wrote the script.
20. See Maes-Jelinek ('Fictional Breakthrough'), who views *A Fringe of Leaves* through the prism of Harris's reading of Conrad, for a discussion of this aspect of the novel.
21. As the text points out (85), his name is German and there is emphasis on the fact that 'all Europe [has] contributed to the making of Kurtz' (71). On Schopenhauer's influence on Conrad, see Knowles and Moore 327–8.
22. Guyana's 'Portuguese' population is usually regarded as distinct from those descended from other European settlers. Most of the country's 'Portuguese' came, as indentured labourers, from Madeira.
23. The phrase is borrowed not only from the title of Conrad's story, 'The Shadow-Line' (1917), where the line in question divides maturity from youth, but also from Amitav Ghosh's novel *The Shadow Lines* (1988), which, while alluding to Conrad, engages in a more thorough-going dismantling of the boundary lines that construct cultural difference. Its most obvious reference-point for this is the politically constructed border that has partitioned Bengal, but as I have argued elsewhere, ' "Shadow lines" are ... far more than just the borders constructed by politicians. They are also the lines of demarcation that separate colonized and colonizer, present and past, self and image. Ultimately they are the signifying acts that construct notions of discrete identity' (Thieme, 'Passages' 65–6). See also Chapter 4 below.
24. See Knowles and Moore (245) for a summary of possible Nietzschean readings of Conrad.
25. Carolyn Bliss points out that White did not admit to having read much Nietzsche. Her footnote on the historical and philosophical sources of *Voss* lists a number of discussions of Nietzsche's influence on the novel, along with references to essays which detect the influence of Hegel, Schopenhauer and Kierkegaard (215–16).
26. Suggestive of Kaieteur Falls, though not named as such.
27. Unlike the exoteric side of the quest, which was concerned with the transmutation of base metal into gold, the esoteric side had a spiritual goal:

that of securing a perfect union with God for sinful humanity and Jung interpreted this in terms of psychic transformation. See Gilkes 46.

28. Cf. Conrad's ironic use of the term in the Eldorado Exploring Expedition of *Heart of Darkness*.

29. Harris's 'new' 1998 Preface to the novel stresses that Mariella 'embodies a plurality of women', but nonetheless associates this 'embodiment' with 'a womb of potentialities' (*Selected Essays* 56) rather than viewing it as a potentiality in itself.

30. Cf. Frye, *Anatomy* 186–206, for a variant, but similar, archetypal account of the heroic quest.

31. See Arnold and Cathy Davidson for a discussion which relates the novel to Frye's account of the archetypal quest plot in *Anatomy of Criticism*; and B. King for a discussion which also mentions Frye in locating *Surfacing* as a mythic novel 'consciously meant as part of a national literary tradition' ('Margaret Atwood's *Surfacing*' 30).

32. Kroetsch's earlier novel, *The Studhorse Man* (1969) is a comic odyssey, in which several episodes are based on Homer's epic.

33. 1972 is the year in which *Surfacing* is set and *Badlands* displays very obvious similarities with Atwood's novel, not simply because of its female quest elements. Atwood's unnamed protagonist and Anna Dawe both search for themselves through a quest for a drowned father. See my article 'Beyond History' for a fuller discussion.

34. He acknowledges a specific debt to *Heart of Darkness* in *Badlands*: 'Yes, I had *Heart of Darkness* in mind when I wrote *Badlands*. ... The river journey that fascinated me from the time when I went up North to work on the Mackenzie River – where I was 21 and fresh out of university. Conrad's work still haunts me.' Personal communication, 10 October 2000.

35. E.g. Johanna H. Smith, in '"Too Beautiful Altogether": Ideologies of Gender and Empire in *Heart of Darkness*' (in Murfin, ed. 169–84), argues that Marlow's description of Kurtz's African mistress 'serves both masculinist and imperialist ends' (174) and that his description of the Intended is equally commodified.

36. See Knowles and Moore (109–10) for a summary of such responses.

37. For a fuller account of other aspects of the text, including the Dawe/Web binary, see my discussion in 'Beyond History'.

38. Though the town's name seems heavily symbolic, it is real enough. Today it is the home of the Royal Tyrrell Museum of Palaeontology, which has seen an upsurge in visitor numbers since the appearance of Steven Spielberg's *Jurassic Park* films.

39. Cf. Kroetsch's travel book *Alberta* (1968): 'The approach – I should say, descent – into Drumheller is an appropriate one for dinosaur country. The road leads down from the green wheatfields into an eroded sun-baked valley that is out of another epoch: that epoch lasting 130 million years during which those extinct reptiles, the dinosaurs, ruled the earth' (80).

40. On Kroetsch's use of the Orpheus myth, see Thomas 88–94.

41. 'Field Notes' was the working title for *Badlands*. It subsequently became the title for Kroetsch's collected long poems.

42. Cf. Kroetsch's comments in Neuman and Wilson 9–10.

43. In 'The Fear of Women in Prairie Fiction: An Erotics of Space', *Lovely Treachery* 73.

44.   *The Double Hook* is the title of Sheila Watson's classic 1959 symbolist novel, set
      in the interior of British Columbia. Kroetsch follows her in making extensive use
      of the figure of Coyote, a trickster/creator in Blackfoot and other Western First
      Nations mythologies. In Hugh MacLennan's 1945 novel, *Two Solitudes*, the
      'solitudes' in question are both personal and the 'equally matched opposites' of
      Anglophone and Francophone Canada. *The Bush Garden* is the title of Northrop
      Frye's 1971 collection of essays on the 'Canadian imagination'. The phrase refers
      to the 'ambiguous' situation of settler Canada.

45.   E.g. Aritha van Herk's view that *'Badlands* is one of Canada's most important
      feminist novels' (quoted in Ricou 123).

3

'On England's Desert Island cast away': protean Crusoes, exiled Fridays

Robinson Crusoe is virtually unthinkable without the colonizing mission that permits him to create a new world of his own in the distant reaches of the African, Pacific, and Atlantic wilderness.

(Edward Said, *Culture and Imperialism* 75)

My Crusoe, then, is Adam, Christopher Columbus, God, a missionary, a beachcomber, and his interpreter, Daniel Defoe. He is Adam because he is the first inhabitant of a second paradise. He is Columbus because he has discovered this new world, by accident, by fatality. He is God because he teaches himself to control his creation, he rules the world he has made, and also, because he is to Friday, a white concept of Godhead. He is a missionary because he instructs Friday in the uses of religion; he has a passion for conversion. He is a beachcomber because I have imagined him as one of those figures of adolescent literature, some derelict out of Conrad or Stevenson, or Marryat. In the poem [Walcott's 'Crusoe's Journal'] he also becomes, in one line, Ben Gunn, the half-crazy pirate who guards Treasure Island, and finally, he is also Daniel Defoe, because the journal of Crusoe, which is Defoe's journal, is written in prose, not in poetry, and our literature, the pioneers of our public literature have expressed themselves in prose in this new world.

(Derek Walcott in Hamner, *Critical Perspectives* 35–66)

I

According to one view, Defoe's *Robinson Crusoe* (1719) is the ur-text of the English novel. Its Preface claims that it is 'a just history of fact' (25) and its method of carefully accumulating a welter of circumstantial details in a linear narrative sequence anticipates the 'realism' that is the dominant mode of the English novel of the next two centuries. Such 'realism' is, of course, a discursive formation, a mode offering the illusion of a transparent representation of a social world,[1] while obscuring the fact that the social reality it purports to represent is linguistically constructed. Nevertheless *Crusoe*'s position at the headwaters of the English realist tradition makes it an archetypal narrative for postcolonial texts to measure themselves against – or contest. If Tiffin is right to suggest that postcolonial con-texts are not 'simply "writing back" to an English canonical text, but to the whole of the discursive field within which such a text operated and continues to operate in post-colonial worlds' (23), then responding to *Robinson Crusoe* can be seen as a particularly appropriate strategy for this metonymic encounter, and less so because of Defoe's novel's concern with colonization in the New World, than because of its generic significance as the archetypal English 'realist' novel.

In non-European societies, where fabulation has loomed larger in traditional storytelling modes and where perceptions of what constitutes social norms have tended to be less settled, the consensus in favour of realism has been decidedly shakier than it has been in Europe. Wilson Harris links 'the rise of the novel in its conventional and historical mould ... in Europe with states of society which were involved in consolidating their class and other vested interests' and more generally with a form of realism which closes down possibilities for 'freedom', even if it offers 'an apparent range of choices' and consequently argues for a more open form in which ' "dialogue" or "dialectic" ' replaces 'elements of "persuasion" ' (*Tradition* 29). While the vast majority of postcolonial writers have not discussed the social implications of the realist novel's ascendancy and the need to find alternative modes this explicitly, nevertheless their practice frequently displays a similar unease concerning the repercussions of using the genre in non-Western contexts. Arguably this disquiet relates to the congruence between the rise of the novel and the emergence of forms of economic individualism that played a key role in the development of colonialism. In his classic study *The Rise of the Novel* (1957), Ian Watt identifies 'the rise of modern industrial capitalism and the spread of Protestantism, especially in its Calvinist or Puritan forms' as the two 'historical causes ... of supreme importance' (63, 62) in the growth of the individualist ethic that characterizes modern society, viewing Defoe's work as offering a 'unique demonstration of the connexion between individualism in its many forms and the rise of the novel' (65). *Robinson Crusoe* is the fictional manifesto of the new mercantilist culture of the late seventeenth and early eighteenth centuries, a text which not only thematizes the capitalist ethic, but also embodies it within the verisimilitude of its Puritan fictional practice. So it is a materialist text in two senses: a work in which the profit motive is the driving force of the hero *and* a text in which everything can be assigned a material value, in terms of its weight, worth or magnitude. As such, and despite its immersion in circumstantial details, it can be read allegorically as a paradigmatic account of early English imperialism and its colonial motifs have, not surprisingly, received considerable attention from postcolonial commentators. At the same time counter-discursive responses to Defoe's novel have frequently pursued other agendas and so, before considering ways in which *Crusoe* has been re-read and re-written, I should like to outline some of the ways in which the novel has been received in the centuries since its original publication.

Paradoxically, despite its apparent simplism, its focus on concrete particulars and the illusion of transposed realism that it offers, *Robinson Crusoe* is a text that has attracted a multiplicity of, often contradictory, readings. On one level it is 'a novel of romantic adventure' (Ross in Defoe, *Crusoe* 7); from another point of view it is a children's adventure story that has been successfully adapted into a pantomime. For political economists such as Karl Marx, Crusoe is an archetype of *homo economicus*, a man for whom everything can be rendered in terms of double-entry book-keeping (Watt 65ff.; Rogers 166–8). For G. A. Starr, the novel is a different kind of Puritan fable: a late example of the popular seventeenth-century genre of the spiritual autobiography, a kind of secular version of Bunyan's *Grace Abounding to the Chief of Sinners* (1666), in which the central defining moment of the story is the hero's conversion. Related to this is the popular eighteenth-century view of the castaway predicament as one of spiritual abandonment: Dr Johnson defined a castaway as 'a person lost or abandoned by Providence'[2] and the spiritual dimension would doubtless have been a significant aspect of *Crusoe*'s appeal to its contemporary readers. For many general readers of all periods, the main attraction of the novel arises from a range of other responses to the desert island setting. For some, such a setting offers escapism, though *Robinson Crusoe* may not be the best example of this aspect of the island novel.[3] For others the fascination of the setting emerges from the challenge to consider 'how on earth we would survive, if all the ready-made supports of a civilized life were suddenly to be swept away' (Moody 11) and on this level the novel is one of the modern world's first great do-it-yourself manuals, as it documents how a novice in manual labour gradually acquires practical skills and argues that 'every man may be in time master of every mechanick art' (85). The invitation to project oneself into a solitary extra-social environment also offers the possibility of playing the role of Adam – or, in the case of a novelist such as Jane Gardam, Eve[4] – in Eden, creating the world over again, a reading that has particular resonance with regard to the New World milieu of the text. And, with the majority of classic desert island stories, from *The Tempest* onwards, having been written by British authors,[5] there is also the appealing thesis that the island may represent a British (in some cases a specifically English) microcosm. Passages that support such a reading of *Crusoe* include an episode in which the protagonist sees himself as eroding class barriers in a fashion that would be beyond his wildest dreams in England. Enacting what can be read as a wish-fulfilment fantasy on his creator's part, he becomes the self-styled 'king and lord' of his island, assuming an aristocratic 'right of possession' and thinking 'if I could convey it, I might have it in inheritance as compleatly as any lord of a mannor [sic] in England' (114). These, then, are some of the numerous ways in which *Robinson Crusoe* has been received and read.

II

Crusoe is shipwrecked in the Caribbean and this chapter is primarily concerned with Caribbean responses to the novel, though Australian and South African *Crusoe* derivatives are also considered. *Robinson Crusoe* has a particular significance for the Caribbean, since, while the man on whom Crusoe is generally considered to have been based, Alexander Selkirk,[6] was cast ashore at his own request in a far less hospitable climate, on one of the Juan Fernandez islands off the coast of Chile, the geographical coordinates given for the island in Defoe's novel clearly locate it within the Caribbean region and it has been popularly identified with Tobago.[7] Given that the text can be read as a blueprint for colonialism, since Crusoe effectively develops an embryonic plantation economy, staffed by a one-man subservient labour force in the person of Man Friday, albeit without the benefit of a market in which to sell his produce, one might expect Caribbean responses to *Robinson Crusoe* to be particularly defined by the colonial encounter, with Crusoe being constructed as arch-colonizer and Friday as colonized Caribbean subject. Equally, one might expect postcolonial responses of the text to accord Friday centrality. However, two of the region's leading writers have focused, not on Friday, but Crusoe as a seminal figure for the Caribbean imagination. In a 1967 essay, 'Columbus and Crusoe', V. S. Naipaul relates 'the heroic legend of Columbus' to the 'enduring human fantasy' of an 'untouched, complete world', subsequently to be persistently pursued in the quest for El Dorado (*Overcrowded Barracoon* 206); and likens the desire to 'imaginatively possess the whole' (203) to the vision developed in Defoe's novel:

> *Robinson Crusoe*, in its essential myth-making middle part, is an aspect of the same fantasy. It is a monologue; it is all in the mind. It is the dream of being the first man in the world, of watching the first crop grow. Not

only a dream of innocence: it is the dream of being suddenly, just as one is, in unquestionable control of the physical world, of possessing 'the first gun that had been fired there since the creation of the world'. It is the dream of total power. (206)

Derek Walcott's response to Crusoe is summed up in a 1965 talk, 'The Figure of Crusoe', from which the second epigraph to this chapter is taken. His main emphasis is on the Protean mutability of the Crusoe figure, seen as a chameleon who takes on a proliferation of roles in changing situations. However, within these multiple stagings of self, Walcott lays particular stress on the figure as a *Caribbean* personification of the Protestant work ethic, emphasizing his ability as a carpenter and particularly associating this with Methodist decency.[8] The distance between this version of Crusoe and Defoe's 'original' is in one sense slight: Walcott's Crusoe shares many characteristics with his Puritan antecedent and in poems about the figure published in his 1965 collection, *The Castaway*, he again places the emphasis on his capacity as a utilitarian craftsman, fashioning a culture from primal raw materials. Thus, in 'Crusoe's Journal', a poem to which 'The Figure of Crusoe' is a companion piece, Crusoe is an Adamic carpenter, writing journals that 'assume a household use', enabling their Caribbean readers 'to shape from them, where nothing was/the language of a race' (*Castaway* 52). Walcott sees Defoe's novel as 'our first book, our profane Genesis' (51), claiming Crusoe as a Caribbean precursor, whose environment demands an art quite different from 'the hermetic skill, that from earth's clays shapes something without use' (52). Another *Castaway* poem, 'Crusoe's Island', also emphasizes the figure's pragmatism, but views the castaway craftsman as building an Eden that combines a religious impulse with the practical necessities of establishing a settlement. Its final section asserts that 'Art is profane and pagan' (57), but although the statement is general, the context gives it a particular resonance for the Caribbean and the poem suggests that the fusion of sacred and secular offers a model for an artistic practice appropriate to the region.

One might be tempted to see Walcott's reworking of Defoe's archetype as simply filiative. He chooses to focus on Crusoe rather than Friday and recreates him as a castaway artist who espouses many of the Puritan virtues of Defoe's 'original'. There is, however, a crucial difference in that Walcott's Crusoe is a *Caribbean* Adam, who cannot allow himself to indulge in the non-utilitarian aestheticism ('the hermetic skill ... without use') that characterizes artistic practice 'elsewhere'. Walcott's Crusoe is creolized to suit a Caribbean context and yet curiously has more affinities with Defoe's shipwrecked mariner than many other reconstructions of the figure. Arguably, this has the effect of redirecting readers back to aspects of *Robinson Crusoe*, which, despite its reputation as an originary novel for the English tradition, make it *untypical* of the genre: as an unashamedly capitalist novel, it lacks much of the middle-class gentility of many later 'realist' novels, where money, and in many cases colonial mercantilism, are the unspoken imperatives that generate the plot.

III

In *Pantomime* (1980),[9] a play written more than a decade after the Crusoe poems of *The Castaway*,[10] Walcott ostensibly offers a different perspective on both Crusoe and Friday, who compete for both dramatic and social primacy in a comic two-hander that explores the prospects for an exchange of roles in the post-independence Caribbean. Written in a similar comic vein to Sam Selvon's slightly earlier novel *Moses Ascending* (1975), which also disturbs former colonial hierarchies through a playful repositioning of Friday and Crusoe, the play is at one and the same time a piece of light comic fun that draws on both English and Caribbean popular performance traditions and a complex investigation of the possibilities for restaging identity in society at large.

Pantomime is about the erosion of the colonizer–colonized divide, but far from dramatizing a situation of postcolonial reversal, the play has its Crusoe and Friday swapping roles in a fluid theatrical exchange that dismantles the very idea of fixed positioning.[11] Harry, a retired English music-hall performer, decides to stage a pantomime performance of *Robinson Crusoe* in the Tobago guest house that he now owns and the action turns upon his attempts to get his Man Friday, Jackson, a Trinidadian ex-calypsonian, to take part. In the course of their exchanges, both characters act out an extended repertory of roles. Jackson insists on his right to be Crusoe as well as Friday, but also spends time subversively reconfiguring Friday as a stereotypically compliant Uncle Tom. Meanwhile the variations on the Crusoe figure are almost as diverse as those in Walcott's 'Figure of Crusoe' essay and include those of Odyssean wanderer, Adamic discoverer and pragmatic Creole. Jackson remembers having heard an auditioning actor claim that he is capable of doing 'all kind of acting, classical acting, *Creole* acting' (131) and, ridiculous though he finds this, *Pantomime* sustains a contrast between these two modes of acting throughout, while moving along a continuum that suggests they are never completely discrete. Just as the Crusoe poems present the solitary castaway as a Creole artist, the play's method fuses hitherto separate forms (pantomime and calypso among them) to create a new artistic practice and once again, though the comic mode is a world away from the meditative seriousness of the poems, the final emphasis is on a creolization of the *Robinson Crusoe* pre-text, in which *both* characters share. So, while Walcott has sometimes been seen as drawing his main inspiration from European models – and in one sense this is a legitimate view here, since he does employ an English 'original' as a starting-point – the end-result is a distinctively Caribbean play that works so many variations on its English intertext that it becomes futile to try to locate it as either filiative or oppositional. What emerges most forcefully is that identity is a series of roles to be donned and doffed at will in the pantomime instituted by colonialism and now continued, with more opportunity for social and other forms of mobility, into the post-independence period. There are moments when Jackson seems to have the upper hand and certainly he comes across as the wittier and more resourceful of the two characters, but ultimately *Pantomime* refuses to allow either of its players ascendancy. The play propounds a view of character as an endlessly mutating process and develops a dramatic technique that is the formal correlative of this, as Harry and Jackson come together, swap roles, overlap and diverge. Throughout there is extensive reference to racial stereotyping, but overall the playfulness and fluidity of the characters' ever-shifting performances enact an identity politics that confounds stereotyping without occluding the social realities of racial difference.

Selvon's *Moses Ascending*, the second novel of his 'Moses' trilogy,[12] is equally comic, but may initially seem to be offering a more directly adversarial response to *Robinson Crusoe*. The narrator/protagonist Moses Aloetta is a member of the '*Windrush* generation', the first generation of post-war Caribbean migrants to Britain, who has now been in London for more than two decades and has become the landlord of a house in Shepherd's Bush. He occupies the 'penthouse' himself and takes on a 'man Friday, a white immigrant name Bob from somewhere in the Midlands' as his 'batman' (4). This suggests what Louise Bennett has called 'colonisation in reverse' (179–80) and the text's inversion of the Friday–Crusoe relationship seems fairly straightforward, as Moses describes Bob as 'a willing worker eager to learn the ways of the Black man' (4) and speaks of 'indoctrinating' him in a manner that fairly obviously alludes to Crusoe's colonization of Friday:[13]

> As we became good friends, or rather Master and Servant, I try to convert him from the evils of alcohol, but it was no use. By and by, as he was so useful to me, I allowed him the freedom of the house, and left everything in his hands so I could enjoy my retirement. ...
> I decided to teach him the Bible when I could make the time. (5)

Later in the novel Moses offers a variation on this joke when he threatens to send Bob back to the Black Country (31), but his relationship with Bob is only one element in the plot and the novel is not simply offering a reversal of the Friday–Crusoe paradigm for the postcolonial period. Numerous other elements, such as Moses' unintentionally letting out his basement to a group of Black Power activists, with whom he has an uneasy relationship, and finding himself a reluctant accomplice in smuggling illegal Pakistani immigrants into Britain, frustrate any attempt to read *Moses Ascending* as oppositional counter-discourse. When, at one point, Moses decides to shift the focus of his narrative from black–white relationships to his Muslim tenants, he wonders 'if I could kill two books with one pen, as it were' (45) and similarly the novel moves between *storylines* in a manner that displaces the framework offered by the Friday–Crusoe opposition from its centre.

What emerges is that there is no way in which Moses can enter into Crusoe's shoes, but he is equally incapable of sustaining the role of Friday. He is a man between worlds, a hybrid subject with aspirations towards an English identity that he is unable to fulfil and vestigial loyalties to his Caribbean roots that he is unable to discard. Like the Marlow of *Heart of Darkness*, though the mode of Selvon's novel is a far cry from Conrad's modernist seriousness, he stands poised on the edge of a breakthrough into a new conception of identity, but fails to realize his capacity to achieve it. His speech, trying to 'kill two books with one pen, as it were', is a particular index of the ambivalent position he occupies. Both as narrator and character, he uses language in a highly self-conscious way, at one point boasting to his long-time associate, Galahad, ' "I will knock them in the Old Kent Road with my language alone . . . . My very usage of English will have them rolling in the aisles" ' (78). In the first volume of the trilogy, *The Lonely Londoners* (1956), Selvon had employed a modified and individualized form of Trinidadian Creole for the main narrative voice of the novel.[14] In *Moses Ascending*, Moses presents himself as composing his 'Memoirs', an individual form of writing which is resistant to fashionable social trends. In compiling them, he once again draws on Creole, but intersperses this with a 'Standard English' that is often stilted and anachronistic and the end product is a register that is uniquely of his own making. In passages such as the following, the racy Caribbean vernacular of the earlier novel is juxtaposed with an archaic English that is formal to the point of being bizarrely at odds with the more colloquial register with which it is juxtaposed:

> I am not getting any younger, and cannot hustle pussy and scout the streets of London as in days of yore. (26)
>
> If I had had time I would of said, 'Unhand me, knave,' but instead I say, 'Let me go man, I ain't done nothing.' (36)
>
> Galahad left me with a nasty taste in my mouth. I could withstand the slings and arrows of misfortune, but when it come to my penmanship, you are treading on dangerous ground. (43–4)

Moses, who, unlike Selvon,[15] is oblivious of the work of prominent black writers of the post-war years, claims that his Memoirs 'will create a new dimension' (43) and *Moses Ascending* achieves something similar through its creation of his highly distinctive narrative voice. Throughout the novel he repeatedly provides ironic reworkings of clichés, but appears to be the *object* of satire when these involve Malapropisms and other language mistakes:

> But my brush with the law only make me realize that I had no friends in the world, that I had to *peddle* my own canoe for survival. (39)
>
> When you read other scribes, or see them television films, at this stage the hero will gird his *lions*, and after a series of breathtaking adventures, successfully overcome the forces of evil. If you think I was about to ditto, you are sadly mistaken. (63)
>
> ... there was no sense in chastising ourselves for anything. *Kay sir rah, sir rah*, as the Japanese say. (66; all italics in original)

The distinctiveness of Moses' use of language does not stop here. The text represents him as a linguistic magpie who, at various points in the novel, uses a parody of Islamic discourse, vague references to Greek mythology, four-letter words, Creole proverbs, Orientalist commonplaces and calypso allusions as part of the uniquely individual hybrid register that he brings into being. However, it remains a matter for debate as to how this is to be read. Selvon's own comments on the style of the novel suggest that he saw it as an extension of the modified form of Creole used in *The Lonely Londoners* and appear to demonstrate little awareness of the potential problems surrounding the hotchpotch of language used by Moses:

> When I was writing *The Lonely Londoners*, it wouldn't come at all in straight, standard English. Eventually I decided to try to set the whole thing down, both the narrative and the dialogue, in this form of Caribbean language. And it just shot along. ...
>
> So in later years when I decided to do this sequel to *The Lonely Londoners*, it came back to me fine. The language worked so well with the first book, I decided I'm going to use it now, but I'm also going to show there's been some kind of development in Moses through all these years he's been living in England. I decided I'm going to use a kind of archaic English together with the dialogue [*sic*] format and see how the two would combine. And I think it has worked very well.
>
> ('"Old Talk"' 74)

Despite this, the novel does contain a critique of Moses' method. Towards the end, the black-power activist Brenda responds to his claim that he is 'writing Literature' (103) by telling him, 'you should stick to oral communication and leave the written word to them what knows their business' (105). The overall effect is one of 'parodic treatment of Moses's aspirations and pretensions' (Nasta 5) and, as Edward Baugh has pointed out, he is a 'victim rather than a master of the Queen's language' (10), an ex-centric individual who is neither Friday nor Crusoe, but someone who has not grasped the positive potential of living in the interstices of cultures. Consequently the view that the novel's counter-discursive subversiveness lies in the 'sophisticated appropriation by "colonial" writing of a literary style formerly reserved to the British-born' (Fabre in King, B. *West Indian Literature* 123) very slightly misses the point. Moses' attempts to 'knock them in the Old Kent Road with [his] language' are clichéd and mannered to the point of being positively bizarre on occasions and are more satisfyingly read either as representing the cultural dislocation of the first-generation immigrant who is exiled from both the Caribbean and more recent forms of Black British culture or as a form of hybridized discourse that allows him to express his own individuality, irrespective of current trends. They cannot simply be read as a manifestation of Friday assuming Crusoe's role through a linguistic appropriation of the former Master's language. Instead the text is concerned with the articulation of new, often incongruously hybridized, forms of expression. An Asian character talks of having ' "left the bonny banks of the Ganges" ' (69); Brenda incorporates Harold Macmillan's 'Winds of Change' rhetoric into her Black Power discourse (81); Bob plays calypsoes by the Mighty Sparrow (21). Everybody within the text seems to exist *between* conventional discursive worlds, bringing something new into being in what Homi Bhabha has referred to as the Third Space of enunciation (36–9). If there is one constant to be found amid this medley of ambivalent and shifting discourses, it is Moses' resistance to causes and essentialist rhetoric. He refuses to espouse the rhetoric of 'black brotherhood' (39), to which many of his associates from the *Windrush* generation and younger Black Britons now subscribe, and is equally hostile to 'woman's lib' (135). He deplores 'how people want you to become involve, whether you want to or not' (14), insisting that ' "Memoirs are personal and intimate. . . . They don't have to be topical nor deal with any social problems" ' (42), and Selvon's novel is written in a similar vein, refusing to be straitjacketed either by the anachronistic English texts that absorb Moses or the adversarial, anti-racist discourse popular in 1970s Britain. By the end, the traditional Upstairs-Downstairs[16] roles of an earlier era have been reinstated: Moses is living in the basement; Bob and his new wife, Jeannie, are in the penthouse, but Moses is plotting to unsettle this situation and the novel's style leaves him poised in a liminal space uniquely of his own making.

IV

A. D. Hope's poem 'Man Friday' (1958) is an earlier response to *Robinson Crusoe*, but it too can be seen to be concerned with a postcolonial experience, if one views Crusoe's island as a paradigm for the colonial situation, since it focuses on what happens to Friday after he has been 'rescued' from the island along with Crusoe. He finds himself an exile, 'On England's Desert Island cast away', and strives to protect his identity as a ' "natural man" ' among 'the cultured' (80). With the passing of the years he is increasingly transformed into an Englishman, but still clings to a dream of his island origins that 'Confounded the fantastic with the true' (81). Despite his acculturation, the climax of the poem has the reality of the *island* supplanting the fantasy of his life in *England* when, on an East Anglian beach, he sees a footprint in the sand that he recognizes as belonging to a member of his own tribe. The image transports him back to the Caribbean and when Crusoe finds his drowned body the next day, he is said to have 'been rescued and gone home' (84). As in Rhys's *Wide Sargasso Sea*, the colonized subject finally finds freedom and symbolic repatriation through suicide. In both cases the twentieth-century perspective invites a postcolonial reading, though the historical action belongs to an earlier period.

Friday also comes to England in the South African J. M. Coetzee's *Foe* (1986), a postmodernist novel that interrogates the ethic implicit in *Robinson Crusoe* in a radically subversive, albeit oblique, way. Although it uses a counter-discursive framework in writing back to Defoe's canonical pre-text, its relationship to *Crusoe* is for the most part tangential and its stance is not overtly oppositional. Instead it undermines the very basis of fictional authority and the Puritan tradition of circumstantial realism that Defoe is credited with having founded. Again 'fantasy' is confounded with 'truth' and fiction with fact − the main metaphor for this in *Foe* involves a contrast between ghostliness and substantiality − but in this case an accretion of metafictive layers problematizes the issue of which is which, to a point where readers may feel that *they* have become the main castaways of the novel.

Foe is mainly narrated by a woman who calls herself Susan Barton and who has been with Cruso (now spelt without the '-e') and Friday during the final year of their time on the island. From the outset this shift from Defoe's method of male fictional autobiography suggests the intertwining of feminist and postcolonial concerns and, as the text develops, it implies that colonial and patriarchal societies operate similar, though by no means identical, discursive hegemonies. As Steven Connor puts it, 'If *Robinson Crusoe* is a cultural myth of the birth of social life in male individuality, then Coetzee's narrative shows the necessary (non)participation of the female in, and as, the sacrifice that enables this supplementary revisionist myth of origin to be generated' (93). The first section of the novel contains numerous allusions to *Robinson Crusoe*, all of which defy unitary interpretation and it quickly becomes clear that *Foe* is neither a sequel to *Crusoe*, nor an account of essentially the same events from another point of view. Cruso is a very different man from Crusoe: Susan estimates he is about sixty years old (roughly *Defoe's* age at the time when his novel was published); and, unlike Defoe's protagonist, he has no desire to leave his island, nor to engage in the kind of practical activities, such as salvaging tools from the wrecked ship or building a boat, that absorb Crusoe — and which render him a Caribbean precursor for Derek Walcott. As María Luz Suárez puts it:

> His values and his island domain are certainly not emblems of omnipresent Empire. None of the myths of the eighteenth-century Protestant society consolidate his "kingdom": hard work, conquering spirit, piety and faith in the progress of civilization. Unlike his ideological father, instead of progressing materially and spiritually, Cruso sinks into silence and sleep — significantly the only piece of furniture he has made is a bed. (85)

If he is any kind of colonist, Cruso belongs, despite his advancing years, to an earlier and more tentative phase of imperialism: he spends his time clearing earth and building terraces in the belief that ' "planting is reserved for those who come after us and have the foresight to bring seed" ' (Coetzee 33). Crusoe throws away what he takes to be a few husks of corn and finds himself providentially supplied with English barley, growing, miraculously, in a climate which he himself admits, 'was not proper for corn' (Defoe, *Crusoe* 94) and he subsequently establishes flourishing plantations. Coetzee's Cruso believes Providence only functions sometimes; Crusoe sees it operating everywhere. Unlike Robinson Crusoe, Cruso does not keep a journal, though Susan puts it to him that if he were he to do so, it would distinguish his shipwreck and predicament by establishing their 'particularity' (18). However, he rejects Susan's thinking and with it the emphasis on contingent detail that is one of the hallmarks of the Puritan materialism of *Robinson Crusoe*. Not that Susan herself provides such a narrative. Try as she will, she is frustrated in her attempts to provide a definitive story, so that, although her behaviour remains within the social conventions of her age, her narrative has more affinities with contemporary postmodernist practice.

Susan's difficulties are compounded by her belief that storytelling is an exclusively male domain and, after being rescued from the island and brought back to England with Friday — Cruso dies at sea on the journey back, seemingly a colonizer who is unable to survive the end of his own imperial rule — she pursues the elusive author figure of Daniel Foe, trying to get him to write *her* castaway story for her. On the island, though she has resisted Cruso's attempts to exercise authority over her, she has become close to him and slept with him on one occasion; and she comes to England, feeling she is his 'wife' and the heir to his story. So, on one level, her belief that she is the carrier of the tale undermines the notion of an exclusively paternal line of influence, but she still feels the story needs a male author to find a pattern in her essentially metonymic narrative. Her relationship with Foe — Defoe's original surname[17] — parallels her relationship with Cruso. This perhaps accounts for the similarity between the two men's ages in Coetzee's text. Susan and Foe spend a good deal of time disputing what is important in the island story. He argues that it is lacking in narrative incident and makes her feel that it is necessary to embellish it by including 'strange circumstances' (67), such as the building of a boat and a journey to the mainland, a skirmish with cannibals and the arrival of a stranger who plants corn — an odd amalgam of episodes that are derived from *Robinson Crusoe* and elements that do not appear there, making the relationship between the two texts even more indeterminate.

Part of Coetzee's academic training was as a linguist and, like most of his work, *Foe* is indebted to post-Saussurean theory. In the opening paragraph Susan slips overboard into the sea and feels that she has become like a floating anemone or jellyfish and the novel's readers are plunged into a world of floating signification. Although the whole text is constructed within this mode, I should like to focus on two characters who particularly typify its indeterminacy. The first is a young woman who appears suddenly in the London sections of the novel and makes demands on Susan Barton. While Susan is trying to persuade Foe to give literary substance to her version of what happened on the island and he seems bent on telling a different tale, even suggesting that the island experience should not be the crux of the narrative at all, she has to contend with the unwanted but insistent intrusion of another story into her life. Prior to being cast away, she has gone to the Americas, to Bahia — Defoe's Crusoe also lives in Brazil prior to undertaking the voyage that leads to the shipwreck — in search of a lost daughter. Now, in London, the mysterious young woman who comes into Susan's life claims that *she* is this daughter, but Susan refuses to acknowledge her as such. The lost daughter motif involves a clear intertextual relationship with another Defoe novel, *Roxana* (1724), where the eponymous heroine deserts a daughter who subsequently tracks her down and harasses her, although there are no explicit references to *Roxana* in *Foe*. Initially the choice confronting readers seems to be whether the young woman is Susan's daughter or an impostor, but as this narrative develops, multiple possibilities, which point up the reductiveness of such a binary formulation, emerge. These include those of the young woman's being Roxana's daughter, but Susan's not being Roxana, although there are some similarities between the two characters, and her being an invention of Foe's, designed to replace Susan's lost daughter. And at this point the dividing line between different levels of fictional creation – between characters in a novel and role-playing in 'real' life – begins to seem a very thin one indeed, as it becomes increasingly clear that identity is staged and plural rather than fixed and unitary. At the same time there is a debate as to whether the story of Susan's earlier life has a place in the story she wants Foe to write, which further problematizes any attempt to view either *Robinson Crusoe* or *Roxana* as the main intertext. Additionally, as if there were not enough ambiguities generated by *Foe*'s oblique relationship to the two Defoe novels, *Foe* also appears to be haunted by other Defoe narratives, among them *Moll Flanders* (1722) and his earlier ghost story, *A True Relation of the Apparition of One Mrs Veal* (1706). The overall effect is one of a constant slippage which leaves readers with no consensual ground on which to base a definitive interpretation – shipwrecked a world away from the illusion of stable, unitary signification offered by circumstantial realism and the authoritative stance of colonial discourse.

The second figure, typifying *Foe*'s indeterminacy on whom I should like to focus is Friday. Where, amid all the relativistic evasions of the text, is the colonized subject, Friday, to be found? In one sense the answer to this, at least until the last pages, is nowhere. Like the 'deaf and dumb' protagonist of Defoe's *Life and Adventures of Duncan Campbell* (1720),[18] he is beyond speech since his tongue has been cut out. And as a listener he responds only to referential language, initially to Cruso's orders and later in England, where Susan effectively inherits him along with Cruso's story, to her similarly practical remarks. Although Susan wants to liberate Friday by teaching him 'his letters' (146), she finds him an unresponsive pupil and even when she engages him in the one area of paralinguistic expression where he seems to communicate, music – he plays a few notes on a flute – she cannot be sure that he is taking part in a duet.

Although Susan takes the view that 'a story entire' could be built out of Friday's 'sorrows' (87), he remains 'a puzzle or hole in the narrative' (121) as far as she is concerned, an absence in the signifying systems with which she is familiar, in much the same way as the anonymous Africans of *Heart of Darkness* belong to a discursive universe that lies beyond Marlow's comprehension. She appreciates that he is a colonial Other who has been constructed from outside because of his lack of access to language: 'Friday has no command of words and therefore no defence against being re-shaped day by day in conformity with the desires of others' (121). Nevertheless she remains powerless to alter this situation, although at one point she takes him to Bristol in the hope that she will be able to effect his repatriation to Africa, a project that she has to abandon when she realizes that he will be exploited by unscrupulous captains. One way of reading this episode is to see it as a metaphor for the situation of the South African white liberal (at the time of the novel's publication in the 1980s), anxious to help alleviate the oppression of the black majority, but unable to overcome the injustice endemic in the apartheid regime. However, such an analogy remains speculative, since the novel remains firmly set within its eighteenth-century frame until the final section and again several other allegorical possibilities suggest themselves.

How Friday has lost his tongue is unclear: Cruso may be responsible, though he has told Susan that slavers did this to Friday, who had been with him before they were shipwrecked *together*.[19] Only one mouth can provide the answer to this particular enigma and it is beyond speech. And this finally is the central problem that *Foe* addresses in its counter-discursive response to *Robinson Crusoe*: the problem of arriving at any kind of definitive or settled meaning in a colonial or postcolonial context. Late on in the novel, Foe lectures Susan on the difficulties of finding appropriate signifiers, telling her the word 'freedom ... is a puff of air, seven letters on a slate', but arguing that this does not negate 'the desire to be free', just as an inability to 'say in words what an apple is' does not preclude the eating of apples (149). On the one hand, the text's concern is with the slippage between signifier and signified that occurs in all forms of discourse, but the emphasis on words such as 'freedom' and the particular focus on Friday's muteness locates this more specifically, in relation to the linguistic dispossession of the colonized subject[20] and debates surrounding white authority to intervene in the construction of alterity in political, social and discursive contexts. The eighteenth-century part of the narrative concludes with Friday dressing himself in Foe's robes and wigs and, seated at the author's table, using his quill to produce smudgy rows and rows of the letter 'o'. Again the significance of this writing is indeterminate. It may be carnivalesque parody, the beginnings of a form of expression that mimics rather than slavishly imitates European discourse,[21] but the section concludes affirmatively, at least from the point of view of the white characters who are trying to break Friday's silence, with Foe saying to Susan, ' "It is a beginning .... Tomorrow you must teach him *a*" ' (152).

However, the novel does not finish here. To conclude on such a note of liberal affirmation, however tentative, would be out of keeping with its postmodernist practice and *Foe* resists closure by providing two further 'endings' in a gnomic short, final section, in which a first-person narrator revisits scenes from the earlier action in the twentieth century. The exact location of these two supplementary endings is blurred, but its opening echoes the beginning of one of the previous sections of the novel, in which Susan has climbed the staircase of a house to which Foe has moved to escape his creditors; and subsequently a blue commemorative plaque confirms that '*Daniel Defoe, Author*' (155) lived here. Inside a room at the top of the staircase, the unnamed 'I' narrator, who appears to be an author figure (a Coetzee surrogate rather than a Defoe figure, but also possibly either Foe or Susan or a mixture of *all* the text's authors) finds a couple who *seem* to be Susan and Foe in bed together. They are apparently dead, while Friday, the only character who is named in this section, is found stretched out in an alcove on his back, but still warm. The contemporary narrator lies down beside Friday and when he parts his teeth puts an ear to his mouth, waiting to see if any sound issues from it. After a time the narrator begins to hear non-verbal sounds, 'the roar of waves in a seashell ... the whine of the wind and the cry of a bird', in short 'the sounds of the island' (154).

And then, this final section appears to make a fresh start. Again the narrator enters the building; again s/he finds Friday in the alcove. This time, however, s/he leaves him there and begins reading a manuscript that s/he finds in the room, which initially appears to be Susan's story, since it reiterates the novel's opening words. Nothing so simple is allowed to stand unchallenged, however, and Susan's originary account (itself a riposte to male myths of origination) is swiftly supplanted by yet another variation on the theme, as the narrator, who once again seems to be a twentieth-century author figure, descends into the wrecked ship of the first part of the text, the Babel-like site of catastrophe which provides the primary impulse for narrative in both *Robinson Crusoe* and *Foe*. At this point it is as if an entry is being made into the missing 'hole' of the story, as the three hundred years that have elapsed between the fictional time of *Robinson Crusoe* and that of this section are collapsed. This ending involves another displacement of earlier narrative elements, including those of the previous ending, as the narrator finds Susan dead in bed with the sea-captain of the ship from which she was originally cast adrift, another patriarchal figure with whom she has slept in the eighteenth-century action. Crawling beneath their bodies, the narrator finds Friday half buried in sand and asks him 'what is this ship?' (157). If this question were answered, the mysteries of the text might be solved in an instant, but the narrator has to conclude:

[T]his is not a place of words. Each syllable, as it comes out, is caught and filled with water and diffused. This is a place where bodies are their own signs. It is the home of Friday. (157)

Again, this can be read as a general comment on the non-transparent nature of language, but it has more specific resonance in relation to the postcolonial agendas of the text. It is the colonized body of Friday that cannot be rendered in language, which defies articulation by the white author who can only speak from outside.

In the final paragraph of the novel, Friday opens his mouth and once again a 'stream' issues from it, which flows out upon the narrator, the cabin, the wreck, the cliffs and shores of the island and ultimately 'northward and southward to the ends of the earth' (157). Yet it remains unclear whether communication has been achieved, whether the 'stream' constitutes words or any form of articulation that is comprehensible to the shadowy author or to another human being of *any* race or gender. Since Friday is being equated with the body, it would not be impossible to see this conclusion as projecting a view in which, as in A. D. Hope's poem, he remains the 'natural man', who exists outside 'civilized' discourse. However, such a view rests on allowing the perspectives of the various author figures of the text (Susan, Foe and the twentieth-century narrator) to stand unchallenged and the final section has effectively completed the work of undermining any right they may have to construct Friday. The stream that issues from his mouth seems rather to suggest the beginnings of a postcolonial discourse, albeit one which the white author cannot share or express. So *Foe*'s dismantling of English canonical discourse adopts a particularly transgressive form, since it radically destabilizes *any* notion of definitive authority. It kills off the hero of *Robinson Crusoe* in its early pages; it instates a female protagonist in his place; it undermines the story of Defoe's colonial masterpiece by allowing other Defoe stories to crowd into the text and vie for primacy; it confuses the relationship between author and character by allowing an elusive and disappearing version of Defoe into the novel and complicating his relationship with the female author, who is the real teller of most of the tale, despite her lack of confidence in her own abilities to be this; and finally it replaces her by an unidentified author who may overlap with her (and the other author figures of the narrative), but ultimately seems to be a twentieth-century figure. Through this labyrinthine series of twists and turns, it refuses, however, to do one thing: to speak for black subjectivity. All three endings of *Foe* conclude with Friday seemingly on the threshold of entering into language, but in each case his utterance is left outside the verbal mode of the fiction, with the white South African author who is finally its originator demonstrating his sensitivity to the need to give voice to silenced black subjectivity, but refusing to attempt to render such discourse himself.

Like *Moses Ascending* and Walcott's 'Crusoe' poems and unlike Walcott's *Pantomime*, *Foe* refuses to see the Friday–Crusoe connection as central. Instead it locates the colonized–colonizer relationship within a range of other contexts, a practice that has the effect of freeing the narrative from an oppositional position, which would, as with the adversarial response of the negritudinists mentioned in the previous chapter, paradoxically leave it defined by the very discourses it is contesting. *Foe's* relocation of the relationship foregrounds the continuing pervasiveness of the colonial legacy, but insists that postcolonial self-definition must emerge from a complex of ambivalent discourses that displace the notion that a single canonical pre-text can provide a departure point.

Just as Robert Kroetsch's displays a Foucaldian scepticism about originary narration, when his two Annas finally turn their back on the 'source' at the end of *Badlands*, *Foe* seems to predicate a similarly layered model of literary influence in which a multiplicity of possible textual antecedents destroy the notion of unitary, linear genealogies. And in the middle of this Babel lies the silenced figure of Friday, the subaltern alterity for which his white South African creator declines to speak.

Notes

1. Catherine Belsey identifies *'illusionism,* narrative which leads to *closure,* and a *hierarchy of discourses* which establishes the "truth" of the story' as the prime characteristics of 'classic realism' (70; italics in original).
2. *Dictionary of the English Language* (1755). This trope persisted throughout the eighteenth century. Cf. Cowper's poem 'The Castaway', dated 'March 20 1799', in which the poet likens his own despondent spiritual condition to that of a 'destined wretch' washed overboard and drowned in the sea (425–6).
3. R. M. Ballantyne's *The Coral Island* (1858) affords a better example.
4. In her novel *Crusoe's Daughter* (1985), in which the eponymous heroine's isolated environment is a lonely house, not a desert island.
5. Johann David Wyss's *The Swiss Family Robinson*, originally published as *Der Schweizerische Robinson* (Zurich, 1812) is a notable exception. It is the best-known example of the genre known as the *Robinsonade*, which flourished in France and Germany in the eighteenth and early nineteenth centuries. Hermann Ulrich's *Robinson and Robinsonaden* (1898) lists 110 translations, 115 revisions and 277 imitations up to 1895 (cited by Rogers 23).
6. An equally important, though less widely acknowledged 'original' for Crusoe was Robert Knox, whose twenty years as a captive of the king of Kandy are described in his *An Historical Relation of Ceylon* (1681).
7. Two of the Caribbean writers discussed in this chapter identify Crusoe's island with Tobago. Derek Walcott's *Pantomime* is set in a Tobago guest house. Sam Selvon's story 'Brackley and the Bed' locates its protagonist by saying, 'Brackley hail from Tobago, which part they have it to say Robinson Crusoe used to hang out with Man Friday' (*Ways of Sunlight* 151).
8. Walcott was brought up as an English-speaking Methodist in the primarily Francophone Catholic island of St Lucia. See my discussion in *Derek Walcott* (78–80) for a fuller treatment of this aspect of Walcott's response to Crusoe.

9. The play was first performed in Port of Spain, Trinidad in 1978.

10. Bruce King (*Derek Walcott* 360) says that *Pantomime* was written while Walcott was staying at Crown Point Hotel in Tobago in late 1977 and early 1978. See King also for details of Walcott's familiarity with pantomime and a review of a 'bad' Trinidadian *Robinson Crusoe* pantomime (361).

11. This discussion is comparatively brief, because I discuss *Pantomime* rather more fully in my *Derek Walcott* (125–30).

12. The other parts of the trilogy are *The Lonely Londoners* (1956) and *Moses Migrating* (1983).

13. For details of passages in *Robinson Crusoe* to which Selvon seems to be writing back, see Mervyn Morris's Introduction to the Heinemann edition of the novel (xiv).

14. Moses' remark, 'I have chronicled those colourful days in another tome' (44), suggests that he is the narrator of *The Lonely Londoners*, but the internal evidence of the earlier novel, in which he is a third-person character, suggests otherwise.

15. See references to George Lamming, Andrew Salkey and James Baldwin (27), to Lamming and Salkey (42–3, 120), to Lamming's *Water with Berries* (138) and Baldwin's *The Fire Next Time* (139). Selvon migrated to Britain on the same ship as Lamming (Lamming, *Pleasures* 211–12) and was associated with both Lamming and Salkey in Britain (Walmsley, *passim*).

16. There is an allusion to the popular 1970s British television series of this name, as Moses pleads with Bob to be allowed to come up to the penthouse to watch the programme in colour (134).

17. Defoe's father's name was Foe. He changed his signature to 'Defoe' when he was aged about forty and subsequently ranged between 'D. Foe', 'D. F.', 'Defoe', 'Daniel De Foe' and 'Daniel Defoe', when signing his name.

18. Campbell was a supposedly deaf and dumb fortune-teller with a considerable reputation in early eighteenth-century London. Whether he was actually dumb or only pretended to be so to attract custom is uncertain. Addison, in *Spectator* 560 (28 June 1714), took the view that he was a charlatan, referring to him as 'the famous conjurer, who according to the opinion of the vulgar, has suffered himself dumb; for which reason, as it is believed, he delivers out all his oracles in writing' (Addison *et al.* 8: 18). This use of writing obviously distinguishes Campbell from Coetzee's Friday in one respect.

19. Cf. Dennis Scott's similar use of a tongueless character in the figure of Rattler in his play *An Echo in the Bone* (in Hill, *Plays*). In this instance the loss of the colonized subject's tongue is directly associated with the legacy of the Slave Trade: in an earlier incarnation Rattler has his tongue cut out on board a Middle Passage slave ship.

20. Within a Caribbean context this could obviously be related to the loss of African languages, cf. Rattler in Scott's *An Echo in the Bone*. The Caribbean dimensions of the silencing of the black subject are not, however, particularly foregrounded in *Foe*.

21. Cf. Homi Bhabha, 'Of Mimicry and Man: The Ambivalence of Colonial Discourse' (*Location* 85–92). Bhabha argues that 'The effect of mimicry on the authority of colonial discourse is profound and disturbing. ... The *menace* of mimicry is its *double* vision which in disclosing the ambivalence of colonial discourse also disrupts its authority' (86, 88; italics in original).

4

Reclaiming ghosts, claiming ghosts: Caribbean and Canadian responses to the Brontës

She seemed such a poor ghost, I thought I'd like to write her a life'
(Jean Rhys on Charlotte Brontë's Bertha, Rhys, 'Inscrutable' 44).

It's only by our lack of ghosts/we're haunted
(Earle Birney, 'Can. Lit.' 138).

I

When I first read Arnold Kettle's Marxist study of the English novel many years ago, it was not too difficult to accept that Hardy's *Tess of the D'Urbervilles* was a *roman à thèse* about 'the destruction of the English peasantry' (Kettle 2: 49), but I found I balked at the suggestion that *Wuthering Heights* was about the state of England in 1847 (1: 139). More mature reading made it possible to see Emily Brontë's binary worlds of Thrushcross Grange and Wuthering Heights as microcosms of broader class distinctions in early nineteenth-century English society and to agree, at least on one level, with Kettle's assertion that 'The people it reveals live not in a never-never land but in Yorkshire' (1: 139). Nevertheless, I still took the view that, like her two sisters, Emily Brontë wrote about an enclosed environment that was a world away from the social milieux of most of the other major novels of the period. This, after all, was part of the Brontës' appeal in their own day and over the last century and a half, the Brontë legend has developed and nurtured the myth of the sisters' isolated and inward-looking upbringing in a Yorkshire parsonage, in a family situation that did comparatively little to foster contacts with the outside world and led them to devise their own self-contained fictional worlds.[1] Although some of the sisters' juvenilia was set in an invented romantic version of 'Africa', implicating their novels in the colonial project seemed still more far-fetched than insisting on their engagement with the state of England: the worlds of *Wuthering Heights*, *Jane Eyre* and *The Tenant of Wildfell Hall* all appeared to be remote from the overt political economies to be found in texts such as *Robinson Crusoe* and *Heart of Darkness*.

It was comparatively easy to read *Mansfield Park* as a Condition of England novel and to see the house itself as a symbol of an exclusive middle-class social world that owed its very existence to West Indian sugar money, and impossible not to appreciate that the plot of *Great Expectations* turns upon Pip's discovery that his status as a gentleman derives not from Miss Havisham, but the transported convict Magwitch's colonial fortune. However, despite their representation of the minutiae of class differences, it remained – and for many, such as those who read *Wuthering Heights* as the timeless, extra-social love-story of Cathy and Heathcliff, it still remains – possible to exempt the Brontë novels from readings that foregrounded their representation of inter-cultural conflicts, apart from class and gender relations. Nevertheless, the construction of both character and place in the Brontë novels is centrally concerned with alterity, possibly *because of*, rather than despite, the isolated material circumstances of the novels' composition. So the sisters' early fascination with 'Africa' and other imagined worlds can be seen as anticipating their adult absorption with otherness.

The central focus of this chapter is on the best-known postcolonial response to the Brontës, Jean Rhys's *Wide Sargasso Sea* (1966), which writes back to *Jane Eyre* in a fairly direct manner by telling the story of the first Mrs Rochester,[2] Bertha, 'the madwoman in the attic' at Thornfield Hall. It also discusses V. S. Naipaul's *Guerrillas* (1975), where Brontëan intertexts are used more obliquely to locate its protagonists' psychologies, and the Canadian novelist, Jane Urquhart's *Changing Heaven* (1990), which engages with Emily Brontë's life and works in a rather different way. Urquhart's novel raises the question of whether romantic fiction encourages escapist fantasizing and this issue is also considered in relation to Margaret Atwood's treatment of the genre in *Lady Oracle* (1976), a novel in which the narrator/protagonist is a writer of sub-Brontëan 'Costume Gothics' and which contains incidental allusions to *Wuthering Heights* and *Jane Eyre*. Some of the broader implications of the use of the Gothic in postcolonial cultures are also discussed with reference to Amitav Ghosh's novel, *The Shadow Lines* (1988), where there are no Brontëan allusions, but the Indo-British encounter is seen as a Gothic site, permeated with Victorian dust.

II

In *Wuthering Heights* the delicate balance between the social worlds of the Lintons and the Earnshaws and their respective houses, Thrushcross Grange and Wuthering Heights, is disturbed by the advent of the figure of Heathcliff. Just as Magwitch's transgressive return from Australia endangers Pip's existence as a gentleman, Heathcliff's arrival threatens the social equilibrium that has been achieved between the two families. He is the catalyst who brings discord into the secluded moorland world of the two houses; order is only restored after his death. But who exactly *is* Heathcliff? For the text's main narrator, Nelly Dean, the old family servant who is the voice of common sense in the novel, his appearance is devilish. Speaking at a time when belief in physiognomy was at its height,[3] she tells the young orphan, Heathcliff, that his eyebrows are Mephistophelean: ' "Do you mark those two lines between your eyes, and those thick brows, that instead of rising arched, sink in the middle, and that couple of black fiends, so deeply buried, who never open their windows boldly, but lurk glinting under them, like devil's spies?" ' (Brontë, E. 97). She continues by encouraging him to escape being demonized by cultivating an angelic appearance and she invents a romantic provenance for his mysterious origins:

> 'You're fit for a prince in disguise. Who knows, but your father was Emperor of China, and your mother an Indian queen, each of them able to buy up with one week's income, Wuthering Heights and Thrushcross Grange together? And you were kidnapped by wicked sailors, and brought to England. Were I in your place, I would frame high notions of my birth.' (98)

At first sight, this appears to be innocent enough chatter on the part of the old servant, who resorts to a mixture of fairy tale and boys' adventure story to instruct her young charge, and nowhere in the text is there any suggestion that Nelly is an accessory to the actions that will disturb the relationship between the two houses and what they represent. Nevertheless, her remarks locate Heathcliff in terms of a romantic – one might argue, Orientalist – construction of 'foreignness' and this is typical of the role ascribed to him in the novel. His mysterious origins are never explained. All that can be said with some certainty is that he is an outsider of unknown ancestry, who belongs to neither of the genealogical family trees that critics have compiled to explain the complications and resolutions of the plot across the two generations of the novel's timespan.[4] Nelly tells Lockwood, the frame-narrator, that Heathcliff's history is that of a cuckoo (76), an intruder whose parentage is unknown, as is the source of the fortune that he subsequently attains as an adult. Again, then, it is an ambivalently positioned orphan who challenges the certainties of the established orthodoxies of the world in which s/he moves.

An interesting extra dimension is added, if one admits as a possibility the suggestion that that the dark 'gipsy brat' who, on his first arrival at Wuthering Heights, keeps repeating 'some gibberish that nobody could understand' (77) may be an *ethnic* 'Other', racially mixed or just possibly actually black, his 'gibberish' a Caribbean Creole. Old Mr Earnshaw has found him destitute in the streets of Liverpool, which was not only the main British terminus of the triangular trade at this time (the late eighteenth century), but also the home of a small community of freed slaves, one of the earliest groups of its kind to become established in Britain.[5] Arguably, though, it makes more sense simply to locate Heathcliff as generically 'foreign' rather than to attempt to ascribe any particular national or ethnic origins to him. Nelly's invention of an exotic Eastern pedigree for him leaves the issue open. So, too, does, Mr Linton's view of him as 'a little Lascar, or an American or Spanish castaway' (91). Both invoke a vague sense of foreign alterity rather than offer a specific explanation of his origins. *Wuthering Heights* suggests the demonic elements inherent in such foreignness, while also allowing Heathcliff to inhabit the role of a Romantic hero, cast in the Byronic mould. Nelly's advice that he should try to replace his devilish potentialities with angelic attributes anticipates the ambivalence that characterizes him in the subsequent action, in which he is alternately a Byronic hero who enlists readers' sympathies and a villainous revenger, finally becoming a Gothic protagonist of another order: a desolate, Frankenstein-like figure, haunted by the ghost of his beloved Catherine. He is both hero and anti-hero, an expression of Emily Brontë's split attitude towards his foreignness, which is depicted as both attractive and destructive, and his liminal ambiguity is central to *Wuthering Heights*'s power as a novel that interrogates the social and literary conventions of its day.

Foreignness is an equally important trope in *Jane Eyre*, where it appears in references to mainland Europe, India and the Caribbean, but lacks the ambiguity attached to it in *Wuthering Heights*. Like Emily, Charlotte Brontë conflates various sites of alterity together, making only minor distinctions between them. Unlike Emily, she demonstrates a fairly general xenophobia, to a point where, as Helen Carr notes, she becomes something of an embarrassment for critics such as Gilbert and Gubar whose 'celebration of *Jane Eyre* as the paradigmatic feminist text ignores Rhys's critique of its chauvinism' (Carr 93). Mainland Europe is the scene of Rochester's early dissipations; when the alternative suitor of the novel, the missionary St John Rivers, wishes to take Jane to India, it is seen as a place of disease. The most negative representation of alterity comes, however, in Charlotte Brontë's comments on the Caribbean and Rochester's white Creole first wife, Bertha Mason. Rochester's brief account of the Jamaican environment to which he has been sent for his prearranged marriage to Bertha is a vision of a hell on earth, 'a world quivering with the ferment of tempest', full of 'the sounds of the bottomless pit' (335), from which he is ultimately redeemed by a 'sweet wind from Europe' (336). This may be a minor element in the novel, but it serves the purpose, not only of partially justifying Rochester, but also, as in more overtly imperialist texts, of cementing a sense of European identity through negative contradistinction. The hell of the Caribbean is the binary opposite of Jane's view of the garden at Thornfield Hall as an 'Eden-like' spot (276); Rochester subsequently seeks an ideal woman who will be 'the antipodes of the Creole' (338). Jane's response to Bertha, while she remains unaware of her identity, is to view her as a ghost and to align her with 'the foul German spectre – the vampire' (311) and her first-person narrative demotes Bertha to the level of beast: 'it snatched and growled like some strange wild animal: but it was covered with clothing, and a quantity of dark grizzled hair, wild as a mane, hid its head and face ... the clothed hyena rose up, and stood tall on its hind-feet' (321). When Rochester is obliged to confess his guilty secret to Jane, he presents Bertha as a human extension of the hellish landscape from which she comes, calling her a 'demon' (322, 335) and contrasting her 'pigmy intellect' with her 'giant' strength (334). The binary oppositions fit into a familiar pattern, with European rationalism being contrasted with non-European bestial passion. There is a hint that Bertha transgresses the borderline between the human and the animal – she is a *clothed* hyena – but her garments seem to be just a superficial accretion and she is as marginalized as the spectre-like Africans of *Heart of Darkness*. Unlike Heathcliff, then, Bertha is the personification of a savage alterity that is unequivocally inimical to 'civilized' English codes and it is no coincidence that her final 'mad' act is to burn down Thornfield Hall, a metonym for the English social order that has imprisoned and dehumanized her. The residents of Sir Thomas Bertram's plantation obligingly stay in Antigua and the spatial dynamics of *Mansfield Park* never open up the possibility that the English country house and its colonial shadow may be intertwined. Charlotte Brontë does venture into this territory, but mainly to locate her Gothic apparition as the product of a non-European world and without any attempt to describe her world in unmythologized terms. Her lack of interest in Caribbean specifics is abundantly evident, when towards the end of his confession to Jane, Rochester distinguishes his 'dissipation' from the 'debauchery' of his 'Indian Messalina' (338). Caribbean Creole heiress, anonymous Indian and dissolute Roman empress are thus conflated. Foreigners begin at Calais and, amid the sensitive special pleading for the governess who is a victim of her society's customary stifling of women's desires and aspirations, the novel displays no interest at all in non-European subjects or the interrelationship of metropolis and colony. *Jane Eyre* implicates itself in the colonial project, to a greater degree than the ostensibly more insular *Wuthering Heights*, through its unequivocal rejection of otherness.

III

Charlotte Brontë's xenophobia appears to have been to the fore in Jean Rhys's mind when she came to write *Wide Sargasso Sea*. Comments she made in interviews suggest that the impetus behind her decision to tell Bertha Mason's story was two-fold: an attempt to reclaim her from the role of shadowy Gothic apparition: 'She seemed such a poor ghost, I thought I'd like to write her a life' (Rhys, 'Inscrutable' 44); and a conviction that Charlotte Brontë had demonstrated an anti-West Indian bias:

> The mad first wife in Jane Eyre [*sic*] has always interested me. I was convinced Charlotte Brontë must have had something against the West Indies, and I was angry about it. Otherwise, why did she take a West Indian for that horrible lunatic, for that really dreadful creature? I hadn't really formulated the idea of vindicating the mad woman in a novel but when I was re-discovered I was encouraged to do so.
>
> (Rhys, 'Fated' 5)

Consequently, in *Wide Sargasso Sea* she is at pains both to humanize Bertha, now referred to as Antoinette, and to develop the cross-cultural theme, implicit in *Jane Eyre*'s ascription of Jamaican origins to Bertha and references to 'other' countries more generally, but little more than an embryo in the pre-text. In fairly obvious ways the novel rewrites the relevant parts of Charlotte Brontë's masterpiece, developing bare details from it in such a way that the view of Bertha/Antoinette as a raving lunatic sprung from a family of congenital idiots (Brontë, C. 333) is no longer sustainable.

Rhys offers a number of possible explanations of Antoinette's mental condition. Rochester's betrayal of her when he sleeps with the servant Amélie, her isolated childhood coupled with the influence of her mother and her Creole predicament – caught between Afro-Caribbean and English worlds, she is abused by the former as a 'white cockroach' and by the latter as a 'white nigger' (Rhys, *Sargasso* 85) – all suggest themselves as contributory factors. In contrast, the notion of congenital insanity is played down as readers see the societal and personal factors that unhinge Antoinette's mother's mind taking shape, witness the psychological effect that Rochester's betrayal has on her and learn that she is, in fact, only the stepsister of her supposed brother, Richard Mason, who Rochester says will probably one day, be 'a complete dumb idiot', like Bertha's younger brother (Brontë, C. 333). Carole Angier, author of the definitive biography of Rhys, points out that '*Wide Sargasso Sea* doesn't deny that Antoinette is mad, it shows us why: because first her childhood, and then an Englishman, have driven her mad' (656) and, although this is a rather reductive summary of the complexities surrounding the treatment of 'madness' in the novel, interestingly it comes in a passage in the biography that discusses Rhys's fear that she herself might be mad. Angier refers to a wartime notebook in which Rhys has recorded a conversation with a policeman, who tells her, '*If the law says you're dangerous you're dangerous, if the law says you're mad you're mad*' (656; italics in original). Such a view of madness as socially – and here, more specifically legally – defined can, of course, be related to *Wide Sargasso Sea*, where the suggestion that Antoinette's madness is hereditary offers itself as just one of a number of possibilities in Rhys's more relativist fictional universe. Additionally, in a novel where the power of language to determine identity is underscored and, amid her musings in the attic at Thornfield Hall in the final section, Antoinette says, 'Names matter, like when he wouldn't call me Antoinette, and I saw Antoinette drifting out of the window with her scents, her pretty clothes and her looking-glass' (147), there is the distinct suggestion that, while it may still be a clinical condition, 'madness' is linguistically constructed. Rhys reclaims the marginalized other from the Gothic margins of the text, epitomized by the ghostly recesses of the attic, to which Charlotte Brontë's 'progressive' text had confined her.

Rochester's insistence on calling Antoinette Bertha is an apt image of his violation of her identity and of his appropriation of the right to speak for Caribbean alterity more generally. However, although the name change very definitely suggests his complicity in the metamorphosis of Antoinette from 'pretty' young woman to the madwoman in the attic at Thornfield, Rhys does not adopt the adversarial strategy of dehumanizing *Rochester* by writing a counter-discursive con-text that simply reverses the positioning of the pre-text. Rochester, never named as such,[6] is also represented as a victim; he is still the impecunious younger son, who has been tricked into an arranged marriage that will secure a fortune for him, and this theme is developed convincingly through the use of his consciousness as the focalizer for most of the long second section of *Wide Sargasso Sea*. Rhys withholds the kind of authorial commentary that one finds in *Jane Eyre*, preferring rather to represent both sides of the tragic divide of the wide sargasso sea[7] and it is crucial to her relativist approach that both her Caribbean and her English protagonists are seen as victims rather than exploiters.

Whether *Wide Sargasso Sea* can stand alone or whether it only enjoys a vicarious existence derived from its relationship to *Jane Eyre* is a question that has split its critics and, of course, it raises crucial issues in relation to ways in which postcolonial counter-discourse functions. Early responses to the novel particularly focused on this aspect. Dennis Porter and Michael Thorpe discussed it purely in terms of the parallel with the Brontëan pre-text (Porter doing so mainly to shed new light on *Jane Eyre*), while West Indian critics such as Wally Look Lai and Kenneth Ramchand (230–6) examined it without *any* such reference. Clearly, their ability to do so demonstrates the novel's autonomy and yet reading *Wide Sargasso Sea* with *Jane Eyre* in mind adds an important extra dimension. Readers who know that Antoinette's journey is moving inexorably towards her incarceration at Thornfield Hall and who take the view that the style suggests events are being narrated from her attic prison are likely to see the novel as employing a curious mixture of proleptic and analeptic elements, with even the early sections both anticipating *and* being haunted by the Gothic conclusion. So an apocalyptic dimension enters into the novel on the levels of both theme and form, if readers see events being structured in relation to the knowledge that they will culminate in the conflagration at Thornfield and through the employment of Antoinette's impressionistic stream of consciousness as the main narrative point of view.

Perhaps the most penetrating comment on the novel's dependence on *Jane Eyre* is John Hearne's 'reflection' on the original nature of this formal indebtedness:

> In form and point of departure, its originality lies in taking the characters from an established work, *Jane Eyre*, back from their literary beginnings and fashioning, credibly, the unwritten history of creatures whom a previous author had invented. Its validity depends on a *book* from elsewhere, not on a basic, assumed life.
>
> And yet, is this not a superb and audacious metaphor of so much of West Indian life? Are we not still, in so many of our responses, creatures of books and inventions fashioned by others who used us as mere producers, as figments of their imagination; and who regarded the territory as a ground over which the inadmissable [*sic*] or forgotten forces of the psyche could run free for a while before being written off or suppressed? (325–6)

Whether or not Rhys conceived *Wide Sargasso Sea* with this in mind, Hearne's comments touch on the crux of the tension that the *Jane Eyre* parallel causes in the novel, a tension staged in Rhys's detailed examination of the relationship between the Brontëan novel, particularly its employment of a characteristically English form of nature imagery, and the tropical ambience.

In a broad general sense *Wide Sargasso Sea* is, superficially at least, a Brontëan novel, a 'poetic' or 'Romantic' novel at odds with the conventional nineteenth-century novel of manners; it is a novel organized around unifying 'organic' imagery rather than narrative development and it also bears a distinct formal resemblance to *Jane Eyre* in its point of view. Though Jean Rhys employs a number of focalizers (Grace Poole and Daniel 'Cosway' as well as Antoinette and Rochester), her method is not markedly different from that of *Jane Eyre*, where the autobiography of the heroine is related not as a comprehensive sequential narrative but as a series of evocative, remembered scenes, recalled by a narrator who is more mature than the earlier self she describes. In *Wide Sargasso Sea* this is replaced by the various first-person narratives, which are dominated by Antoinette's own, more fragmentary memoir of her earlier life. Her account takes the form of a highly selective, impressionistic interior monologue, which, while it has a basic affinity with the mode of *Jane Eyre*, is also influenced by modernist fictional techniques such as stream-of-consciousness. To embody a consciousness such as Antoinette's that has been shaped by its highly emotional response to the West Indian landscape and alienated Creole predicament, the narrative form of the fictional autobiography undergoes a modification, with the result that the text becomes a kind of 'Victorian' anti-novel, which has affinity with later, more fragmentary fictional modes. In this sense it could be seen as performing the role that Helen Tiffin assigns to counter-discourse: not 'simply "writing back" to an English canonical text, but to the whole of the discursive field within which such a text operated and continues to operate in post-colonial worlds' (23). There are, though, problems with this view, in that *Wide Sargasso Sea* is not so very different in this respect from a roughly contemporary English 'liberal' novel such as John Fowles's *The French Lieutenant's Woman* (1969) and subsequent British novelists, like Julian Barnes, Peter Ackroyd, Jeanette Winterson and Graham Swift, have taken the anti-canonical counter-discursive novel considerably further. Also, in important ways, the novel does look backwards for literary influences: to the modernist period when Rhys's writing sensibility was shaped, particularly during the period of her life when she lived in Paris. So one view might suggest that, although the novel is oppositional in its response to *Jane Eyre*, it is more comfortable with other British intertexts that may not have been deemed canonical during Rhys's earlier career, but had come to be regarded as such by the time she came to write the final version of *Wide Sargasso Sea* later in life.[8] Seen in this light, the novel is a late modernist text that is more concerned with providing multiple perspectives on the interior lives of its characters than with feminist or postcolonial identity politics.

Aspects of the style of *Wide Sargasso Sea* owe a clear debt to the stream-of-consciousness novel, but less to, say, Benjy's monologue in *The Sound and the Fury* than to the account of Stephen Dedalus's early life in *A Portrait of the Artist as a Young Man*: Antoinette's monologue is closer to Joyce's child's-eye view than Faulkner's tale told by an idiot. Passages such as the following where the training of her convent education punctuates her vividly remembered sense impressions demonstrate an affiliative response to Joyce's style that is markedly different from the combative response to the pre-text of *Jane Eyre*:

> The smell of soap as you cautiously soaped yourself under the chemise, a trick to be learned, dressing with modesty, another trick. Great splashes of sunlight as we ran up the wooden steps of the refectory. Hot coffee and rolls and melting butter. But after the meal, now and at the hour of our death, and at midday and at six in the evening, now and at the hour of our death. Let perpetual light shine on them. This is for my mother, I would think, wherever her soul is wandering, for it has left her body. (47)

Antoinette's fragmentary narrative is, then, less an index of madness than of her distance from the values of early Victorian England[9] and Rhys makes this abundantly clear by taking over many of the central images of *Jane Eyre*, while deploying them in a quite different way. How much of this, though, relates to her modernist inclinations; how much to her response to the 'West Indian' location? In fact, the two elements come together, in a mode that unsettles the fairly comfortable relationship between language and landscape that characterizes the Brontëan 'Romantic' novel.

Just as Achebe humanizes Conrad's African 'darkness' in his village novels, Rhys inverts the hell and devil imagery that is used to locate the Caribbean in *Jane Eyre*. Three times in *Wide Sargasso Sea*, Antoinette has a nightmare, which she explicitly refers to as a dream of being 'in Hell' (51). This becomes 'real' at the end of the novel in the 'cardboard world' (148) of her attic prison, which she refuses to believe is in England. In contrast, the Caribbean is a lost Eden for Antoinette and both the garden of her childhood home at Coulibri – 'Our garden was large and beautiful as that garden in the Bible – the tree of life grew there. But it had gone wild' (16) – and Granbois, the house where she spends her honeymoon with Rochester, are regarded by her as possible prelapsarian refuges from life, so much so that when Rochester betrays her at Granbois by sleeping with Amélie, she regards the desecration of the place as more important than the violation of the sanctity of their relationship (121).

Rhys's portrayal of Rochester's attitude to Granbois is consistent with Charlotte Brontë's account of his reaction to the West Indies, but here, too, she humanizes the sparse detail given in *Jane Eyre* to suggest psychological tensions in the character's mind. His initial reaction to Granbois is that it is a place of excessive colours, 'Not only wild but menacing' (58), and though he says it is 'Not the end of the world' (55), even the suggestion that it might be is, of course, the antithesis of Antoinette's Edenic view. Throughout most of the second section of the novel, the landscape that Antoinette loves so much is a 'nightmare' (99) to him and he is repeatedly disturbed by the scent of night-blooming flowers, an image not only of tropical nature but also of Antoinette. Towards the end of his section of the narrative, however, there is a marked change in the mode of expression: the syntax becomes more broken, the line of thinking more elliptical, the logic more associative. At this point he contemplates the possibility of reconciliation with Antoinette and this change of attitude is complemented by a new sympathetic response to the landscape, no longer viewed as a hell on earth, but as the loveliest place he is ever likely to see (135). He even longs for the time when the moonflowers that he has previously found repugnant will open (139). So for an instant the possibility of healing the breach with Antoinette seems real enough, but when he looks at her and sees hatred in her eyes, his own hate springs up again in return and his reaction against the landscape is total: 'If I was bound for hell let it be hell. No more false heavens. No more damned magic' (140). In short, Charlotte Brontë's Rochester's reductive and totally negative mythologizing of the Caribbean as hell is replaced by an account of ambivalent and vacillating responses, culminating in a final view that suggests his own sense of lost Adamic innocence: 'She had left me thirsty and all my life would be thirst and longing for what I had lost before I found it' (141). Again, while reversing some of the patterns of *Jane Eyre* to dramatize her heroine's predicament, Rhys does not do so at the expense of the other side of the novel's central duality. Like Antoinette, Rochester finds himself shipwrecked in a sargasso sea of competing discourses.

Central to the imagery of *Jane Eyre* is an antithesis between fire and stone[10] and again, this is a pattern that is reconfigured in *Wide Sargasso Sea* as a means of defining the characters' relationships to one another. In *Jane Eyre* the heroine is torn between the elements personified by the stony restraint of St John Rivers and the fiery passion of Rochester and she ultimately achieves some kind of synthesis through her marriage to a 'stone-blind' (454) Rochester. Bertha is also linked with fire, but in an extreme form that seems to exist outside the human continuum that has Rochester and St John Rivers as its two poles: as indicated above, she is constructed as a subhuman animal, completely ruled by her passions. Rhys also associates Antoinette with fire, but with its positive not its destructive aspects. This becomes clear in the final section of the novel, where her dream of accidentally setting fire to Thornfield initiates her into a new world of action. Hitherto she has been almost entirely passive, but now as the fire rekindles the bright colours of her West Indian girlhood in her imagination, she sees it as a liberating force and the dream concludes with her symbolically crossing the divide of the wide sargasso sea to be reunited with her mirror image, Tia, the black friend of her childhood from whom she has been irrevocably separated in the novel's earlier scene of arson, the burning of Coulibri. Once she wakes up, it simply remains for her to act out the dream and the text concludes with her feeling a sense of a purpose about to be completed as she makes her way along the passage with a lighted candle in her hand. Her imminent act of incendiarism is no longer seen as simply destructive: her suicide promises to be a positive existentialist act through which she will achieve release through an imaginative leap back to the lost Eden of her childhood, while at the same time burning down the Great House that represents everything that has stifled the spontaneous expression of her Caribbean subjectivity.

So the distance between Charlotte Brontë's attitude to the West Indies as a trope for uncontrolled desire and Jean Rhys's response to this negative depiction is crystallized in their differing uses of fire imagery. In *Jane Eyre*, Rochester is the personification of fire/desire and Jane is only able to accept him once the impediment of his first marriage has been removed and he has been maimed in the burning of Thornfield; Bertha is no more than a two-dimensional symbol of the destructive nature of uncontrolled fiery passions. In *Wide Sargasso Sea*, Rochester is a very different man, torn, like Jane Eyre, between conflicting forces, but ultimately a creation of stone rather than fire, as Antoinette points out to him after his betrayal (122). Wilson Harris comments perceptively: 'The stone-masked Rochester is an ambiguous yet shrewd alteration by Jean Rhys of the stature – of the almost Gothic stature – of Charlotte Brontë's creation' (*Explorations* 127). The once-fiery Byronic hero finds himself both physically and psychically displaced in the Caribbean and becomes a precursor of a certain kind of postcolonial subject, as he is forced to recognize the presence of conflicting strands within his own mental make-up, but is unable to reconcile them. Meanwhile Antoinette's association with fire represents the tragic predicament of the character who totally commits herself to the instinctive life of the tropics despite alienation from the mainstream experience of the black populace.

Wide Sargasso Sea is, then, a very carefully constructed response to the dominant patterns of *Jane Eyre*, and nowhere more so than in its detailed reworking of its pre-text's imagery. In addition to the Eden/hell and fire/stone oppositions, Rhys also employs images of colour, dress, landscape, bird and animal life and physiognomy (especially eyes), all patterns that are central in *Jane Eyre*, as narrative devices that delineate the relationship of her novel's world to that of Charlotte Brontë. The total effect is not only a criticism of the attitude taken towards the West Indies in *Jane Eyre*, but also of the 'poetic' or 'Romantic' novel, which itself departed from the dominant realist norms of nineteenth-century realist fiction (particularly in the case of *Wuthering Heights*). Charlotte's 'Romantic' reaction to the natural world is now made to appear cloistered through the subversive relocation of her kind of novel in a West Indian setting. Aldous Huxley's famous essay on the impossibility of Wordsworth in the tropics (1–10) seems relevant here, for *Wide Sargasso Sea* is pervaded by the same sense of the inadequacy of English Romantic literature in a tropical context. This motif emerges very clearly in the early part of Rochester's account of his time at Granbois, when he examines the books on a shelf in his dressing-room and finds 'Byron's poems, novels by Sir Walter Scott, *Confessions of an Opium Eater* [sic], some shabby brown volumes, and on the last shelf, *Life and Letters of* . . . . The rest was eaten away' (63). Again, Rhys is working very close to *Jane Eyre*, where Byron and Scott are specifically alluded to, as well as being important influences on the novel, but beyond this particular inversion lies the general disaster that is befalling English Romantic literature in the tropics and this is a metaphor for the process that is occurring in the novel as a whole, as the English book flounders in the liminal world of Rhys's textual sargasso sea.

As part of the process of eroding the monocultural optic of its canonical pre-text, Rhys's novel also turns to other contexts and intertexts, most notably another novel about the white Creole experience, *The Orchid House* (1953), by her fellow-Dominican Phyllis Shand Allfrey, and her own early life in Dominica, as can be seen from her 'unfinished autobiography', *Smile Please* (1979). Rhys had become friends with Allfrey in England in the late 1930s and kept in correspondence with her after she returned to Dominica in the 1950s (Angier 369). Critics have, however, been hesitant to claim *The Orchid House* as even a partial source for *Wide Sargasso Sea*. Elaine Campbell, for example, notes certain parallels, but concludes that 'coincidence and conjecture are all we can summon to support the hypothesis that Allfrey's *The Orchid House* helped to inspire Rhys's magnificent West Indian novel *Wide Sargasso Sea*' (Allfrey ix–x). Karina Williamson simply asserts, 'Clearly the central idea and setting of *Wide Sargasso Sea* owed nothing to *The Orchard House* [sic]' (5). Nevertheless the evidence for arguing the opposite case is persuasive. Names of servants (Christophine and Baptiste) in Rhys's novel are taken over from *The Orchid House*; Rhys's Granbois is distinctly similar to Allfrey's eponymous house, L'Aromatique; and a focus on the fragility and sensuality of the Dominican landscape and the threatened existence of a white Creole family also strongly supports the conclusion that the earlier Dominican novel is an antecedent for some of the main themes of *Wide Sargasso Sea*, where flowers, including orchids, are used as an index of the transience both of natural phenomena and the relationship between Antoinette and Rochester. And, given that Rhys remained in regular contact with Allfrey, it seems likely that her Dominican friend's novel inspired her to situate the long central section of her novel in the island of her birth. The Caribbean scenes in the prehistory of *Jane Eyre* are set in Jamaica and Rhys stays true to Charlotte Brontë's 'original' in locating the first part of *Wide Sargasso Sea* there, but the scenes which loom largest, both in terms of bulk and imaginative power, are set on an unnamed Windward island, which can be identified as the Dominica of Rhys's early years,[11] while even the Jamaican scenes draw on her Dominican childhood.[12] Prior to writing *Wide Sargasso Sea*, Rhys had only turned to Dominica for parts of her novel *Voyage in the Dark* (1934) and a number of her short stories, otherwise setting her novels in London and Paris. Allfrey's example appears to have given her the confidence to locate Dominica at the centre of her counter-discursive response to *Jane Eyre* and she also appears to have been indebted to *The Orchid House* for particular incidental details and some of her main patterns of imagery. Charlotte Brontë's novel remains the most obvious pre-text for *Wide Sargasso Sea*, but Rhys's response is mediated through a Caribbean text that further shifts the ground away from an adversarial response to the canonical English novel. At the same time, as in all her fiction, her own life provided raw material for a fictional practice that displays scepticism about the privileged status of literary pre-texts. The difference in *Wide Sargasso Sea* lies in its turning to her early *Dominican* life as a starting point for her most thorough-going interrogation of European values.

IV

V. S. Naipaul's remarks on *Wide Sargasso Sea* in a 1972 article on Jean Rhys succinctly sum up the novel's 'nightmare' quality:

> An order has collapsed and some people are 'marooned' ... a world that appeared simple is now seen to be diseased, and is no longer habitable. Across the sea there is England, no longer home: an attic, imprisonment, flames. *Wide Sargasso Sea* remains in the mind as a brilliant idea for a nightmare; and it completes Jean Rhys's world. It fills in the West Indian scene and makes more explicit the background to that journey, which turns out not to have been from innocence to darkness, but from one void to another.
>
> There is no innocence in Jean Rhys's world; there has always been loss.
>
> (Naipaul, 'Dog's Chance' 29)

These comments could equally well be applied to Naipaul's own novel *Guerrillas*, which is loosely based on the 'Michael X' murders that Naipaul discusses in his book *The Return of Eva Perón with The Killings in Trinidad* (1980).[13] The novel is set in the Caribbean in the revolutionary climate of the 1970s, in a social situation where 'order' appears to have 'collapsed' and the three main characters — Jimmy Ahmed, the Michael X character, the Englishwoman Jane and Roche, a white South African exile — seem ' "marooned" '. For Jane, England is 'no longer home'; and, as in *Wide Sargasso Sea*, the movement of the novel suggests it will culminate in a fiery apocalypse. A sense of existential 'void' pervades the whole novel, while allusions to English novels set in rural landscapes — *Wuthering Heights*, *Jane Eyre* and Hardy's *Woodlanders* — suggest a more particular 'loss' of innocence, in which city sprawl and the psychic anomie that accompanies it are in marked contrast to the imagined security of the English settings of the Brontës and Hardy. Nevertheless, despite the two novels' shared emphasis on dislocation, Naipaul's focus is markedly different from Rhys's, since his references to *Jane Eyre* and *Wuthering Heights* mainly serve to point up the shortcomings of his characters. I have discussed this aspect of *Guerrillas* elsewhere[14] and so am refraining from re-examining it in any detail here. However, brief discussion of the representation of Jimmy Ahmed will perhaps help to show how Naipaul uses the canon in this instance. As with his affiliative identification with Conrad, his response to the Brontës foregrounds Caribbean distance from the world of English literature, but the stance is neither adversarial nor complicitous. The two pre-texts are employed, more incidentally than *Wide Sargasso Sea* uses *Jane Eyre*, as reference points that help to locate the Caribbean action in a situation where 'order has collapsed'.

The most obvious Brontëan allusion in *Guerrillas* is Jimmy Ahmed's choice of the name Thrushcross Grange for the house attached to the agricultural commune he has founded. As Jane and Roche drive towards the commune at the beginning of the novel, Roche comments:

> 'I don't think it means anything. I don't think Jimmy sees himself as Heathcliff or anything like that. He took a writing course, and it was one of the books he had to read. I think he just likes the name.' (10)

Roche's view of Jimmy is borne out by later details, which suggest he is a semi-literate mimic, of the same order as Ganesh Ramsumair, the protagonist of Naipaul's first novel, *The Mystic Masseur* (1957), whose absorption with books mainly takes the form of a fascination with bindings, typefaces and the physical space they occupy. In *Guerrillas*, Naipaul's touch is subtler, but Jimmy, too, is seen as a misguided aspirant to culture. The sardonic tone of the earlier novel, which appears to have a superficial affinity with *Guerrillas* as a study of a leader who betrays his followers, is, however, replaced by an approach to Jimmy as a limited man who is as much victim as victimizer. Like Malik in 'The Killings in Trinidad' essay, he becomes another version of the colonial subject entrapped within the discourse of the colonizer, again particularly represented by his attachment to books. Not that Naipaul presents the issue in quite this way. His view, as expressed in an interview, is that a mimic man like Malik may have been seduced by an alien discourse, but nevertheless 'wounds a certain section of the society' ('Portrait' 15) through his cynical manipulation. Where Jimmy Ahmed is concerned the presentation is more compassionate. Although Naipaul suggests the futility of Jimmy's aspirations to culture, he puts more emphasis on his personal tragedy than his exploitation of others. His failure as a man of letters comes out most clearly through his attempts at fiction, fantasies based on a partly written novel of Malik's (*Return* 36–7, 60–3). He endeavours to order his life through the process of writing, but Naipaul's Caribbean is a world without order, in which such an endeavour seems doomed to failure, even if Naipaul's achievement in the novel itself affords evidence to the contrary.

Jimmy is, then, seen as only semi-literate and one might assume that his use of the name Thrushcross Grange indicates his inability to measure up to the yardstick of the Brontëan pre-text. Such a view would be entirely consonant with Naipaul's dismissive attitude to what he sees as Caribbean mimicry. However, Roche's assumption that his choice of the name represents no more than a vague yearning for culture is mistaken. It later becomes clear that Jimmy *does* identify with Heathcliff. In one of his fictions he has his female narrator, a fantasy-version of Jane, envisage a crowd's recognition of him as a messianic redeemer in the following terms:

He's the leader they're waiting for and the day will come of that I'm convinced when they will parade in the streets and offer him the crown, everybody will say then 'This man was born in the back room of a Chinese grocery, but as Catherine said to Heathcliff [sic] "Your mother was an Indian princess and your father was the Emperor of China", we knew it all along' and that was in the middle of England mark you, in the days when they had no racial feeling before all those people from Jamaica and Pakistan came and spoiled the country for a man like him. They will see him then like a prince, with his gold colour. (62)

Yet, even though the identification with Heathcliff is explicit here, it involves a number of ironies. Wuthering Heights would surely be a more appropriate name for a projected revolutionary base than Thrushcross Grange, but Naipaul inverts the pattern of Emily Brontë's novel by making the high ground, the Ridge, where Jane and Roche live, the home of the bourgeoisie. Similarly, Jimmy's notion of an idyllic English past in which racism was unknown is, of course, belied by the facts[15] and the remark he attributes to Cathy is a slight misquotation of Nelly Dean's remark to Heathcliff (quoted above). For all this, the basis of his identification with the dark outsider of *Wuthering Heights* is sound enough in certain respects, especially if one admits the possibility that Heathcliff may be an ethnic other in the wild, but parochial world of Emily Brontë's novel.

The complexity of the passage is compounded by the angle of focalization Jimmy adopts: it is written from the point of view of an Englishwoman whom he names Clarissa, and who, like Cathy in *Wuthering Heights*, appears to be a projection of Jane in his fantasy. The fictional narrative itself is partly based on a story of a gang rape of a white girl, which Jimmy remembers from his youth, and this appears to suggest that his desire to be recognized by Jane is counterpointed by a desire to dominate and violate her. It contains the seeds of the subsequent action in the novel at large: when a version of the fiction is acted out, Jimmy sodomizes Jane prior to ordering her murder.

Given Jimmy's rape fantasies, it seems no coincidence that the name of his fictional heroine is the same as that of the most famous canonical English novel on this subject, Richardson's *Clarissa* (1747–48), and Jimmy shares Lovelace's ambivalence as a sexually disturbed man, torn between competing desires, for love and dominance. Since Richardson's male and female archetypes were an influence on the Brontës, particularly Charlotte,[16] it seems reasonable to suggest that part of Naipaul's project in *Guerrillas* involves a reworking of one of the classic encounters of English fiction, especially since his white characters have been given the names Jane and Roche. Naipaul's disturbing novel seems to begin with a desire to suggest the impossibility of Victorian pastoral in the Caribbean. It ends as a fable about murder and violation that is every bit as disturbing as *Clarissa*, with which it at least in part identifies, even if Jimmy lacks the dubious 'heroic' elements in Lovelace that Richardson had taken from Milton's Satan, via Rowe's Lothario. The total collapse of order prevents the restoration of harmony that is achieved at the end of both *Jane Eyre* and *Wuthering Heights*, but it would be wrong to suggest that Naipaul adopts an oppositional position in relation to these novels. *Guerrillas* uses its Brontëan intertexts altogether more incidentally and yet, like *Wide Sargasso Sea*, concludes with an individual tragedy that has its roots in the Gothic relationship between the canon and the postcolonial world.

V

Jean Rhys's decision to reclaim 'the first Mrs Rochester' from having been depicted as 'such a poor ghost' is not only indicative of a strongly felt need to give voice to the silenced colonial other; it also unsettles the relationship between pre-text and con-text by taking issue with Charlotte Brontë's use of Gothic elements in her construction of alterity. Rhys's reply to *Jane Eyre* is typical of a large number of postcolonial texts that invert such usage by representing the local world as a Gothic site haunted by the spectre of *English* culture. Naipaul's more indirect riposte also enacts the ultimately fatal consequences of a Gothic encounter with the canon.

Amitav Ghosh's novel *The Shadow Lines* does not refer to the Brontës, but it provides a particularly powerful account of Gothic aspects of the colonial relationship, particularly in passages where the Bengali narrator views himself as the mirror image of an English character he has never seen, locating himself in an inferior relationship to England and Englishness:

> Nick Price, whom I had never seen, and would, as far as I knew, never see, became a spectral presence beside me in my looking glass; growing with me, but always bigger and better and in some ways more desirable. … I would look into the glass and there he would be, growing, always faster, always a head taller than me. … And yet if I tried to look into the face of that ghostly presence, to see its nose, its teeth, its ears, there was never anything there, it had no features, no form. (49)

So an English alter ego has become the 'ghostly' other, with whom the colonial subject sees himself as strangely twinned, albeit in a manner never to be reciprocated by his unseen doppelgänger, whose own socialization has left him altogether less aware of umbilical connections generated by the colonial encounter. As in Nirad Chaudhuri's *Autobiography of an Unknown Indian* (1951), England pervades a Bengali consciousness in a way that Bengal can never pervade the consciousness of an English person who has 'stayed home'. Like Chaudhuri, Ghosh's narrator becomes conversant with the minutiae of aspects of English life without ever leaving Bengal. Prior to travelling to the 'Mother Country', he familiarizes himself with the locale in which the Price family live by studying the relevant square of an A-Z London street atlas and, when he eventually does makes his pilgrimage to England, he has internalized every aspect of these particular shadow lines so thoroughly that he is able to make his way to their house in West Hampstead with little difficulty. Once inside the house he astonishes its occupants, who include his cousin Ila, by his similarly detailed knowledge of its interior. In fact it is Ila who has provided him with this information many years before during a visit to an old family house near Calcutta. On this occasion she has taken him into a dark basement room and beneath a huge Victorian table, enshrouded by a sheet until she removes it — Miss Havisham's room and *its* draped dressing-table appear to be an intertext — she has re-enacted a game called 'Houses' (48) that she has played with Nick Price in London, by drawing the floor plan of the West Hampstead house in the dust. So the narrator's intimate knowledge of a corner of England has been attained in this underground Gothic site, where, as in Satis House or the attic at Thornfield Hall, time has been arrested. The table itself suggests the lingering presence of Victorian imperialism in Calcutta — Ila's grandfather has bought it at an exhibition at the Crystal Palace in the 1890s — and the novel subsequently sets a key scene at Calcutta's Victoria Memorial, which the narrator, who believes 'that a place does not merely exist, that it has to be invented in one's imagination' (21) comes to regard as 'a haunted site' (167). The underground room suggests a similar haunting by the Gothic tracings of a legacy written in dust. Basement may have replaced Brontëan attic, but the use of the marginalized recesses of an ancestral house as a trope for the hidden presence of the other side of the colonial relationship metonymically expresses the relationship between Ghosh's novel and English pre-texts such as *Great Expectations* and the Conrad novella, from which it takes its title. The text itself becomes a haunted site, a palimpsest written on its buried English intertexts, in much the same way that the Memorial has been superimposed on Indian soil. At the same time there are clear indications that, while such Gothic traces haunt the contemporary Indo-British encounter, particularly the middle-class Indian experience, and nowhere more so than in Calcutta, they are a buried level of ancestry that points to the impossibility of transplanting and maintaining anything more than the vestigial shadow lines of British culture in India, not just in the present, but even in the late Victorian heyday of Empire. The table has been shipped to India in pieces and left neglected in the underground room ever since.

So, while the narrator's attitudes frequently suggest a filiative colonial psychology, the text undermines this by a recurrent stress on the arbitrariness of its many shadow lines, which include the invisible frontier that has partitioned Bengal, the lines of demarcation that separate colonizer and colonized and the borders between present and past and self and image. Ultimately shadow lines are the signifying acts that construct notions of discrete identity and Ghosh's own practice, in all his writing to date, is based on an *affiliative* excavation of a labyrinthine network of traces which undermines essentialist versions of national and regional cultures and enables him to construct his own inter-cultural tradition. He wrote his Oxford doctoral thesis on the history of weaving and, as Robert Dixon, points out, the interweaving of cultures is a central 'organizing figure' (9) in his early work: literally so in *The Circle of Reason* (1986), which takes a young weaver from his home village near Calcutta to work in the Gulf; metaphorically so in *In An Antique Land* (1992), where Ghosh suggests that medieval trade routes functioned as a mobile intercontinental network that was largely unaware of Oriental/Occidental bifurcations. In *The Calcutta Chromosome* (1996), a novel which moves between the nineteenth century and the near future, this figure appears in two new forms: the World Wide Web and a cult of Silence, which challenges Western beliefs in discrete subjectivity through its attempt to evolve a technology for transmitting knowledge 'chromosomally, from body to body' (Ghosh, *Chromosome* 107).[17] This counter-epistemology represents a direct challenge to Western intellectual hegemonies, here specifically represented by the 'official' historiography of late nineteenth-century malaria research, and in so doing posits the possible existence of subaltern discursive systems that can dismantle the oppositional relationship between colonizer and colonized and along with it pre-texts and con-texts. In Ghosh's work, the West's presence still looms large, both as a Gothic trace of colonialism and, more insidiously, in contemporary American-dominated forms of globalization such as the Internet, but it is overwritten by so many interweavings that it is impossible to sustain a narrowly filiative or an oppositional reading of cultural interactions.

VI

In the hands of postcolonial writers such as Rhys and Ghosh, the main ground of the encounter with English culture is, then, a haunted site, to which they respond in different ways. However, it is not difficult to find instances of an opposite, ostensibly more filiative impulse, particularly among New World writers who bemoan the absence of cultural ghosts. While early New England authors such as Charles Brockden Brown and Nathaniel Hawthorne used the Gothic genre to engage with local cultural legacies, twentieth-century Canadian writing has more frequently agreed with Earle Birney's view that 'It's only by our lack of ghosts/we're haunted' (138). Such a view certainly appears to underpin Jane Urquhart's more recent Brontëan derivative, *Changing Heaven* and Margaret Atwood's playful treatment of popular Gothic fiction in *Lady Oracle*.

Urquhart's novel is an imaginative, if 'self-indulgent',[18] tour de force centred on the stories of a contemporary Canadian academic, Ann, who is writing a book about the 'emotional weather' (Urquhart 232) of *Wuthering Heights*, and a balloonist, Arianna Ether,[19] who dies in 1900, when her parachute fails to open as she jumps to earth over the Yorkshire moors, and finds herself engaged in a dialogue with the ghost of Emily Brontë.[20] The novel's 'Emily's' comments on her life and writing provide a further narrative strand, as do the stories of the men with whom Ann and Arianna have relationships. Gradually these various narratives converge to a point where, in a passage reminiscent of Lockwood's dream of being visited by Catherine's ghost in the third chapter of *Wuthering Heights* (Brontë, E. 66–7),[21] the ghosts of Arianna and 'Emily' listen outside a window to hear an explanation of the mystery of Arianna's death being given to Ann by a contemporary Yorkshire storyteller. *Changing Heaven* is not, however, a novel in which plot is paramount. It uses a collage of references to landscape, weather, obsession and culture to provide a modern-day meditation on issues raised by the life and writing of Emily Brontë, both *Wuthering Heights* and her poetry.[22]

Initially at least, the text seems to view Emily Brontë's work as a positive escape from the anomie and urban sprawl that both Ann and the novel more generally[23] present as characteristic of contemporary Canadian life. Early on, the building of a new highway[24] signals the end of both Ann's childhood and any clear-cut division between the urban and the rural:

> The highway.
> Its arrival in the province has, for Ann, heralded the end of an era. And the beginning of another where four lanes sew the disparate parts of her life together like a long, grey thread. The highway connects everything: the countryside and the city, the known and the unknown. ... It connects the house in the city with Ann's mother's past – a village and a farm in a rural landscape that becomes, with the advent of the highway, a miraculous hour and a half away. An hour and a half of grey speed and you are able to enter the nineteenth century; its general stores, its woodstoves, its large high-ceilinged rooms, its dusty gravel roads. (44)

Along the highway, there are 'ugly subdivisions ... where it was once green' (86) and perhaps the most telling image of all of the loss of earlier, supposedly organic landscapes is that of the shattered glass dome of a Catholic church, which Ann sees from the interstitial world of the highway. It is an image that relates directly to the novel's title, which is taken from an Emily Brontë poem, as Ann reflects that 'After the broken dome, Heaven changes' (47) and the dome's splintered shards reflect the loss of her childhood sense of the wholeness of experience, along with her belief in the self-contained completeness of Canadian rural environments.

To escape from this 'ugliness' as a young girl, Ann fantasizes she is Catherine in *Wuthering Heights* and turns to the emotional terrain of Emily

Brontë's moors to find release in a world where passion can transcend death: 'Hearts cracked open. The weather and the landscape a suitable reflection of a province in the mind' (69). When a 'hurricane' rages outside during her Toronto childhood, it is less real to her than the storms and winds of *Wuthering Heights* (18–19). Later, when she goes to a church dance, she knows she will find no Canadian Heathcliffs there[25] and returns home determined to spend a lot more time with the Heathcliff of Emily Brontë's novel (68–70). More generally, she is struck by the incongruity that 'in order to visit culture, [she] and her mother must travel into the dark heart of cities' (32). Her absorption with *Wuthering Heights* continues into adulthood and she travels to Haworth to research her book, identifying with Catherine's ghost, and 'straining towards ether' (125) in the belief that the wild weather of the West Yorkshire moors may blow away the emotional baggage she has brought with her, enabling her to return to Canada, 'light, unencumbered, without any burdens at all' (125).

Like Ann, Urquhart's novel seems to share Earle Birney's belief that Canada suffers from cultural barrenness and *needs* to be haunted by ghosts. So just as Ann's obsession replaces her everyday world with the emotional landscape of *Wuthering Heights, Changing Heaven* appears to develop an affiliative relationship with Emily Brontë's novel. Contemporary Ontario communities may have British 'origins', but there is little sense in the novel of an uninterrupted filial link with England. So, in the late twentieth century, British culture represents such a small part of the Canadian national mosaic that both Ann's identification with the world of Emily Brontë and the text's response to her work are a matter of affiliative choice. Needless to say, the passionate engagement with Emily Brontë's landscape that leads Ann to make an actual pilgrimage to West Yorkshire represents a highly personal response to her fiction, albeit one that is in keeping with the *Wuthering Heights* myth fostered by a thousand and one adaptations, ranging from William Wyler's classic 1939 Hollywood film to Kate Bush's surreal 1978 pop song. Nevertheless, to contemporary British readers, struck by the commercialization of Haworth and its surroundings as a tourist site and more generally by England's almost total lack of wilderness space, it may seem ironic that a *Canadian* novel should focus on contemporary West Yorkshire as a landscape of ethereal freedom.

Urquhart's novel is, however, subtler than this. Patsy Stoneman points out that its view of place is constructivist (251): 'Emily' claims to have built the landscape that she and Arianna Ether are haunting (Urquhart 179) and the text's 'devotion to mutability is combined with a remarkable sense of history' (Stoneman 250). For Ann, *Wuthering Heights* and Emily Brontë's poetry offer a landscape of desire and transcendence, which exists apart from the social reality of the 'dark satanic mills'[26] that have disturbed the natural balance of the moorland world, but these are not ignored in Urquhart's vision. Even 'Emily' comes across as an incipient ecologist when she complains, '"There is dirt everywhere. Nothing is pure."' (101). And yet history finally takes a secondary place in *Changing Heaven* and the novel does not put its main emphasis on its constructivist view of place. It is not ultimately about the state of England in 1900, or any of the other years in which individual scenes may be set, but rather about the power of the romantic vision to rise above temporal situations; and, although its imaginative audaciousness complements Ann's obsession with the Brontëan 'ether', this threatens to leave all its characters as disembodied ghosts floating, like 'Emily' and Arianna, in dehistoricized air.

Ann sees herself as 'locked ... in the perpetual present of her own emotional landscape' (219) and this raises the issue of whether the kind of romantic escapism that she indulges in is an unhealthy form of fantasizing, an issue that has troubled feminist critics in recent decades, particularly in the 1980s. Quoting a 1982 *Guardian* article, which noted that in 'the past decade, the rise of feminism has been paralleled almost exactly by a mushroom growth in the popularity of romance fiction' (Charlotte Lamb quoted by Jones in Radford 195), Ann Rosalind Jones discussed the apparent contradiction between 'Mills & Boon and the faith that a woman's greatest happiness lies in love and marriage' and 'feminism, which questions the social construction of that faith and the viability of that institution' (198). Romantic fiction of the Mills and Boon variety has, of course, seen changes in recent years, but if one accepts Jones's summary of the values it promotes as a working definition, its origins can be traced back to the novel of romantic courtship, in which the lower-class heroine is elevated into the ranks of the gentry through marriage, a genre that is generally seen to have begun with Richardson's *Pamela* (1740), which influenced several major British women novelists, among them the Brontës, particularly Charlotte. Following in the footsteps of *Pamela*, *Jane Eyre*'s famous conclusion, 'Reader, I married him' (474), seems to open the floodgates for the fantasies particularly associated with Mills and Boon in Britain and Harlequin[27] in North America, raising questions about how such fiction differs from supposedly serious earlier writing on the same theme? In 'Write, She Said', Michèle Roberts talks of 'wondering why it was apparently all right to enjoy reading Jane Austen and the Brontës and Mrs Gaskell but not the twentieth century novels their work subsequently inspired', such as the fiction of Georgette Heyer and Victoria Holt (Radford 222).

Changing Heaven seems to be 'serious' fiction and it certainly departs from the rags-to-riches 'marriage' formula. Moreover, it is altogether more knowing in its self-conscious use of *Wuthering Heights* to comment on the romantic psychology and along with it the discourse of transcendental romantic love. Nevertheless it remains a novel which begs the question of whether romance can function as 'one of the few widely shared womanly commentaries on the contradictions and costs of patriarchy' (Radway 18) and whether fantasy can provide an alternative discourse that liberates female desire from the inherently patriarchal codes of realist fiction.[28]

This question may seem to depart from the postcolonial issues with which this book is primarily concerned, but this is not altogether the case, since the novel's investigation of gender and fantasy is directly related to its representation of places and, of course, gender is never discrete from other determinants of identity. Colonial relationships do not figure prominently in the text in any obvious sense, but inter-cultural relationships *are* central and the main male characters are as caught up in fantasies of place as Ann, Arianna and 'Emily'. Ann's lover, Arthur, is an art historian, who since adolescence has had an obsession with Tintoretto that parallels her absorption with Emily Brontë. His fascination is as much with Tintoretto's character as the artist's paintings and he is drawn to 'the concept of the passionate inner man combined with the practical outer one' (61). This fascination stems directly from the two main elements in his parentage: the 'stiff repression' of his 'ordinary Canadian' (59, 58) father,[29] who runs a laundry and dry-cleaning business' and the 'dancing, sentimental' (59) nature of his Italian mother. Again, then, there is a contrast between Canadian Puritanism and a more catholic European world of Romance. Arthur may be more captivated by Tintoretto's character than his art, but when he travels to Venice to study the two cycles of his paintings in the Scuola San Rocco, his concern is with aspects that loosely match those that Ann finds fascinating in Emily Brontë – lightning, thunder and angels among them – and at one point Ann tells Arthur he has enabled her 'to stand in Emily Brontë's landscape and think about Tintoretto. His lightning was there' (226). Again, there is a strong emphasis on the constructivist nature of artistic representations of place and even Tintoretto is seen as a fantasizer of idealized pastoral backgrounds, when it is pointed out that he never left Venice, an 'architectural' city, in which 'apart from gardens there is no landscape' (105). The predominant pattern, however, has European sites providing the Canadian imagination with romantic possibilities absent from the unhaunted local world.

Canada is, though, allowed to offer one possibility for romantic fulfilment. Arianna's lover, Jeremy, has Arctic fantasies, which are directly mapped onto an imagined version of the Canadian landscape shared by the real-life Emily Brontë, who was fascinated by polar exploration and invented her own Arctic continent, which she called '*Parry's land*' (Urquhart 108; italics in original)[30] after the explorer, Sir Edward Parry.[31] Jeremy has effected a Svengali-like transformation of the identity of Arianna (née Polly Smith), capitalizing on her ethereal beauty to make her the centrepiece of his balloonist performances.

Prior to this, however, he has been their main protagonist, a self-styled 'Sindbad of the Skies', who tries to elude both the constrictions of a social existence and the entrapments of romantic love and resents Arianna's having '"taken the sky from [him]"' (10). He finally realizes his goal in the closing sections of the novel, in which he flies further and further north, finding solace in a world of Gothic whiteness that evokes the final sections of Mary Shelley's *Frankenstein* (1818) and Edgar Allan Poe's *Narrative of Arthur Gordon Pym* (1838). He dies amid the Arctic snows: as in Poe and Melville, white rather than black is the colour of Gothic.

And this finally lends a particularly Canadian dimension to the text's romantic constructions of place. As wilderness space disappears even in North America, recent decades have seen an increasing number of writers turning to the North as the last Frontier. The Arctic has taken this role over from the West, particularly in the work of Prairie authors such as Rudy Wiebe, Aritha van Herk and Robert Kroetsch,[32] but also in a varied range of writing from Ontario and Québec, including Gwendolyn MacEwen's verse drama *Terror and Erebus* (1987),[33] Mordecai Richler's novel, *Solomon Gursky Was Here* (1989), which deals with the Jewish 'discovery' of the Arctic, Margaret Atwood's short story 'Age of Lead' and Atwood's critical study *Strange Things: The Malevolent North in Canadian Literature* (1995). Urquhart's novel also seems to construct the North as the final Frontier, and hence the last site for possible romantic fulfilment within North America, but *Changing Heaven* suggests throughout that place is invented and her main sites of romance are firmly located within the Old World, and particularly the landscape of Emily Brontë's moors.

Wuthering Heights and Emily Brontë's poems are, then, complemented in Urquhart's novel by other romantic sites such as Tintoretto's Venice and his imagined pastoral landscapes – and beyond this there is the insistence that romance belongs in the upper atmosphere, in the ethereal world that claims the lives of Arianna and Jeremy and through which the ghosts of 'Emily' and Arianna can seemingly move at will. *Changing Heaven* presents its readers with a range of variations on the issue of Romantic fantasizing, to a point where it is less about such fantasizing itself than the textual construction of fantasy. So, while Urquhart may be right to accuse herself of having been 'self-indulgent' in the novel, it remains a world away from the wish-fulfilment fantasies of Mills and Boon.

VII

In Atwood's *Lady Oracle*, the heroine, Joan Foster, is a writer of 'Costume Gothics', who also engages with a range of other escapist discourses; and the issue of whether her romantic escapism is a form of self-evasion or a potential source of positive liberation, for both Joan and her readers, is central to the text. Produced for 'Columbine Books' (156), a playful fictionalization of the name of Harlequin Books, Joan's Gothics are certainly formula fiction, written in the romantic novelette vein, as can be seen from her breathless account of the plot of the latter stages of her book, *Escape from Love*:

> Samantha Deane was kidnapped precipitously from her bedroom in the house of the kindly guppy man; threatened with rape at the hands of the notorious Earl of Darcy, the hero's disreputable uncle; rescued by the hero; snatched again by the agents of the lush-bodied, evil-minded Countess of Piedmont, the jealous semi-Italian beauty who had once been the hero's mistress. Poor Samantha flew back and forth across London like a beanbag, ending up finally in the hero's arms, while his wife, the feeble-minded Lady Letitia, died of yellow fever, the Countess now quite demented, plunged to her death off a battlement during a thunderstorm and the Earl was financially ruined by the Pacific Bubble. (175–6)

This pastiche brings together numerous Gothic ingredients that typically beset the heroine: the 'feeble-minded' wife who is an impediment to the union of the hero and heroine draws on Charlotte Brontë's Bertha; the name of the villain comes from *Pride and Prejudice*, even if the character bears little resemblance to his namesake in Austen; the fate with which Samantha is threatened can be traced back to Richardson's use of rape as a pivotal plot element. And, when the book appears, its jacket depicts Samantha with 'her hair rippling like seaweed against an enormous cloud; Castle DeVere turreted with menace in the background' (176): the architecture of the Gothic house, another staple of the Gothic form from Horace Walpole's *Castle of Otranto* (1764) onwards, is redolent of Thornfield Hall and the Manderley of Daphne du Maurier's *Rebecca* (1938) – and, again typically, is invested with gender attributes.

One's first inclination is to dismiss such writing as parody, while enjoying the comedy. However, Atwood's treatment of the genre is more complex than this. Writing Gothics provides Joan with a secret life apart from her husband Arthur, who is presented as a product of the repressive, Calvinist aspects of Canadian Maritime culture (23–4, 168). Writing an ironic reworking of popular Gothic provides *Atwood* with a means of subverting conventional gender stereotypes. Throughout *Lady Oracle*, there are links between the fiction Joan is writing and the novel itself and towards the end the distance between inner and outer novels collapses totally, as the main Gothic of the text, *Stalked by Love*, refuses to be contained by the formula. Joan feels an involuntary force is controlling the composition of this novel, as she slips from using her significantly named Jane Eyre-like protagonist, Charlotte, who is typical of all her heroines, as the focalizer, to telling the story from the point of view of Felicia, the lascivious first wife of the Rochester-like hero, Redmond. She stops writing, telling herself, 'It was all wrong' (319), but it is fairly clear that, as in *Wide Sargasso Sea*, the 'Bertha' character is usurping the 'Jane Eyre' role. Joan resists this shift, but when she returns to *Stalked by Love*, Felicia has completely taken over as the narrative consciousness and *she* goes into the maze in the grounds of the Gothic house, which the servants have been warning *Charlotte* about all along. Entry into this labyrinth promises a resolution of all the romantics complications in the 'central plot' (341) and Felicia now meets several former wives of Redmond, who emerges at this point as more of a Bluebeard than a Rochester, though, if one takes the view that con-texts generate re-readings of pre-texts, one could contend that this angle of vision simply refracts back on the Bluebeard aspect of Rochester's character that is present in the 'original'.

The conventional ending of the popular Gothic undergoes a feminist metamorphosis, as Felicia is welcomed into this sorority of victimized wives. At the same time a number of other distinctions are dismantled, as the former wives are given characteristics earlier ascribed to Joan and Redmond is eventually referred to as Arthur. The thin dividing line that has separated 'fact' and 'fiction' throughout the novel — Joan has *lived* a number of fictional identities and the text consistently stresses the performative aspects of identity — now disappears entirely and, although Felicia/Joan is left struggling with Redmond/Arthur as *Stalked by Love* finally breaks off, there is a strong sense that Joan is able to draw positive sustenance from her multiplicity of roles and is no longer evading the realities of her social existence. In one sense, then, the romance formula of *Jane Eyre*, as mediated by Mills and Boon and Harlequin, is subverted by elements that reverse its central premises. This is achieved through the transformation of the Gothic form in the inner novel and a playful admixture of genres in the main novel, which is primarily social comedy. However, Gothic is not simply parodied: both the conclusion to *Stalked by Love* and the overspill of Gothic elements into novel at large suggest that, read from a certain con-textual viewpoint, it can be a liberating mode. The overall effect, then, is that of a reworking that foregrounds the positive potential of fantasy. *Lady Oracle* may seem a far cry from *Wide Sargasso Sea* and yet in its reclamation of the figure of the first wife, part of a more general process of interrogating female stereotypes, it occupies similar territory. Atwood may seem to be more concerned with gender than cross-cultural debates, but like Urquhart's novel, her contemporary Gothic takes Joan to Italy and, as in *Changing Heaven*, this clearly offers a Romantic alternative to Canadian Puritanism.

Of the four novels discussed in this chapter, only *Wide Sargasso Sea* offers anything resembling an adversarial approach to its English pre-text, but they are all concerned with reading across cultures and introduce motifs that refract back on Charlotte and Emily Brontës' representation of equivocal 'foreignness'. Irrespective of whether gender or cultural identity is to the fore and regardless of their geographical settings, all four novels shift the ground of their 'originals' by creating a discursive space in which Gothic and romance elements are refashioned, as a necessary correlative of their exploration of alternative versions of identity. *Guerrillas* stands apart from the other three novels in that it gives little sense of the positive gains to be made from such refashioning, but even Naipaul is at pains to put distance between himself and the world of the Brontës and demonstrates the need for postcolonial fiction to create its own new territory.

Notes

1. While quite young, the three sisters and their brother Branwell made up a series of tales and legends that owed much to their reading of the *Arabian Nights*. These were peopled by Branwell's wooden soldiers and set in an invented magical city they called Glass Town. In adolescence Charlotte and Branwell composed stories about the fictional kingdom of Angria, which, like Glass Town, was set in an exoticized version of 'Africa'; Emily and Anne set their tales in 'Gondal', a wilder landscape that bore more resemblance to the local moors (Gérin, *Charlotte Brontë* 26–7, 78–80, 87–8).
2. *The First Mrs Rochester* was a working title for the novel (Angier 500, 502).
3. There were numerous English translations of the Swiss pastor, Johann Kaspar Lavater's *Essays on Physiognomy* (1789–98), on which Goethe collaborated, in the late eighteenth and early nineteenth centuries.
4. E.g. David Daiches, Introduction to the 1965 Penguin edition (16).
5. I am indebted to Denis Judd for this information.
6. I am grateful to Louis James for emphasizing this to me.
7. This is only one interpretation of the title. Never mentioned in the text itself, it evokes the seaweed sea in the North Atlantic, which encompasses the Bermuda islands and has a particular place in early European mythologies of the New World. Columbus, who crossed it on his first voyage, welcomed it as an indication of the proximity of land, but other early European navigators thought it was hazardous to shipping and mistakenly believed their vessels would become entangled within it. It lies between latitudes 20° and 35° N and longitudes 30° and 70° W and is a biological waste area, since it lacks the plankton on which fish feed. In Rhys's novel it suggests the cultural divide that obstructs contacts between the Caribbean and England. This relates most obviously to the relationship of Antoinette and Rochester, which metaphorically flounders in mid-Atlantic, but alternatively it can be viewed as a metaphor for Antoinette's split psyche, from which she is only able to escape when her

portentous dream of her final suicidal leap allows her imaginatively to reinhabit the Caribbean world of her childhood.

8.   She wrote the novel between 1957 and 1966, after being 'rediscovered', when the BBC broadcast a dramatization of her novel *Good Morning Midnight*, in 1957. She had, however, worked on an earlier version entitled *Le Revenant*, which was half completed by 1945. Her accounts of the genesis of the novel vary considerably, but she appears to have embarked on *Le Revenant* in 1938 or 1939 (Angier 370–1).

9.   Rhys sets her novel in the period immediately after Emancipation, whereas, given the retrospective nature of Rochester's account of his time in Jamaica, the latest possible date for Bertha's marriage to Rochester in *Jane Eyre* puts it in the pre-Emancipation period.

10.   See Lodge (114–43) for a discussion of the fire imagery.

11.   Numerous general details suggest this; the use of the place-name Massacre (55) confirms it beyond doubt.

12.   Aspects of her description of Coulibri are based on the garden of Geneva estate, where her mother had been born and where an earlier estate house had been burnt by freed slaves in the period immediately after Emancipation (Rhys, *Smile Please* 33).

13.   The 'Killings in Trinidad' essay was originally published in two parts in *The Sunday Times Magazine*, 12 May 1974: 16–35 and 19 May 1974: 24–41.

14.   Thieme, *Web of Tradition* 163–78.

15.   See, e.g. Bolt, *passim*.

16.   Tillotson 149. Jane's situation at Thornfield can be read as a subtler version of Pamela's predicament in the household of Mr B.

17.   See Thieme, 'Discoverer' for a fuller discussion.

18.   Urquhart's own phrase. *Profile: Jane Urquhart*. By Beverley Slopen. Digital Bookworld. Online. www.digitalbookworld.com/bookworld/topinterviews.html. 6 January 2001.

19.   Cf. Jane Eyre's ethereal surname.

20.   Hereafter referred to as 'Emily' to distinguish her from her real-life original.

21.   Urquhart paraphrases part of this passage earlier in the novel, in a section where Ann 'enters the structure called *Wuthering Heights*', as she reads Catherine's cry ' "*Let me in, let me in. I've been lost on the moor for twenty years*" ' (48; italics in original) and also at the beginning of Part Two of the novel (123). Cf. Brontë, E. 67.

22.   The epigraphs to the whole novel and Section I are taken from poems by Emily Brontë (*Poems* 70–1 and 73–4). The novel's title is taken from the first poem, 'How still, how happy', dated 7 December 1838. The epigraphs for the other two sections are taken from women poets who could be seen as similar to Emily Brontë in temperament: another Emily – Dickinson – and Stevie Smith. Another Canadian writer, Dorothy Livesay, offers a precedent for linking Emily Brontë and Emily Dickinson in her poem, 'The Three Emily's' (David and Lecker, eds: 226), where the third Emily is the Canadian Emily Carr.

23.   Cf. Naipaul in *Guerrillas*, where there is a similar opposition between postcolonial urban sprawl and the imagined harmony of an organic, English landscape, associated with *Wuthering Heights*, as well as *The Woodlanders* in Naipaul's case.

24. The 401, specifically the section going east from Toronto towards Belleville and Kingston.
25. Cf. Margaret Atwood's narrator in *Lady Oracle*, asking 'Was every Heathcliff a Linton in disguise?'(269).
26. The Blake phrase is explicitly cited on one occasion (135) and indirectly alluded to on another (172).
27. See the discussion of Atwood's *Lady Oracle* below.
28. See Jackson and Radway, *passim*.
29. Cf. the representation of the (identically named) Arthur's father in *Lady Oracle*.
30. Gérin explains the 'mysterious and prolonged incidence of the name "Parry", "Parrysland", "Parry's Glasstown", "Chief Genius Parry" as personifications and pseudonyms for Emily in the Brontë juvenilia" (*Emily Brontë* 12).
31. Cf. a later passage in *Changing Heaven*, where Emily contrasts Parry with Sir James Clark Ross, seeing Parry as a visionary explorer who dreamt of the Northwest Passage and the North Pole and which mentions that he lived in Halifax, Nova Scotia (240–1). Cf. also 202. Gérin points out that Ross was Anne Brontë's 'hero' (*Emily Brontë* 15).
32. See, for example, Wiebe's *Playing Dead: A Contemplation concerning the Arctic* (1989) and *A Discovery of Strangers* (1994), van Herk's *The Tent Peg* (1981) and *Places far from Ellesmere* (1990) and Kroetsch's *Gone Indian* (1973) and *The Man from the Creeks* (1998).
33. Originally a radio play, broadcast by CBC around 1963 (Atwood, *Strange Things* 24).

5

Turned upside down? Dickens's Australia and Peter Carey's *Jack Maggs*

The man, after looking at me for a moment, turned me upside down, and emptied my pockets. There was nothing in them but a piece of bread. When the church came to itself – for he was so sudden and strong that he made it go head over heels before me, and I saw the steeple under my feet – when the church came to itself, I say, I was seated on a high tombstone, trembling, while he ate the bread ravenously.

(Charles Dickens, *Great Expectations* 36; quoted by Jolley 23)

Do gentlemen make convicts? Then a convict will 'make' and 'own' a real gentleman, not a colonial facsimile. He will show the truth about gentility: It can be bought.

(Robert Hughes 585)

I

Throughout this study I have tried to emphasize the diversity of the ways in which counter-discursive texts have re-read the English pre-texts with which they engage, and argued against the simplism of seeing canonical discourse as unitary. Postcolonial responses to Dickens are, however, especially complex, since he is variously seen as occupying a central role in the canon and as an outsider who could be a trenchant critic of the dominant social codes of his day. His extraordinary international popularity during his lifetime – the stories of the crowds on the New York docks clamouring to learn the fate of Little Nell are but the tip of an iceberg – is an index of the extent to which his fiction transcended cultural differences. Among the many reasons one may posit to explain it are his gifts as a storyteller, his broadly drawn comic characterization and his social reformism, which often touched a chord in the experience of his overseas readership; and, while his sentimentalism was also clearly a significant factor in his popular appeal, many of his readers found as much realism as romanticism in his writing. One can see virtually all these elements at work in his influence on a writer such as Henry Lawson, who played a central role in the evolution of the Australian Legend of the 1890s and came close to achieving an ambivalent canonical status within Australia,[1] comparable to Dickens's in Britain. As Xavier Pons argues in a Freudian study of Lawson's life and works, the Australian writer, despite his general reluctance to acknowledge influences, saw Dickens as a father figure (53). In Dickens's fiction, Lawson found a model for a technique that combined romanticism and realism, as well as bringing together humour and pathos and 'an awareness of social issues born out of personal experience of poverty and injustice', which he hoped to emulate, by doing for Australian society what Dickens had done for England (Pons 259). If one follows Pons's reading, Lawson's debt to Dickens seems, to use Said's terms once again, to constitute a filiative relationship rather than an affiliative identification (*World* 174). However, since the debt is elective – Lawson could have chosen any of the literary greats, or not-so-greats, of his day as a father figure in preference to Dickens, had he been so minded – it clearly is an *affiliative* choice. The borderline between colonial complicity and postcolonial contestation begins to look especially porous in a case such as this, once again pointing up the reductiveness of seeing the English canon as a unified body of texts operating against the interests of the colonized society, even during the heyday of British cultural imperialism.

Other colonial and postcolonial writers may not have seen Dickens in quite such a paternal light, but he has frequently provided an affiliative touchstone for writers around the globe, who have found it easier to identify with the cultural and social politics of his reformist fiction than the work of many of his more middle-class contemporaries. Outside America and Britain, nowhere was his popularity higher than in Australia, where his reputation was ensured after a pirated edition of *The Pickwick Papers*, published in Hobart in 1838, sold 30,000 copies (Lansbury 69). This chapter is mainly devoted to Australian responses to Dickens, which particularly react to the two principal constructions of Australia to be found in his writing: his view of the colony as 'Botany Bay', the site of convict transportation, which is dominant in his early fiction and once again to the fore in *Great Expectations*, the main Dickens reference point for this chapter; and his alternative view of it as a New World Arcadia offering certain kinds of free emigrants, such as Mr Micawber, Mr Peggotty and Little Em'ly in *David Copperfield*, opportunities of a kind denied to them in English society. The central focus of the chapter is on Peter Carey's 1997 novel, *Jack Maggs*, which responds to *Great Expectations*, albeit obliquely, by taking a returned convict, reminiscent of Dickens's Magwitch, as its protagonist, while also, like Coetzee's *Foe*, engaging with elements from the writer's other novels and the figure of the author himself. Elizabeth Jolley's *Miss Peabody's Inheritance* is also examined, as another Australian novel in which *Great Expectations* is a significant, though less central, intertext.

Before considering Dickens's representation of Australia and Carey's and Jolley's responses in more detail, I should, however, like to underscore the particularly ambivalent nature of Dickens's reception and influence outside Britain by looking briefly at work by other postcolonial writers that develops a relationship with his fiction that is more complicitous than adversarial, though again there is seepage between the two positions. Such a primarily filiative response is particularly prominent among novelists who have identified not only with Dickens's social reformism, but also his comic mode or his distinctive blend of realism and romance. The South Indian novelist R. K. Narayan is a case in point. Talking about the various English books he consumed voraciously during the vacations of his Mysore schooldays, Narayan records how he 'picked up a whole row of Dickens and loved his London and the queer personalities therein' (61) and V. S. Naipaul has seen Narayan's novels as bringing together social comedy – in the Dickensian tradition of the English novel – and Hindu fable, while viewing the latter element as the dominant, underlying mode of Narayan's fiction (Naipaul, *India* 18–27). Naipaul himself is interestingly ambivalent about his own response to Dickens in an early essay about his boyhood difficulty in adapting 'foreign' books to his native Trinidad. In this essay, 'Jasmine', he discusses passages in Dickens that he could imaginatively adapt to the 'reality' of his Port of Spain boyhood and aspects which simply would not work in this context:

> All Dickens's descriptions of London I rejected; and though I might retain Mr Micawber and the others in the clothes the illustrator gave them, I gave them the faces and voices of people I knew and set them in buildings and streets I knew. ... Dickens's rain and drizzle I turned into tropical downpours; the snow and the fog I accepted as conventions of books.
>
> (Naipaul, *Overcrowded Barracoon* 24)

He goes on to describe how he found himself able to envisage Trinidadian equivalents for chapters of *Oliver Twist*, *Nicholas Nickleby* and *David Copperfield*, but was unable to do the same for Pickwick and his club. When the process of imaginative transformation was successful, he still felt troubled by the illustrations in his Dickens editions, which he felt rendered his adaptations absurd (25). Towards the end of the essay, Naipaul talks about his current attitude to Dickens and his adult inability to dismiss the alienness of the illustrations. His conclusion is that 'All literatures are regional' and that 'perhaps it is only the placelessness of a Shakespeare or the blunt communication of "gross" experience as in Dickens that makes them appear less so' (28–9). So, if Dickens was sometimes able to work across cultures in a way that the majority of writers did not for Naipaul, in his case it was not because of any subtlety of style; rather the opposite. Yet Dickens had provided a touchstone for him in other more specific ways, possibly because, as he also writes in 'Jasmine', the 'only social division I accepted was that between rich and poor' (24). In this case, it is Dickens the critic of the English class system, who speaks across cultures to the 'colonial' author.[2] Naipaul's early masterpiece, *A House for Mr Biswas* (1961), completed just a few years before 'Jasmine' was written, displays an obvious debt to Dickens. While the most important single intertext of the novel is H. G. Wells's *The History of Mr Polly* (see Fido; Shenfield; Carthew; Thieme, *Web* 71–4), a novel which itself displays a strong Dickensian influence, *Mr Biswas* also exhibits clear parallels with *Great Expectations* (Boxill 131–3); and the Dickensian intertexts are foregrounded by passages that actually bring Mr Biswas's fascination with Dickens into the text:

> Then it was that he discovered the solace of Dickens. Without difficulty he transferred characters and settings to people and places he knew. In the grotesques of Dickens everything he feared and suffered from was ridiculed and diminished, so that his own anger, his own contempt, became unnecessary.
>
> (Naipaul, *Biswas* 337–8)

Such a practice of diminution through caricature was a method Naipaul himself had employed in his first novels, *The Mystic Masseur* (1957) and *The Suffrage of Elvira* (1958). *A House for Mr Biswas* is more complex in tone. Although there is occasional sardonic satire, ridicule is less prominent and arguably this shift in tenor generates an approach that is closer to Dickens's varied use of caricature, which blends social criticism and sentimentalism. In any case, despite his expressed reservations about the grossness of Dickens's approach, the early Naipaul is another 'colonial' who finds him a writer with whom he shares affinities and this appears to relate to his identification with Dickens as a social outsider who challenged the assumptions of genteel English society. Naipaul's relationship with the English canon is seldom adversarial, but his customary response points up the social distance between those who inhabit a supposedly secure middle-class world and those who struggle to rise from lowly origins, whether they be working-class British or, as in the case of Jimmy Ahmed,[3] colonial. However, in Dickens's case such distance does not seem to intrude.

Like many other postcolonial writers and despite his reservations about aspects of Dickens's method, Naipaul finds rather more common ground than alien territory in his fiction.

II

While it would be far-fetched to claim Dickens as a postcolonial writer, his mode of writing challenged many of the canonical orthodoxies of his day; and his imaginative response to Australia, part of his crusading zeal against social injustice within Britain and in particular within the English penal system, is in keeping with this. His work engages with both of the main Victorian constructions of the antipodes: those of convict hell and site of Arcadian promise (see Gibson; White, R.; Lansbury). He considered emigrating to Australia in 1841 (Wilde *et al.* 217)[4] and, particularly in the middle of his writing career, seems to have seen the colony as offering its free settlers egalitarian possibilities that were impossible in class-ridden Britain. However, in *Great Expectations*, the main pre-text to which Carey's *Jack Maggs* responds, Australia is mainly constructed as the invisible penal colony, to which convicts are sentenced for life. As in much of Dickens's work, 'New South Wales' is the site of transportation, the place to which Britain has been sending its surplus prison population. Magwitch apart, transported convicts in his novels include Wackford Squeers in *Nicholas Nickleby* and Uriah Heep in *David Copperfield*, as well as characters in *The Pickwick Papers*, *Martin Chuzzlewit* and 'Somebody's Luggage'; in *Hard Times* transportation is Bounderby's solution to trade unionism (White, R. 17) and in *Our Mutual Friend* Jenny Wren threatens her delinquent father with transportation. As a site for punishment, Australia becomes a repressed shadow image of English society's criminality – not just a physical locus for penal servitude, but also a psychic escape valve that allowed middle-class England to persuade itself that society could be purified by the banishment of 'evil' to the hellish, nethermost regions of the earth. A case of out of sight, out of mind? Not altogether. The figure of the returned convict haunted middle-class English society throughout the early and middle parts of the nineteenth century (White, R. 20–1) and Pip's shock when Magwitch returns to tell him that he, and not Miss Havisham, is his benefactor is an apt metonym of this fear.[5] Beyond this, this central peripeteia of *Great Expectations* provides one of Dickens's most powerful expressions of his view that the lives of the respectable and the criminal classes are inextricably entwined: not only is Pip's status as a gentleman dependent on Magwitch's money, Estella is revealed to be his biological daughter. At the same time the gentleman criminal, Compeyson, who has initiated Magwitch into his life of crime, is presented in a far more villainous light than Magwitch. From *Oliver Twist* onwards, Dickens had been concerned with the criminalization of the poor, but with the exception of *Bleak House*, none of his novels erodes the distance between supposedly law-abiding and criminal classes to the same extent as *Great Expectations*.

Over a decade before he wrote the novel, Dickens had also become influenced by another popular nineteenth-century English view of antipodean life, which envisioned Australia as a workingman's paradise, an Arcadia for the yeoman classes dispossessed by the Industrial Revolution (Lansbury *passim*, particularly 92–107; Hughes 559).[6] He had also been strongly influenced by a contemporary English 'authority' on Australia, Samuel Sidney (the pen name of Samuel Solomon), who published the influential *Sidney's Emigrant's Journal* (1849–50) and a number of books on the practicalities of settling in the new country, and the Catholic philanthropist, Caroline Chisholm (Lansbury 60–78; Hughes 557–8), whose campaigning on behalf of new migrants was informed by first-hand experience of New South Wales; and disseminated their opinions in the issues of *Household Words*, the journal that he edited from 1850 to 1859.

Ostensibly *Jack Maggs* is more concerned with writing back against negative representations of Australia as antipodean penal colony than with depicting the colony as a workingman's paradise. Magwitch is transformed into the ex-convict Jack Maggs, who is reclaimed from the margins by being accorded *textual* centrality. However, the ending of the novel, which allows him a far happier ending than Dickens provides for Magwitch, can be related to the alternative, Arcadian discourse. Nicholas Jose has described *Jack Maggs* as 'an Antipodean revenge on one of Albion's literary glories' (15) and Carey's reworking of both convict and Arcadian motifs is consonant with such an interpretation. Yet, reading the novel in this light, as straightforwardly oppositional counter-discourse, ignores the fact that a 'revenge' element is already present in *Great Expectations*, in the revelation that the fearsomely described Magwitch is the puppet-master who has pulled the strings of Pip's life, the hitherto absent impresario who has created an English gentleman, despite being exiled from both the mother country and his creation's memory. As Robert Hughes says of Magwitch:

> His energy is demonic, his thirst for revenge insatiable. And it turns out that his anonymous, obsessively prompted generosity to Pip is another kind of revenge, a black joke against English and colonial class relations. Pip will be his revenge on the Exclusives, who still spurn him as a risen felon. Do gentlemen make convicts? Then a convict will 'make' and 'own' a real gentleman, not a colonial facsimile. He will show the truth about gentility: It can be bought.
>
> (Hughes 585)

In short, if Magwitch is seen as the representative Antipodean character, *Great Expectations* itself already exacts a revenge on the injustice of the English class system.

At the outset *Jack Maggs* holds out the promise of a narrative that will involve a rewriting of the later sections of *Great Expectations*, from the 'Magwitch' point of view. The novel opens with the eponymous Jack, an ex-convict, whose history parallels Magwitch's in a number of respects, returning to London to find his own self-made gentleman. He has, however, previously sent the gentleman, Henry Phipps, a letter from Dover and this has allowed Henry, who, unlike Pip, knows only too well who his benefactor is, to leave his lodgings in Great Queen Street, Covent Garden and go into hiding in his club in nearby Floral Street. So Maggs arrives to find Henry's house vacant and, rather like Susan Barton in Coetzee's *Foe*, finds himself spending much of the text trying to track down his quarry. Maggs shares several of the characteristics of Dickens's Magwitch. From the first he is characterized by his physical size, a visage that looks as though it has been 'scrubbed' and 'burnished' by life and eyes that have 'a bruised, even belligerent quality' (1). His threatening appearance is reminiscent of Magwitch, who is a figure of terror to Pip not only in the opening scene in the graveyard, but also on his return to London; and it soon becomes clear that, like Magwitch, he is a potential threat to the manufactured gentleman's very existence. It is one thing to be set free in Australia; it is another to reappear from oblivion to make claims on the land of one's birth, from which one has been sent into supposedly permanent exile.

Conveniently, Jack is taken in as a footman by another kind of gentleman, the nouveau riche Percy Buckle, who owns the house next door to Henry's. This general situation established, *Jack Maggs* then leaves other possible parallels with Magwitch aside until the latter stages of the novel. Jack remains the central, though by no means the only, protagonist of the text, but in the present he inhabits a London from which the Pip surrogate appears to be absent. He writes an autobiographical account of his early life for Henry, sitting at his desk in the empty house, after having crossed the roof from next door, but this deals with his boyhood and events that occurred prior to his first meeting Henry – as it were the pre-history of *Great Expectations*.[7] It is only late on in the novel that he tells the text's Dickens-like novelist, Tobias Oates, how he came to meet Henry. It is a story that again bears a close relationship to *Great Expectations*, although it is located in a blacksmith's forge (reminiscent of Joe Gargery's) rather than the graveyard that provides the setting for the opening chapter of *Great Expectations*. Henry, a self-styled 'orphing' (263), has given Jack a pig's trotter, when the coach which is taking him on the first stage of his journey of transportation stops at the forge. Jack has sworn to him that he will come back to take him from his orphanage and ensure that he has a better start in life than he had himself. He has subsequently fulfilled this vow, though not in person and without the anonymity that shrouds Magwitch's patronage of Pip in *Great Expectations*. This account, when it occurs three-quarters of the way through the novel, is clearly strongly redolent of Dickens's novel, in which Pip steals the 'wittles' (37) that Magwitch has demanded from his sister's pantry. However, coming this far into the narrative, it seems comparatively incidental. By this point Jack has already established himself as a much more solid presence than Henry Phipps. So much so that roles have effectively been reversed, with the absent Henry replacing the convict as the shadowy offstage figure and Jack, at least partially, assuming the role of Pip, as he writes the autobiography of his own early life, in which Henry's part is comparatively incidental.

Readers harbouring expectations that Jack's meeting with Henry in the present action of the novel will be the pivotal encounter of the text find themselves frustrated, as Jack himself is, until close to the end, and when Jack finally does discover the whereabouts of his vanished protégé, it leads to a non-encounter in which his 'son' tries to shoot him. His fantasy of playing the role of father to his own reinvented version of England is dispelled in an instant and with it, one might say, the text finally sunders its bond with its English 'original'. Hitherto, there has been an appearance of filial/paternal role reversal, but, again like *Foe*, *Jack Maggs* refuses definition in relation to an English pre-text. Jack returns to Australia and, as he does so, Carey's novel, which has insisted all along on telling a plurality of stories, confirms that it is staking out different territory for postcolonial fiction.

Great Expectations takes the form of Pip's autobiography. Jack, too, tells his own story, but this is only one of the angles of vision employed in Carey's novel, where the technique departs significantly from the mode of Dickens's novel. *Jack Maggs* does not simply change the basic agenda of *Great Expectations* by telling the story, like Jean Rhys, from the 'other side', to arrive at different conclusions. Of course, it does do this, but it is far more than a Magwitch surrogate's version of events that can be mapped, however imprecisely, onto those of its supposed English pre-text. The unitary storyline of *Great Expectations* is replaced by a multiplicity of plots, most notably those of the Dickens-like novelist, Tobias Oates, and the maid of the household into which Jack is taken as a footman, Mercy Larkin. And with the protagonist encountering the writer who created his supposed 'original' and other Dickens texts, as well as non-Dickensian intertexts, finding a place within the novel, the effect, again as in *Foe*, is to destabilize the very basis of fictional authority − and with it linear, filial lines of influence between metropolis and former colony.

III

Although he has no success in tracing the elusive Henry Phipps until close to the end of the narrative, Jack Maggs encounters the Dickens figure, Tobias Oates, early on, when Tobias attends a dinner party at Percy Buckle's house. Subsequently Tobias persuades Jack to become a subject for his experiments in animal magnetism, a popular early nineteenth-century form of mesmerism, soon to be discredited as a pseudo-science, albeit a forerunner of more modern hypnotic techniques. Tobias's life and career fairly obviously parallel those of the young Dickens, up to the point when the action of the novel takes place, in 1837. Once again the relationship is oblique and it is as if Carey is holding a distorting-mirror up not only to *Great Expectations*, but also to the pre-text of *the author's life*. 'Dickens' is reconstructed in a manner that makes him a fictional invention and consequently denied the authority usually associated with writers as the prime movers of their creations. Parallels with Dickens include: Tobias's having already achieved popular success with a novel entitled *Captain Crumley*,[8] reminiscent of Dickens's success with *The Pickwick Papers*; his insecurity about his family background and particularly his father's transgressions; his having been a newspaper reporter; his penchant for dramatic performance; his fascination with 'the Criminal Mind'; his love of dinner parties; references to the later popularity of his public readings; his age – twenty-four as opposed to Dickens's twenty-five in April 1837; and the circumstances of his domestic life, particularly his love for his wife's sister, who is living with the couple.[9]

One could go on at some length, spotting such parallels and analysing the way they invariably function in an oblique or transformative manner. However, to do so would be to obscure the extent to which *Jack Maggs* moves beyond its Dickensian 'original' and emphasizes the postmodernist provisionality of fiction-making. The text follows *Foe* in representing a number of stories competing for primacy, though it differs from Coetzee's novel in providing narrative closure, of the kind one finds in most Victorian novels, for several of its central characters. Carey repeatedly suggests the coexistence of parallel stories, each of which has more or less equal validity, even if they initially seem to belong to different levels of 'reality', especially for readers who come to the text looking for correspondences with *Great Expectations* and Dickens's life. Such readers quickly find themselves caught up in a web of *possible* intertexts, parallels that almost fit, but cannot be neatly matched with their supposed antecedents. If *Jack Maggs* were simply writing back to *Great Expectations*, Jack should be solely based on Magwitch, but his account of his early years owes more of a debt to *Oliver Twist*. So too with the use of elements from Dickens's life. Tobias has a sexual relationship with his wife's sister, which leads to her death after an illicit abortion. Dickens was passionately fond of his sister-in-law, Mary Hogarth, and, in Peter Ackroyd's words, his grief at her death, *in 1837*, at the age of seventeen 'was so intense ... that it represented the most powerful sense of loss and pain he was ever to experience' (225), but his biographers doubt that his desire for her took the form of physical expression.

So, although it has all the qualities of the traditional well-made novel, including consistent characterization, with only the occasional incursion into Dickensian caricature, and a carefully crafted plot, *Jack Maggs* engages in a playful postmodernist interrogation of the nature of fictional authority. One way in which it does so is by allowing Jack to stand as a rival to the more obvious author figure of Tobias. The names assigned to the two characters are revealing concerning the text's attitude to authorship. Jack's name appears to be taken from 'magsman', a colloquial Australian term for a confidence trickster that first appeared in the early nineteenth century. The word appears three times in the novel: twice in sections that deal with the Fagin-like character of Silas Smith (77 and 214), who is Jack's early benefactor, and once in connection with Jack himself, or rather the version of him that Tobias proposes to invent for his novel about Jack (129). *The New Oxford Dictionary of English* defines 'magsman' as 'an informal Australian term for a confidence trickster; a person who likes telling stories; a raconteur'. So the term links the activities of the storyteller and the conman, in a manner not dissimilar to the title of Carey's earlier novel, *Illywhacker* (1985), one of the greatest shaggy dog stories in Australian literature. In *Illywhacker* an epigraph from G. A. Wilkes's *Dictionary of Australian Colloquialisms* (1978) provides a definition of the meaning of the word, 'A professional trickster, esp. operating at country shows', and goes on to incorporate a definition from Sidney J. Baker's earlier *Popular Dictionary of Australian Slang* (1941) that identifies an illywhacker as a 'trickster or spieler' (7).

If it requires a degree of detective work for the average non-Australian reader to locate the meaning of 'magsman', the choice of the name Tobias Oates is still more puzzling. It seems to be a distorted echo of Titus Oates,[10] the Anglican priest who fabricated the story of the Popish plot of 1678, which alleged that Jesuits were planning the assassination of Charles II in order to bring his Catholic brother, who later became James II, to the throne. One can only speculate on the significance of this possible echo, but one appealing explanation is that it locates the novelist Tobias in relation to a storyteller who very clearly falsified evidence and Tobias is both less than honest in his dealings with several of the text's characters and also guilty of appropriating the experiences of others for his fictional ends. Such an interpretation relates directly to his treatment of Jack. A self-styled 'cartographer' of the 'Criminal

Mind' (90), Tobias seems at the very least to be treating Jack as a case-study in alterity and his practice in the mesmerism sessions can be seen as analogous to the various forms of colonial appropriation that Said describes in *Orientalism*. It takes only a slight stretch of the imagination to see parallels between Tobias's supposedly scientific investigation of the criminal mentality and the slightly later Victorian project of trying to identify the salient features of the *'primitive'* mind, through such activities as the dismemberment and measuring of Aborigines' skulls, as a way of lending legitimacy to the sub-Darwinian thinking that attempted to find a scientific basis for racial discrimination. After the first of the sessions, Jack decides that he has been 'burgled, plundered, and he would not tolerate it' (32). Later, when he reads Tobias's account of the Canary-Woman of Islington, one of his journalistic 'Character Sketches' that earn him a quick five pounds, he relates such appropriation of other people's experience to Tobias's profession as a writer and, becoming increasingly aware of and resistant to the fact that he, too, is being subjected to such a process (226–9), charges him with both theft and, distortion through caricature. Relating this to *Dickens's* representation of Australia in his fiction, one might ask not only whether Magwitch is allowed to become more than two-dimensional as he exacts his revenge on the English class system, but also, following Richard White, whether the fact that something finally does turn up for Mr Micawber in Australia reflects at all well on the colony:

> The system did not allow him to succeed in England, but nor did Dickens see him as deserving of the success he had in the colonies. The joke rubs off on Australia; it might be a haven for the poor but, as a society where someone like Micawber could make a splash, it cannot be taken seriously.
>
> (White 39–40)

Carey, though, clearly reverses this situation, with Jack's annoyance at Tobias's covert theft and over-simplification of the characters of others, foregrounding the issue. This annoyance erupts into violent anger when Jack realizes Tobias has stolen the image of his first love, Sophina, for his fictional ends and forbids him ever to use her name again (280–2). So Tobias comes off altogether worse than Jack, as he is likened to a thief, an analogy that generates two possible ironies: the transported felon, Jack, has been a more obvious burglar; and the self-reflexivity of an author depicting writing as theft is compounded by the extent to which *Jack Maggs* demonstrates a debt to Dickens in its narrative mode as well as its theme, even though Carey has been described as a magic realist and the novel, as already suggested, is a postmodern pastiche, employing multiple optics.

However, Tobias is a complex character and Carey's making him the focalizer for central sections of the action where his life is plunged into crisis tends to enlist at least a modicum of sympathy for him. Moreover, the text frequently suggests parallels between its different characters' experiences: for example, Tobias's distress, when his sister-in-law, Lizzie, dies after aborting the child they have conceived, has a parallel in the story of the young Jack, who has experienced a similar situation when Sophina has been forced to abort the child *they* have conceived. This said, *Jack Maggs* does not simply engage in postmodernist relativism by playfully suggesting unresolved parallels between different levels of experience and narrative. Some characters are clearly to be preferred to others and Tobias's authorial appropriation of the experience of others does come across as particularly manipulative, going beyond the attractive, transformative aspects of trickery that have been associated with such behaviour at least as far back as Melville's *Confidence-Man* (1857) and, from a Jungian point of view, can be seen as central to the role of the trickster in many ancient cultures.[11] In the early stages of the novel, long before Jack becomes aware of the extent to which such appropriation is part of Tobias's writing method as well as his practice as a mesmerist, he believes in the accuracy of the transcripts of the sessions he has with Tobias. However, the third-person narrator of the novel, who for the most part assumes the manner of a typically Victorian authorial voice, makes Tobias appear doubly culpable, by pointing out that Tobias's 'transcriptions' of the mesmerism sessions have been 'fabricated by the writer to hide the true nature of his exploration':

> There were, as in all crooked businesses, two sets of books, and had Jack Maggs seen the second he might have recognized scenes (or fragments) more familiar to him .... . For the writer was stumbling through the dark of the convict's past, groping in the shadows, describing what was often a mirror held up to his own turbulent and fearful soul. (91)

Tobias's manipulations are not confined to the mesmerism sessions and his activities as an author. He is also a keen conjuror and actor, whose party piece is playing the role of Sir Samuel Spence, a Regency doctor. At one point he assumes this guise to place Percy Buckle's household under quarantine, thereby inflicting a kind of imprisonment on them, which could be seen to parallel the penal servitude imposed on transported convicts such as Jack. This piece of play-acting has fatal consequences, when Buckle's butler, Spinks, dies and, given that Tobias's behaviour towards Lizzie contributes to *her* death, this is not the only killing for which he could be held accountable. The implications are never forced home. Indeed it verges on overstatement to call Tobias a jailer and murderer, but it remains possible to see him as both, literally as well as metaphorically.

Quarantine may seem a far cry from imprisonment, but Jack, who after all is an expert in penal servitude, sees the connection immediately and links the regime that Tobias imposes on Percy Buckle's household with his mesmerism sessions, his behaviour as an author and the power he is achieving through acting the role of Sir Samuel Spence:

> This doctor, with his twisted red mouth and wild bright eyes, was incredible, ridiculous, and yet he *existed*, given life by some violent magic in his creator's heart. The jerky little writer was thus made invisible. A glaring demon had taken his place, and this being took Jack's jaw in its dry square hands and made as if to thrust a metal spatula down his throat. ... the convict's heart fell prey to a new anxiety – a blood-dark feeling in his gut – that he had become the captive of someone whose powers were greater than he had the wit to ever understand. (146–7; italics in original)

Jack's seeing Tobias as a demonic figure is an interesting reversal of *Great Expectations*, where the accounts of Magwitch's physical appearance tend to demonize *him*. Again, *Jack Maggs* draws on Dickens's representation of Magwitch, as in the initial account of Jack's appearance as he first arrives in London, but shifts the balance by suggesting that *Tobias's* behaviour is more terrifying. Carey puts his main emphasis on authorial megalomania and Tobias is the nearest equivalent in the novel to the two contrasted megalomaniacs of *Great Expectations*, Magwitch and Miss Havisham, who both attempt to realize their own unfulfilled desires vicariously, though fashioning and controlling someone else's destiny – Pip's and Estella's respectively. Writers, Carey's novel wryly suggests, are the worst megalomaniacs of all, controlling their self-created fictional worlds and characters in a quasi-colonial exercise of authority.

The quarantine section, in which Tobias's authoritarian tendencies are most obviously to the fore, still seems a strange episode. Jack even disputes Tobias's view of what quarantine is and sets about implementing a different quarantine regime by nailing the front door of Percy Buckle's house shut, leading Percy, who rushes off to fetch a dictionary to tell him, ' "You misunderstand the meaning of the word" ' (147). A partial explanation may lie in an apparent Australian literary in-joke. Percy Buckle is in the habit of reading to his maid and lover, Mercy Larkin, at night. On one occasion when he has been reading from Hazlitt to her,[12] he imagines that he hears Jack's footsteps on the stairs and his unease at the 'convict's' possible presence leads Mercy to remark, ' "This is even worse than Hasluck" ' (113). Percy corrects her, but nonetheless an allusion to the Western Australian writer, Nicholas Hasluck, the author of a novel entitled *Quarantine* (1978), has been slipped in. In Hasluck's novel, a law student and his fellow passengers on board a ship bound for England are mysteriously quarantined in a deserted port in the Middle East. Left in a state of suspended animation, they are given no explanation for their situation. Carey's aside may represent exasperation at the gnomic quality of *Quarantine*; equally it may relate in some way to the ambivalence of the characters' predicament, caught as they are en route from Australia to England, but unable to make progress towards the 'Mother Country'. More obviously, it suggests the impotence of those trapped by unseen forces which they are unable to combat. Jack's situation in relation to Tobias, during the mesmerism sessions, represents this kind of enthralment and equally it could be seen as a paradigm for the subjection to authority exercised by writers.

In any case, Jack's attempt to implement a different kind of quarantine regime establishes him as a rival to Tobias at this point and in recording his narrative of his early life, he occupies this role on another level: along with Mercy Larkin, who also tells her 'history', he is an alternative author figure within the novel. As the first-person narrator of the story of his past life, Jack in some ways takes over Pip's role in the supposed pre-text. Initially this is a history that bears rather more relationship to *Oliver Twist* than *Great Expectations*. The three-day-old Jack has been found in the mudflats underneath London Bridge and entrusted to the care of a 'great Benefactor' (92), Silas Smith, who runs a school for boy thieves, reminiscent of Fagin's. Later he is sent to steal silver in Kensington The details never correspond to *Oliver Twist* in any precise way – as in every other respect Carey holds a distorting lens up to his pre-texts – but the choice of *Oliver* as a departure point for the narrative of Jack's early life is interesting in a number of respects: it is an earlier Dickens novel and thus fits the chronology of the period in which *Jack Maggs* is set rather better; it is a text that is explicit in its criticism of the penal system; and it is a work that achieves its resolution through securing Oliver's place amid the gentry. Transposing these patterns onto the account of Jack's life, it is of course clear that he has suffered a very different fate. Unlike Oliver and unlike Pip, who rises from *his* orphan beginnings to become a gentleman (thanks, of course, to Magwitch's intervention), Jack remains in the lower echelons of English society until his eventual transportation. Yet in one important respect Jack is, at least in part, the Pip figure in Carey's novel: he is the first-person narrator of his own story. No longer relegated to being constructed from outside as the embodiment of fearsome, if redeemable criminality, and of colonial alterity, he becomes a narrative agent in his own right.

However, the nature of his writing is very different. It is a secret counter-discourse, written in the form of letters to Henry Phipps, that has particular antipodean resonances. Jack crosses the roof to Henry's deserted house, where seated at his desk, he writes his own story. To do so he uses invisible ink and writes from right to left across the page, as he puts it himself, 'back to front like a Chinaman' (158). Although the simile does not directly refer to the antipodes, it certainly involves a reversal of Western scribal norms, which is arguably necessary for the expression of subaltern utterance. Jack's situation in Britain is as parlous as Magwitch's – he needs to remain an invisible man since he has been transported for the term of his natural life – and so resorts to a secret mode of expression and this can be seen as a metonym for the text's stance. Carey sidesteps any kind of adversarial encounter with Dickens – indeed in many ways the novel can be read as a homage to his work – and by instating Jack as the first-person narrator of his own story allocates the role occupied by Pip in *Great Expectations* to him, even if he is only the author of one of the text's narrative strands. His assumption of the role of author, as he sits at Henry's desk, is very reminiscent of Coetzee's Friday sitting at Foe's table and writing with his quill.[13] By this point Jack has, one might say, taken over the roles of both his self-created middle-class alter ego *and* the author who created him, but, of course, this argument loses some of its force if one does not connect him with Magwitch, Henry with Pip and Tobias with Dickens. What remains, however, is a character who realizes that an established Dickens-like novelist intends to use him as grist for his authorial mill and who is fiercely resistant to this appropriation. Should one, then, pursue the Dickens parallels or do such identifications have the effect of limiting the imaginative range of *Jack Maggs*? Put more generally, this again relates to one of the central questions raised by the use of canonical counter-discourse, that of whether it locks the respondent into agendas previously determined by the canonical author. In addition to the invisible ink and the 'back to front' format, there is another dimension to Jack's secret writing which helps to clarify the text's position. In order to read his letters, Henry will need to brush lemon juice across the page and then use a silver-handled mirror that Jack sends to him. In his first letter to Henry, Jack, an expert on hallmarks since his childhood days as a thief, says Henry, 'will read a distinguished story on the mirror's handle', but he 'will read a different kind of story in the glass, by which I mean – mine own' (74). Similarly, *Jack Maggs* seems to bring a hitherto invisible dimension into being, by holding an antipodean mirror up to Dickens.

As well as employing trickery in the mesmerism sessions and in playing the part of Sir Samuel Spence, Tobias has 'a great talent for all kinds of dialects and voices, tricks, conjuring, disappearing cards, pantomime performances' (83). While such attributes are perfectly consonant with Dickens's theatricalism, they also suggest an engagement with the ludic side of postmodernism, which tends to emphasize the performative nature and fictiveness of all discourse. This fits with the notion of the novelist as a liar[14] and, if one makes the link between Tobias's name and that of Titus Oates suggested above, it is possible to interpret this in a negative way, rather than simply as an expression of the postmodernist view of the provisionality of all discourse. Certainly, there is much in Tobias's behaviour to support such a reading and equally the text suggests that Jack is an alternative author figure. Far from being a simple, unlettered convict – he is familiar with *Macbeth* (43,144) and *Lear* (227) – or a repository of an oral storytelling tradition, he is rather the exponent of a different kind of *written* narrative, a subaltern who emerges from the Gothic shadows of the canonical text to tell another side of the story.

IV

Along with the interpolated story of Jack's early life, the novel includes the parallel history of Mercy Larkin, Percy Buckle's maid and mistress. The reader who searches for a Dickens connection to place Mercy is, however, likely to be frustrated; and in the closing chapter the authorial voice more or less confirms the futility of such a quest by pointing out, 'There is no character like Mercy in *The Death of Maggs*' (327), the novel based on Jack's life that Tobias is to publish years later, after having put the subject aside for three decades. The dating[15] and the few details provided concerning *The Death of Maggs* encourage a comparison with *Great Expectations*, rather than *Oliver Twist*, since it appears to be a novel about an ex-convict. However, again there are significant alterations: Tobias's Maggs dies in a fire reminiscent of Miss Havisham's end in Dickens's novel; and it seems that Tobias, like Carey, has accorded him a centrality not given to Magwitch; and Mercy has no equivalent in either Tobias's fictional or Dickens's actual novel. Just possibly, her name has another provenance: Mercy is the name of the child of the spiritual union of Voss and Laura Trevelyan in Patrick White's *Voss*,[16] an orphan who becomes the symbol of a new direction for Australian cultural identity. Carey may or may not have this in mind, but his use of the name has a similar Bunyanesque allegorical ring to it and, as in *Oscar and Lucinda* (1988), the novel emphasizes the female as well as the male line of Anglo-Celtic Australian ancestry.

Jack Maggs does not explicitly identify White's novel as an intertext. It does, however, locate Mercy very precisely in relation to an English novel that Percy Buckle reads to her, Samuel Richardson's epistolary novel, *Pamela* (1740). The narrative of Mercy's early life describes the desperateness of her family's situation after her father's death, and she is on the verge of prostitution when she is rescued by Percy. In her present position, as a servant within his household, she identifies strongly with Pamela, and Percy, too, sees her situation through a Richardsonian filter: 'Neither servant nor master ever discussed their attachment to the novel, but it was clear as day to her that she, like Pamela, might one day be mistress of the house wherein she had been called to serve' (151).

To those who deny Defoe and his predecessors the title of 'novelist', usually on the grounds of their failure to provide sustained plot development, *Pamela* is the first English novel. It is recognized for its skilful use of the epistolary technique, even though Pamela's letters dissolve into a journal when she appears to have no means of getting them to their addressees, her parents, a situation closely paralleled by that in which Jack finds himself when he is unable to make contact with Henry Phipps and *his* letters turn into a journal. The most interesting aspect of the *Pamela* analogy in *Jack Maggs* is, however, the obvious one: Mercy's identification with Richardson's servant heroine, which gives her *her* strong sense of 'expectations'. Richardson's work may initially seem a far cry from Dickens's, but along with his contemporary, Henry Fielding, a novelist with whom he is often paired in an oppositional binary, he played a major part in laying the groundwork for subsequent treatments of class and inheritance in the English novel. Both developed plot structures that were to remain popular throughout the eighteenth and nineteenth centuries in England *and* which exercised a potent influence on Australian colonial fiction, albeit not without numerous complicating factors. Specifically, both Richardson and Fielding, developed plot paradigms in which resolution was achieved through the protagonist's elevation into or confirmation within the gentry. Fielding's critique of Pamela as a scheming social climber who inveigles her way into the gentry through trapping her master into marriage[17] suggests the class distance he put between himself, as an old Etonian gentleman, and the middle-class printer Richardson, whose theme represented the rise of a very different stratum of English society, just as his method followed Defoe in introducing a new kind of 'realism' into the English novel. Fielding's fiction finally displays none of Richardson's concern with upward social mobility, but initially it may seem to do so, for the heroes of both *Joseph Andrews* (1742) and *Tom Jones* (1749) appear to be low born and it takes a revelation concerning their hidden parentage to promote them into the ranks of the gentry and secure their good fortune in the novels' predictably happy endings. Richardson provided a very different outcome in *Clarissa*, but in novels where a comic resolution was assured, fulfilment invariably took the form of the confirmation of class status (the main male paradigm) or a marriage that involves at least a degree of social elevation for the heroine (its female equivalent). The famous opening sentence of *Pride and Prejudice* (1813), 'It is a truth universally acknowledged, that a single man in possession of a good fortune must be in want of a wife' (1), signals Jane Austen's ironic attitude towards such a materialistic view of marriage and the text as a whole is at pains to establish distance between moral probity and the material determinants of human behaviour. Nevertheless, the comic providence that presides over the novel and ensures a happy ending for Elizabeth Bennet does so by promoting her to become the mistress of Pemberley, providing an instance of 'Virtue Rewarded' (the subtitle of *Pamela*), in material terms and in *this*, not the afterlife. Even Jane Eyre becomes an heiress as well as Rochester's wife, though here there is an interesting variation on the pattern, in that Jane's coming into an inheritance of her own gives her an independence shared by comparatively few eighteenth- or nineteenth-century novel heroines, albeit with little legal security (prior to the passing of the Married Women's Property Act of 1882).

In short, just as marriage is a pivotal subject in the English novel before and during Dickens's era, inheritance is frequently a trope for success and happiness, as the complications of the plot are resolved through the elevation of the hero or heroine to the status of gentleman or gentlewoman. In Dickens's fiction, where orphans abound, this motif undergoes a range of metamorphoses. Oliver Twist's happy ending is achieved when he is adopted by Mr Brownlow. However, *Great Expectations* moves in the opposite direction and the central epiphany, Pip's discovery that Magwitch, not Miss Havisham, is his benefactor, sunders his connection with genteel society, as well exposing 'the truth about gentility' as something that 'can be bought' (Hughes 585). The hierarchical class values of English society did not, of course, readily transport themselves to Australia and a strong egalitarian streak was central to the process of national myth-making that took place in the century following the beginnings of European settlement in 1788. Nevertheless class issues continued to exercise settler Australia's imagination and much of Dickens's nineteenth-century antipodean appeal can be attributed to his engagement with the topic, as well as his more specific critique of the English penal system that had played a fundamental role in the colony's genesis.

A text which has often been regarded as the most significant Australian novel of its period, Marcus Clarke's *His Natural Life* (1870),[18] has these issues at its centre. Carey's engagement with Australian intertexts is even more oblique than his response to his English pre-texts, but there are hints of references to Clarke's novel in *Jack Maggs*, where the phrase 'for the term of his natural life', the revised title[19] by which the novel has been generally known, is used twice (128 and 324).[20] Whether or not one views *His Natural Life* as an intertext for *Jack Maggs*, its treatment of convictism and inheritance makes it interesting to read alongside Dickens and an obvious forerunner for *Jack Maggs*. Clarke's novel is best known for its uncompromising indictment of the convict system, but is arguably even more fascinating as a study of the colonial psyche wrestling with the competing claims of English and Australian society, a conflict that led the author to produce two different endings for the novel. Even to call the novel 'Australian' is problematic, since it was written by an

English expatriate who, in Laurie Hergenhan's words, 'remained in two minds about life in colonial Australia' (49), a man whose own early life had much in common with the vicissitudes of a Dickensian hero. Clarke had received a privileged English education and was looking forward to a diplomatic career and a private fortune in the region of £70,000 when he was effectively disinherited by the sudden death of his father (Murray-Smith 8). His solution to this predicament was a Micawber-like emigration to Australia, where he found a niche for himself as a journalist in post-gold rush Melbourne. Writing at a time when crime and its penal consequences had, Dickens apart, produced such classics as Dumas *père*'s *The Count of Monte Cristo* (1844), Hugo's *Les Misérables* (1862) and Dostoevsky's *Crime and Punishment* (1866), he was particularly influenced by Charles Reade's *It is Never Too Late to Mend* (1856), a novel set in Australia, which also depicted two possible versions of the country: as a land of financial possibilities and as the site of penal transportation. Clarke's novel was published at a time when transportation to eastern Australia had been abandoned twenty years before (Murray-Smith 10), but he discovered his great theme in an account of the recent convict past. *His Natural Life* first saw the light of day over a period of two years as a serial in the Melbourne *Australian Journal* (1870–72) and was subsequently published in 'revised' book form in 1874, in a much shorter version and with a different ending. In the revised version, the protagonist Richard Devine is the illegitimate son of English aristocrats. Expelled from his home by his mother's husband, he is an archetype of the disinherited Englishman and his cup of woe *seems* complete (though there is worse to follow!), when he is wrongly accused of theft and, having assumed the name of Rufus Dawes, transported to Australia 'for the term of his natural life', becoming a first-hand victim of and witness to the brutality of the penal regime. So the inheritance motif has a particular Australian inflection and Devine/Dawes's situation is altogether more desperate than that of, say, Tom Jones – or even Oliver Twist. His dual name provides an expression of his double identity, but this dualism lacks the positive potential associated with the schizophrenic imagination by more recent postcolonial authors, such as Derek Walcott, Nayantara Sahgal and Wilson Harris. Clarke's hero may be the convict 'Rufus Dawes' for much of the novel, but his filiative relationships are with England. In Australia he sees himself as a Johnsonian spiritual castaway, 'a person lost or abandoned by Providence',[21] likening himself to Robinson Crusoe in this respect.

Clarke's masterpiece is, then, a *colonial* classic. The struggle depicted is between Devine/Dawes's choosing to identify himself as an English gentleman or as an Australian victim and he prefers the former identity, though Clarke produces variations on the theme in the different versions of the novel. Indeed, examining its textual history makes for a fascinating study of the issue of authorial affiliation. Most notably, the revised book edition of 1874 replaced the happy ending of the longer serialized version, in which Dawes like Tom Jones and Joseph Andrews comes into his inheritance, with a tragic ending in which he dies in Australia. In both instances, the stance remains filiative, but the revised text's failure to provide a return to England and to resolve the narrative complications by restoring the protagonist to his 'true' parentage represents a significant departure from the Fielding paradigm of social and literary inheritance that had become the convention within the English novel. Fielding's novels appear to suggest a proletarian questioning of the status quo, but finally leave it unchallenged; death in exile opens up an altogether different can of worms. Beyond this, as Elizabeth Perkins has pointed out, the revised version of Clarke's novel 'heightens the representation of the convict system as a violation of the social family' (Bennett and Strauss, eds 62). Orphan status, illegitimacy and disguised parentage dominate pre-twentieth-century English and colonial treatments of this family, but resolutions that reaffirm the social order are usually achieved. For the postcolonial writer, the very nature of the family is under question and membership is at best a matter of *affiliation*.

In the dénouement of *Jack Maggs*, Jack finally 'meets' Henry Phipps, who shatters his conviction that he belongs in an England in which he can triumph over the class system by making Henry his 'son', when this prodigal attempts to murder him. Mercy, whose finger is blown away by Henry's bullet, thus linking her with Jack in 'deformity' (327), has previously told him he should return to his 'real children' (312) in Australia and the novel concludes with his taking this more practical view of fatherhood. His fantasies concerning Henry dispelled, he leaves London the same night, along with Mercy. They marry in Australia, where she becomes the stepmother of his two 'real' sons and they have five more children together. Interestingly, the text puts its emphasis on parenthood not childhood, with Jack's elective choice concerning whose *father* he will be, not whose *son*. Despite its setting in the nineteenth century, *Jack Maggs* suggests a coming of age for the transplanted subject, who escapes the infantilization engrained in filial models of the relationship between metropolis and colony.

Carey's novel concludes by providing a Victorian happing ending for Jack and Mercy *in Australia*, as parents of 'That race' (327), but denying Henry Phipps and Tobias any such providential closure. One might say that Jack has become Micawber rather than Magwitch at this point: he becomes a pillar of society in the 'new town of Wingham' (327), where he is twice president of the shire and president of the cricket club. Mercy becomes an even more famous member of local society, renowned for the 'grand mansion' (328) over which she presides and, since she is the character with no obvious Dickensian antecedent, this seems to represent the text's most comprehensive assertion of autonomy from its English 'originals'. Carey employs a range of Dickensian and other pre-texts and in so doing problematizes the very notion of unitary influence, but ultimately *Jack Maggs* stakes out its own fictional territory, by reversing the pattern of a colonial novel such as *His Natural Life*, where there is a continuing filiative relationship with the Mother Country. As an incursion into the heart of Dickens's darkness, it is set almost entirely in nineteenth-century London, but it remains a distinctively 'Australian' novel in its orientation and outlook. So it is fitting that Jack – and the narrative – should finally settle in Australia and that Jack and Mercy should achieve prosperity and happiness in an environment where there is no need to disguise identity. The colonial, affiliative stance of *His Natural Life* has been turned upside down.

V

The first epigraph to this chapter is taken from Elizabeth Jolley's 1983 novel, *Miss Peabody's Inheritance*, in which the title character is an English spinster, who divides her time between a humdrum office job and caring for her elderly mother and feels that her life has 'become a series of clichés and platitudes' (68). She has entered into a correspondence with an Australian novelist, Diana Hopewell, to whom she has sent a fan letter and who sends her extracts from her current work-in-progress, a novel about a post-menopausal lesbian headmistress, Miss Thorne, and her entourage, whose comic adventures include a journey to Europe. Jolley begins her novel with the words, 'The nights belonged to the novelist' (1) and Miss Peabody's secret nocturnal correspondence provides her with an emotional outlet lacking in her daytime life. The exact nature of her fascination with Diana's fiction is debatable and one obvious interpretation is that it introduces her to an aspect of her own sexuality that has hitherto lain dormant. After reading an account of Diana's characters having a water fight in the shower of a Western Australian motel in her 'airless and virginal bedroom' (11), she adds a little of her mother's medicinal brandy to her cup of hot milk. After receiving Diana's next letter, which describes how three unmade motel beds cause 'thoughts of hitherto unknown erotic adventures to race and surge within the indignant breast' (18–19), she departs from her routine by taking a bath on an uncustomary night and shocks her listening mother by singing ' "I'm a little prairie flower," ... / "Growing wilder every hour" ' (20), as she does so. However, while the discovery of previously buried aspects of her sexuality is part of her awakening, it is by no means the only element. She also rediscovers the pleasure of literature that she once knew as a girl and, on one level, the novel is a comic investigation of the writer–reader relationship, located, as in *Jack*

Maggs, in a cross-cultural context. When she was a child, her parents read her a range of stories, including Hans Christian Andersen's tale of the ugly duckling and Kingsley's *The Water-Babies* (1863), a classic of the discourse of cleanliness that was foisted upon both the English working classes and the colonies during the Victorian period, and both of these texts now seem relevant to her present response to the excitement of water. She has also had several canonical English novels read to her, among them *Robinson Crusoe, Jane Eyre* and *Great Expectations*. The last of these becomes the most significant fictional intertext in Jolley's novel. She remembers how her father loved Dickens and particularly recalls the opening scene of *Great Expectations*, in which Magwitch turns Pip upside down in the graveyard where, as an orphan, he is looking at his parents' tombstones. This encounter defines her own relationship with Diana, whose letters are effectively turning *her* life upside down. She thinks of Diana as a mythical figure, associating her with her namesake in the Roman pantheon, and borrows a book from the public library, which makes her more aware of the attributes of the Diana/Artemis figure:

> The Lord of Free Nature. She goes hunting on the mountains with her group of nymphs. She lives with them in the grove and in the paddock. She is related to the cultivation of trees and is the Goddess of Fertility. (73)

These attributes perfectly match her invented image of Diana Hopewell: to Miss Peabody, Diana is the embodiment of free *Australian* nature and, in this latter-day version of the Arcadian myth, she envisages her riding on horseback in her 'paddock', a signifier that she particularly associates with Diana's world (7, 99), as a kind of antonym to the restrictions of her own claustrophobic suburban life. The implications with regard to writing and reading are particularly interesting and represent another antipodean inversion that can be related to the episode of Pip's being turned upside down at the opening of *Great Expectations*, since it is the English character who is left hanging on every word of the Australian author, awaiting Diana's letters as eagerly as Dickens's nineteenth-century readers awaited the next instalment of his serialized novels. Australia has become the site of writing, England of semi-passive reading – or so it would seem. In fact, Jolley's novel's treatment of the writer–reader relationship is every bit as complex as that of Carey's in *Jack Maggs*. In the latter stages of *Miss Peabody's Inheritance*, Miss Peabody's mother dies and she resolves to journey to Australia to meet Diana, reversing the journey that Diana's Miss Thorne and her entourage have been making in the inner novel. What she discovers comes as something of a shock to her, but it makes sense of a puzzling earlier fragment in one of Diana's letters (87–8) which refers to a series of hospital operations that bear no relationship to the novel about Miss

Thorne, nor to the details of her own life that she has sent Miss Peabody. The mystery of this fragment is now solved. Far from being a free-ranging horsewoman, Diana has been a patient who has undergone several operations, since being thrown from a horse years before. Just prior to Miss Peabody's arrival, she has died in the nursing home where she lives. So the expected encounter between the writer and reader figures within the text is once again frustrated and at the same time other details are now seen in a new light. Diana has told Miss Peabody how much she values her letters and the significance of this is now clarified by the revelation that she has been living a life that is even more confined than Miss Peabody's. And with this disclosure, it becomes clearer to readers of the novel that simply to view Miss Peabody as a reader, as the passive recipient of literary work is inadequate, since the correspondence has been a two-way one, an exchange in which each participant has contributed something to the imaginative and emotional life of the other. The novel ends with Miss Peabody sitting in Diana's room in the nursing home, reading a letter that Diana was writing to her when she died. It contains the final instalment of the inner novel about Miss Thorne and her ménage and as Miss Peabody puts it down at the very end of the text, she is on the verge of assuming the mantle of the author. She thinks that the matron of the nursing home will know where to get a typewriter and feels that 'All she really needed to enter into her inheritance was a title' (157). So, as in *Jack Maggs*, the novel ends in Australia and, while it would be an overstatement to say that the view in either of the two novels is utopian, in both cases it is closer to the nineteenth-century view of Australia as Arcadia than the construction of the colony as a penal hell. In *Miss Peabody's Inheritance*, the inheritance motif relates most obviously to literary inheritance and Miss Peabody, the passive suburban nobody, becomes an author by virtue of having responded to the imaginative promise of Diana's Australian vision. Like Pip, she is propelled into a new life by an Australian intervention; unlike Pip, she comes into 'expectations' that are imaginative rather than material. The closing lines of the novel show her contemplating a visit to the farm where Diana lived before her accident, but realizing that this is unnecessary. It is her own invention of a new psychic geography for Australia, initiated by her response to Diana's writing, that will enable her to complete Diana's work-in-progress. Like *Jack Maggs*, *Miss Peabody's Inheritance* sidesteps an adversarial response to *Great Expectations*, preferring to use it as an intertext for pointing up a series of literary, social and sexual relationships. This said, both novels finally depart from Dickens by locating the fulfilment of the protagonist's expectations (albeit fairly provisionally in the case of *Miss Peabody's* open ending) in Australia.

Notes

1. He was popularly known as 'St Henry' and the Apostle of Mateship. Commenting on 'the extent of the Lawson legend in his lifetime', *The Oxford Companion to Australian Literature* notes that he was the first Australian to be granted a State funeral, and cites his commemoration by a statue in the Sydney Domain and his appearance on the Australian ten-dollar note when decimal currency was introduced in 1965 as evidence of his enduring popularity as 'Australian literature's most famous son' (Wilde *et al.* 409).

2. Naipaul styles himself as a 'colonial' in much of his early writing, e.g. 'To be a colonial was to know a kind of security; it was to inhabit a fixed world' (Naipaul, *Return* 216).

3. See the discussion of *Guerrillas* in Chapter 4.

4. Two of his sons did migrate to Australia, where they enjoyed rather less good fortune than Mr Micawber (Lansbury 136–7).

5. An interesting, albeit unverifiable, Australian tradition adds an extra irony to this. Miss Havisham is said to have been based on the figure of the Sydney recluse, Eliza Emily Donnithorne, who, after she was jilted in 1856, reputedly immured herself within her house for the remaining thirty years of her life (Wilde *et al.* 217).

6. Richard White locates the emergence of this stereotype of Australia in the period 1830 to 1850 (29), i.e. before the gold rush of 1851.

7. Cf. Rhys's inventing the pre-history of Bertha/Antoinette in *Wide Sargasso Sea*.

8. If there is a skewed Dickensian echo in the name used here, it would seem to be to Captain Cuttle, a character in the later *Dombey and Son* (1846–8).

9. See below and Ackroyd 225.

10. The name Tobias could just possibly allude to the title of a proposed Australian imitation of *The Pickwick Papers*, *Tobias Twickenham* (Wilde *et al.* 217).

11. See, for example, Joseph L. Henderson, 'Ancient Myths and Modern Man', Jung *et al.* 103 ff.

12. Apparently from the *Liber Amoris* (1823), though this is not mentioned by name.

13. Subsequently, when he undertakes a journey to Gloucester with Tobias, he takes up *Tobias's* quill to continue his account to Henry (238).

14. Helen Daniels discusses both Carey and Hasluck in *Liars* (1988), a study of 'new' Australian fiction that interrogates the boundaries between both truth and fiction and writing and reading.

15. Tobias does not begin the novel again until 1859 and the first chapters are published in serial form in 1860 (328). *Great Expectations* was serialized in *All the Year Round* during 1860 and 1861. Other references to editions of *The Death of Maggs* also relate closely to the publishing history of *Great Expectations*.

16. See Chapter 2 above.

17. See the parody of the early sections in *Joseph Andrews* (1742) and more obviously the anonymous prose work, *Shamela* (1741), now generally agreed to have been written by Fielding.

18. Introducing the 1929 edition, Hilary Lofting called it 'the only great novel that Australian literature has produced' (xi). Laurie Hergenhan describes it as 'the best novel produced in nineteenth-century Australia' (47). More recent revisionist accounts of early Australian writing have been rather less enthusiastic. See, for

example, John Docker's comments on its reception as part of the 'metaphysical ascendancy' that dominated the post-war, academic construction of Australian literary studies (168) and the more marginal role accorded to it in recent histories, e.g. Bennett and Strauss, eds.

19.   First used in an 1882 edition of the novel.

20.   Cf. a similar possible allusion to the title of another classic Australian novel, Joseph Furphy's *Such is Life* (183). In both cases the phrases are commonplace enough to allow readers to spot or deny allusions as they choose. The possible link with Nicholas Hasluck's more recent novel, *Quarantine*, discussed above, is also tenuous, though the mention of Hasluck's name (113) seems unambiguous.

21.   See Chapter 3, note 2.

6

Encountering other selves: re-staging
The Tempest

Caliban is [the] convert, colonised by language, and excluded by language. It is precisely this gift of language, this attempt at transformation which has brought about the pleasure and paradox of Caliban's exile. Exiled from his gods, exiled from his nature, exiled from his own name! Yet Prospero is afraid of Caliban. He is afraid because he knows that his encounter with Caliban is, largely, his encounter with himself.

(George Lamming, *Pleasures* 15)

There is now a fashionable, Marxist-evolved method of analysing figures from literature as if they were guilty. These analyses, we have seen them happen in brilliant re-creations, to Prospero as the white imperialist, and to Caliban as the ugly savage.

(Derek Walcott in Hamner, *Critical Perspectives* 36)

I

Like Crusoe and Friday, Prospero and Caliban have become synonymous with the figures of colonizer and colonized for many postcolonial writers and theorists.[1] Viewing *The Tempest* as an allegory of colonialism is, of course, nothing new; and ultimately its long genealogy can be traced back to Shakespeare himself. Like many of his contemporaries, Shakespeare was fascinated by both the commercial and the imaginative possibilities of the trope of the New World and this interest particularly informed the writing of his last play. It is generally agreed that he knew the 'Bermudas Pamphlets', a group of narratives describing the wreck of a ship bound for the recently established colony of Virginia in 1609, and was also familiar with other travel narratives about the New World.[2] The shipwreck was an event which excited considerable interest in early seventeenth-century England, not only among those with vested interests in the Virginia plantation and the imperial adventure more generally, but also among those who viewed the Americas as a tabula rasa, a 'natural' environment in which sophisticated European values would be reassessed.[3] The marooned settlers lived in a state of nature for nearly a year before managing to refloat their ship and proceed to Virginia in May 1610; and the Jacobean imagination saw their situation as a living enactment of longstanding debates about the relative merits of Nature and Art. In Frank Kermode's words, 'Ancient problems of poetry and philosophy were given an extraordinary actuality' (xxv), as the colonists found themselves living out the age-old pastoral theme of the contrast between primitive innocence and cultivated experience. For Shakespeare and his contemporaries, the narratives of their experience crystallized many of the ethical issues surrounding the colonization of the New World, but unlike Montaigne, whose essay 'Of Cannibals' (1580) is a clear intertext in *The Tempest*, Shakespeare's play declines to construct a simple opposition between utopian nature and corrupt nurture. As in several of his earlier comedies, the wilderness environment in which the play takes place provides an extra-social space in which the nature/nurture debate can be conducted, but there is no comfortable, pastoral sentimentalization of the natural life. *The Tempest*, however one decides to stage it, reveals at least a degree of scepticism about, if not a wholesale rejection of, the possibility of savage nobility. Nevertheless the 'salvage and deformed slave'[4] Caliban is the tearing-point of the play, 'the natural man against whom the cultivated man is to be measured' (Kermode xxiv) and understandably, along with Prospero, he has attracted more attention in postcolonial reworkings of motifs from *The Tempest* than any of the play's other characters, although Miranda and Ariel have also figured prominently in some of the con-texts that have engaged with Shakespeare's 'last will and testament' (Lamming, *Pleasures* 95).

This chapter mainly concerns itself with examining the perspectives adopted in a selection of Caribbean and Canadian responses to *The Tempest*, which, given their origins in very different postcolonial societies might be expected to produce divergent reactions to Shakespeare's pre-text. The Caribbean con-texts are: George Lamming's non-fictional work, *The Pleasures of Exiles* (1960), which, in addition to dedicating a chapter specifically to *The Tempest*, makes numerous other references to the play, seeing it as having been written 'against the background of England's experiment in colonisation' and as 'prophetic of a political future which is our present' (Lamming, *Pleasures* 13); Lamming's novel, *Water with Berries* (1971), a novel about Caribbean 'exiles' in London, in which this political future *has* become the present; and Edward

Kamau Brathwaite's poem, 'Caliban' (1969), which offers variations on the Caliban figure that embody three distinctively different Caribbean perspectives. The Canadian texts are: Robertson Davies's *Tempest-Tost* (1951), in which a provincial Canadian theatre company's decision to mount a production of *The Tempest* generates a series of comic storms in teacups; and Margaret Laurence's *The Diviners* (1974), where *The Tempest* is ostensibly a more incidental intertext.

Of course, looking at such a limited number of case-studies does little more than scratch the surface of the vast body of postcolonial texts that have in some way engaged with Shakespeare's last play, but the texts concerned promised a variety of outlook that, I anticipated, might lend them *some* kind of representative significance, particularly with reference to the contrast in approach one expected to find between Caribbean and Canadian *Tempest* derivatives. And to some extent the con-texts examined did fulfil this expectation. I also began with another expectation: that there might be cross-fertilization among the con-texts themselves – it would, after all, be an unusual postcolonial writer who could come to *The Tempest* without an awareness of at least some of the pre-existing literature on this subject – and again this turned out to be the case. What I was not prepared for was the discovery of a close relationship between a Caribbean and Canadian response to *The Tempest* of a more individual kind, between Laurence's references in *The Diviners* and Lamming's *Tempest* writings. The discovery that Laurence had also been strongly influenced by O. Mannoni's classic study of the psychology of colonialism, translated into English as *Prospero and Caliban* (1956),[5] lent further weight to the belief that the volume of writing that had used *The Tempest* as a paradigm for colonial relationships was frequently casting a long shadow over the individual writer's response to the play and its archetypes.

II

While the view of *The Tempest* as colonial allegory can be traced back to Shakespeare himself, it took on a new urgency in the second half of the twentieth century, particularly during the period when the European empires were being dismantled, and Lamming's commentary on the play is written against the background of a body of work by Francophone writers. Around the middle of the century, this group of writers revitalized the supposedly oppositional pairing of Prospero and Caliban as archetypes of the colonizer and colonized, placing particular emphasis on the psychological consequences of colonialism and Caliban's response to the imposition of Prospero's language. Mannoni focused on Caliban's dependence complex; Frantz Fanon in *Black*

Skin, White Masks (1952) suggested the extent to which psychology constructed the colonizer/colonized relationship as 'normal', thereby alienating Caliban from integral aspects of his personality. Rather later, the distinguished Martinican poet, Aimé Césaire produced a revisionist dramatic *Tempête* (1969); and, as Diana Brydon points out (76), the Haitian-Canadian writer Max Dorsinville, in *Caliban without Prospero* (1974), used Shakespeare's two archetypes as a paradigm for discussing a broader range of postcolonial writing, focusing particularly on Québecois and African American writing and arguing that Caliban's aesthetic emancipation is doomed to fail so long as he accedes to Prospero's agendas. Again, it is a view that has obvious implications for the counter-discursive project: simply to adopt an oppositional stance is to fall into the negritudinist trap of leaving colonized subjects inscribed within European definition, since, despite the attempt at reclamation from negative construction through reversal, the rules of engagement remain unchanged.

Lamming's *Pleasures of Exile* does not refer directly to Mannoni or Fanon,[6] but he, too, reads the play as a template for the psychological aspects of the colonial 'experiment', placing more emphasis on its contemporary relevance than its early Renaissance aspects and demonstrating a particular concern with the ways in which Caliban's encounter with Prospero engenders a sense of existential exile. On the most obvious level, the 'exile' of the book's title is that of the Caribbean migrant to post-war England, particularly that of the West Indian artist, and Lamming talks at some length about the London experiences of the *Windrush* generation of writers. But exile is also seen as a psychological consequence of colonialism, as the text discusses the forces that have motivated the writers' migration to the metropolis. The exile of the colonial is primarily Caliban's exile, but Lamming insists on the interdependence of Caliban and Prospero, seeing himself as a descendant of both figures:

> I am a direct descendant of slaves, too near the actual enterprise to believe that its echoes are over with the reign of emancipation. Moreover, I am a direct descendant of Prospero worshipping in the same temple of endeavour, using his legacy – not to curse our meeting – but to push it further. (15)

So, like Derek Walcott, who aligns himself with both Friday and Crusoe, Lamming lays claim to a dual ancestral legacy. However, while he views contemporary Calibans as sharing Prospero's characteristics, contemporary Prosperos are seen as less versatile and Lamming goes further than Walcott in *Pantomime*[7] in demonstrating the superior adaptability of the Caliban/Friday archetype. Just as Shakespeare, in Lamming's view, wrote *The Tempest* as 'an apology for any false dividends which Art ... may have brought home'

(*Pleasures* 95), personifying such disquiet in Prospero's situation, the end of the colonial era seems to usher in the need for a similar transition in the former colonizer, in a future which 'threatens to reduce Prospero to madness or impotence' (85). 'Colonised by his own ambition' (85), Prospero is seen as terrified by the uncertainty of the future, needing to be re-educated by the altogether more adaptable figure of Caliban. Although Caliban remains Prospero's other, an Ishmael constructed by the colonizer's gaze, alterity proves to be a condition that enables him to reinvent himself at will and the Caribbean artist in particular is represented as a figure who can quickly size up situations and metamorphose himself to meet Prospero's requirements of the moment: 'He will then proceed to offer the self which they are looking for; and each self changes with the white need and the white situation which wants to exploit or embrace him' (87). Consequently, Caliban is not only an aspect of Prospero; his capacity for 'chameleon transformation' also makes him an Ariel (87) who can play all the parts in the colonial repertory. Most notably, he is also an alter ego for *The Tempest*'s other child of nature, Miranda: 'Miranda is the innocent half of Caliban; Caliban is the possible deformity which Miranda, at the age of experiment might become' (15).[8]

In addition to offering a detailed reading of aspects of the play (95–117), Lamming sustains the *Tempest* analogy in a remarkable range of situations – Caribbean, European and African – reclaiming Caliban from being constructed as a savage child of nature by assigning him a multiplicity of roles and demonstrating the extent to which the seemingly passive colonized subject can play all the available roles, while the colonizer's former monopoly of the Word has left him imprisoned within a singular identity. Lamming's Caliban is, however, more than just a brilliant mimic: in a chapter on the Haitian revolution, he becomes Toussaint L'Ouverture, as celebrated by C. L. R. James in his classic study, *The Black Jacobins* (1938), a compassionate military genius who emancipates himself from the passive status conferred on him by his colonial role to become a protagonist who 'orders history' (118–50). Elsewhere, Caliban is the Haitian peasant who takes part in the Ceremony of Souls, a communion rite that releases the dead from the 'purgatory of Water' (9). This is a trope which Lamming has deployed on several occasions in his writing,[9] but in *The Pleasures of Exile* it takes on particular force, since the water in question is both the Middle Passage and the sea in which the shipwreck of *The Tempest* occurs. The implication is, of course, that Caliban and Prospero – and indeed all the other characters of the play – share the same predicament. At the moment of postcolonial transformation, with which Lamming seems to be concerned in virtually all his fiction, there is a need to achieve communion with the dead and Caliban seems to be altogether better equipped to undertake this task, through the mediation of an Afro-Caribbean rite of passage. So, although *The Pleasures of Exile* is centrally concerned with depicting the exploitation, stereotyping and denial of human dignity from which African diaspora subjects have suffered, it is far from pessimistic in its counter-discursive reversals of the *Tempest* paradigm and, although the meeting with Prospero is still seen as the single most important determinant of Caliban's predicament, it also avoids the trap of promoting an oppositional aesthetic. 'Caliban reorders history', but he does so by insisting on his right to play all roles, as it were to stage his own one-man pantomime of *The Tempest*.

Water with Berries is less optimistic about Caliban's capacity to restage history and identity in this way. One of its protagonists, Derek, is an actor who finds himself repeatedly playing the role of a corpse, after a single moment of glory when he had a season as Othello at Stratford.[10] Othello may be a hero, but he is inescapably a tragic hero and the novel only offers tragic possibilities for its three exiled artists: Derek, the composer Roger and the painter Teeton, the character who links the text's various strands. It begins in a restrained low-key manner and initially its subdued naturalistic mode almost obscures the extent to which Lamming, as always, is developing an allegory about the legacy of imperialism, though there are incidental hints of this: the real name of Teeton's landlady, the Old Dowager, is Mrs Gore-Brittain (35); a pub that Derek and Roger visit has 'a clown's head of John Bull grinning from the wall' (57). However, as the novel gathers momentum and apparent understatement gives way to a catalogue of violence that compares with the sensationalist horror of Shakespeare's younger Jacobean contemporaries, unmistakable allusions to *The Tempest* overtly locate the action in such a context.

These references mainly seem to belong to a 'sub-plot',[11] which acts as a kind of supplement to *The Tempest* by developing motifs that are either absences or bare hints in the play. After hearing of the suicide of his wife, Randa, in their 'home' island of San Cristobal, a fictional composite of several Caribbean countries, from which he has fled years before, Teeton goes walking on the nearby heath in the night. The area of London in which *Water with Berries* is set is recognizably Hampstead, but the heath has less affinity with the terrain that inspired Keats's 'Ode to a Nightingale' than with the elemental moorland of the central scenes in *King Lear*. In this extra-social setting, Teeton meets another Miranda figure and an intimacy develops between the two, which leads her to tell him the story of her past during a subsequent night meeting. Anonymous at this point, this woman is subsequently named as Myra and, as she tells Teeton about her past, her history bears an obvious relationship to Miranda's in that she has lived 'alone' with her father, who has been her only teacher, on an isolated island, since she was just three (145).[12]

In *The Pleasures of Exile*, Lamming comments on three undeveloped elements in *The Tempest,* and in *Water with Berries* he supplements these aspects through a series of violent and disturbing details that run directly counter to the pastoral mode of the pre-text. The first is Prospero's charge that Caliban has tried to 'violate' Miranda (*Tempest* I, ii, 348) and Caliban's retort that, if he had not been prevented from doing so, he would have 'peopled else/This isle with Calibans' (I, ii, 351–2). In *The Pleasures of Exile,* Lamming comments on the extraordinariness of a slave's speaking to his master in this way, laying particular emphasis not on Caliban's desire 'for the mere experiment of mounting a piece of white pussy' (102), but on his belief that he could have become the founder of a race. Why, Lamming asks, should any offspring of Caliban and Miranda not be Mirandas as much as Calibans? Perhaps the answer lies in his playing on Prospero's fears of miscegenation. 'Did Caliban really try to lay her?', Lamming continues. If he had, 'the body' would have provided proof, since 'it is most unlikely that Prospero and his daughter could produce a brown skin baby' (102). So along with the charge of rape comes the mischievous suggestion of possible incest; and in *Water with Berries* both elements are present. The Myra that Teeton encounters on the heath is a ravished, syphilitic woman who has been gang-raped and subjected to bestiality on the island by her father's 'servant and his men' (150) during a terrifying night of arson. This seems to represent Caliban's living up to Prospero's construction of him as a subhuman other, as it were acting the role of the proverbial dog that has been given a bad name. At the same time, however, Lamming's central chapter on *The Tempest* in *The Pleasures of Exile* is entitled 'A Monster, A Child, A Slave', which has the effect of identifying *Prospero* as the real monster of the play. The novel also refers to Myra's 'father' in this way (224), albeit through the mouthpiece of an unreliable narrator, and in a passage that clearly refers to the sexual brutalization of women during the slave era he is charged with having provided ample precedent for his servant's behaviour by virtue of having 'made this devil's crime a common sport upon his servants' (228). And there is even a veiled hint of an incestuous relationship between Myra and her 'father', when she is said to have 'continued to share his bed even when she was grown almost his equal in height' (146). *Water with Berries,* then, realizes Prospero's worst nightmares, offering an alternative scenario in which Caliban orders history, but everyone is a loser and Miranda is the most brutalized figure of all.

Lamming's second supplemental development of a motif in *The Tempest* relates to the identity of Miranda's mother. In *The Pleasures of Exile,* he comments that, unless he is mistaken, there is only one reference to her in the play, in the passage where Prospero tells Miranda that her mother 'was a piece of virtue', who 'said thou wast my daughter' (*Pleasures* 104; *Tempest* I, ii, 56–7). This may be no more than a casual joke for the groundlings and, to be fair, it is a response to Miranda's having asked him if he is her father. Nevertheless, it foregrounds not just the physical absence of Miranda's mother – and by extension maternal genealogies more generally – but also the lack of any information concerning who she may have been. Lamming's riposte insists that gender is inseparable from race as an aspect of identity and the text develops the motif of the absent mother to provide a narrative variant in which maternal ancestry is equally prominent. Indeed, although her parentage is European, Miranda is effectively a white Creole, similar in background to Rhys's Antoinette, though she was not born on the island.[13] As the play's other child of nature, she complements Caliban and Lamming seems to be insisting that she be given a mother to balance her patriarchal father. After all, even Caliban's mother is identified in *The Tempest* – as the witch, Sycorax.

In *Water with Berries*, the closing chapters reveal that Myra's mother is Teeton's landlady, the Old Dowager. However, Mrs Gore-Brittain does not know her daughter is still alive, having been told that she has perished in the storm that killed her father; and only Teeton has the information that could link the various elements of the plot. The Old Dowager is a Britannia figure who represents the more benign aspects of the colonizer's side of the colonizer/colonized relationship, again suggesting that the connection between black male and white female is potentially less troubled than the Prospero–Caliban bond. *Water with Berries* takes its title from the speech in *The Tempest*, in which Caliban, in addition to claiming 'This island's mine', speaks with nostalgic fondness of the first phase of the colonial encounter, when Prospero treated him more humanely and he in turn introduced his new master to 'all the qualities o' th'isle' (I, ii, 332–45).[14] Within a novel that devotes comparatively little space to representing the benevolent aspects of the colonizer/colonized opposition, it is Teeton's relationship with the Old Dowager, a game played according to carefully observed rules, in which Teeton takes on the role of a son, that most obviously expresses the 'water with berries' trope and the suggestion seems to be that such a bond is impossible between Prospero and Caliban. This is also reflected in Teeton's first encounter with Myra on the heath, when he tells her that he would not have spoken to her in such a situation if she had been a man (108). In fact, there is no clear Prospero figure in the present action: Myra's 'father' has, like Coetzee's Cruso, died before returning to Europe; and no other character can fulfil the role of Prospero without complications. Again, as in *Foe*, the absence of Prospero in Albion seems to signal the beginnings of an era in which he is an anachronism.

Racism is, however, alive and well in Britain, as becomes clear in the closing sections when Teeton and the Old Dowager, take flight to *another* island, a remote spot in the Orkneys. This section allows Lamming to supplement a third element in *The Tempest* on which he comments briefly in *The Pleasures of*

Exile. In the earlier work, he refers to the 'logical treachery' (103) of Prospero's brother, Antonio, the usurper who has seized his dukedom in the pre-text, and berates Prospero for having neglected his responsibilities as a ruler in favour of 'the Book' (116), without formally abdicating. In the meantime Prospero has, of course, asserted his right to rule *the island*, as a 'Philosopher-King' (106),[15] and in so doing demonstrated the extent to which culture and imperialism are opposite sides of the same coin. In *Water with Berries*, Teeton and the Old Dowager are conveyed to the island in the Orkneys by a mysterious and silent pilot, whose house they share on arrival. He proves to be the Old Dowager's brother-in-law and, when he finally breaks his silence, it is to reveal that he has been her lover and is Myra's biological father. So, like so many postcolonial protagonists, Myra has in effect been brought up as an orphan. Even Prospero's claim to fatherhood is challenged, albeit by a character who stigmatizes Teeton as a monster and, in a racist diatribe, simply equates him with the servant who has been responsible for Myra's rape.

At this point, identities are becoming very blurred, suggesting the impossibility of sustaining the hierarchical and unitary definition of roles that was one of the linchpins of the cruder forms of colonial discourse. Like Derek and Roger, Teeton is a character who cannot be simply labelled as Caliban: as an artist working in a metropolitan context, he can effect Ariel-like transformations of his identity and play the part of Prospero as well as Caliban. The revelation that the pilot is the brother of Myra's supposed father suggests that Prospero is being replaced by Antonio, and the implication seems to be that the authoritarian colonizer has been a worse tyrant than the European usurper. When the pilot tells Teeton his version of events, it corrects and completes the story that Myra has told him on the heath. In her narrative, the island experience has been altered by the arrival of her father's 'partner', Fernando, with whom she falls in love but from whom she is irrevocably separated after her rape. The pilot now reveals that he was the supposed 'partner', venting his anger on the brother who has lied to Myra about his identity and telling Teeton he was responsible for his death. In effect, then, Fernando combines the *Tempest* roles of Ferdinand and Antonio. The possibility of a brave new world that remains ahead at the end of Shakespeare's commentary on the first phase of the colonial 'experiment' is, of course, completely unsustainable at the end of Lamming's novel. His allegory of the *end* of the colonial era leaves us with a 'mad', violated and syphilitic Miranda, who has been denied what would have been an incestuous relationship with a Ferdinand who is actually her real father, but appears to have had one with her uncle. Worse still, the pilot Fernando is, despite his indictment of his brother's imperialist and patriarchal mentality, at least in part, a madman and an overtly racist Prospero himself. He has his own secret cell on the remote Orkneys island and resents Caliban's intruding into a space that he seems to feel should be left untouched by the aftermath of the colonial tempest. In the dénouement, the Old Dowager murders Fernando when he threatens Teeton's life, but when Teeton tells her he holds the secret of her daughter's whereabouts, her liberalism collapses. She resents Caliban's assumption of superior knowledge, which breaks the rules of the game they have played together – and Teeton kills *her*.

In the closing stages, Teeton holds the information that links all the strands of the plot, and is a potential puppet-master who could resolve all the entanglements. But the novel suggests events have gone too far for any such resolution: Prospero may be an anachronism, but it is not possible for a hitherto silenced Caliban to right past wrongs. Teeton remains constructed as an other and, although it is clear that he has the knowledge and the capacity to play all the parts of *The Tempest*, there is no possibility of his being allowed to do so in Albion in the period immediately after the end of Empire. In the less-than-brave new world of the late 1960s and early 1970s, there is only the possibility of joining the revolution back 'home' – and Teeton has been a member of a secret 'Gathering' that plans to effect change in San Cristobal – or the romance of violent revenge within Britain.[16]

The Tempest intertexts may initially seem to belong to the Myra 'sub-plot', but as the various elliptically rendered narrative strands converge into a single story towards the end, it becomes clear that this plot cannot be separated from the account of the lives of the three exiled artists. In Teeton's case this is obvious, since he is privy to the details of the tangled histories of Myra, the Old Dowager and Fernando, but Roger and Derek are also contemporary Calibans and Lamming has said, 'The three characters really represent three aspects of Caliban making his journey to Prospero's ancestral home – a journey which was at the beginning a logical kind of development because of the relationship to Prospero's language' (quoted in Pouquet 84). As artists, they have become heirs to Prospero's legacy, but they are denied their share of this inheritance, because they are still stereotyped in terms of the negative characteristics ascribed to Caliban in *The Tempest*. Derek is only allowed to play Othello or 'the corpse', until in his final performance he resurrects himself from his current death, in a play entitled *A Summer's Error in Albion*, to commit a violent rape that seems to re-enact the earlier rape of Myra on the island and leaves the shocked audience feeling that 'some dragon of legend had been released on the stage' (242). Similarly, Roger can be seen as an anguished Prospero, tormented by the prospect of his white American wife, Nicole, having their racially mixed child, a fear that seems to relate to Lamming's comment on Prospero's fear of miscegenation in *The Pleasures of Exile*.[17] Nicole apparently commits suicide in Teeton's room, causing his flight to the Orkneys

with the Old Dowager, and an inconsolable Roger turns to Calibanesque
incendiarism, burning down the rooming house where he lives, the pub he
frequents and the nearby station and, in so doing, evoking memories of the
arson that has accompanied Myra's rape. Lamming refrains from quoting the
words most frequently associated with Caliban's response to the linguistic
construction of the colonized subject: 'You taught me language; and my profit
on't/Is I know how to curse' (*Tempest* I, ii, 364–5), but *Water with Berries* in
effect responds to the legacy of the English canon by cursing. Its action, which
includes murders, arson, rapes, bestiality, madness, suicides and apparent
incest, provides a terrifying catalogue of violence. Its language and narrative
mode, which begin in a subdued enough manner, increasingly suggest the
impossibility of postcolonial rapprochement, as actual violence is complemented by metaphors and similes that intensify its effect by adding an extra
dimension of brutality:

> God, God, the monsters. How they took her body, *like cannibals feeding
> on some carcass they had never hoped, never dreamed they might ever taste.*
> (228; my italics)
> Suddenly the air was *raped* by gun shot. (230; my italics)
> He had *made arson* on the Old Dowager's body. (247; my italics)

In each case, then, the violence is compounded by this extra turning of the
linguistic screw, which one might say adds insult to injury, as the narrative
persona adopts the tone of Caliban's curse.

When Teeton kills the Old Dowager, the possibility of complicity with liberal
Albion seems to have completely disintegrated. The only grounds for optimism
lie within the Caribbean, in the activities of the Gathering, or through a rite that
could provide absolution for Prospero as well as Caliban, the Ceremony of Souls.
Teeton describes this ceremony to Myra on the heath, but since their encounter
is an incognito meeting conducted under the cover of night and they remain
unaware of crucial aspects of each other's identities and since there is no mention
of the Ceremony in the latter stages of the text, it is hard to see this as offering
the same promise as it does elsewhere in Lamming's work. Instead, the novel
ends with the three artists all awaiting 'trials' (249), two of them for murder.
Caliban may have exacted a kind of revenge for the traumatic legacy of
Caribbean history, but *Water with Berries* does not offer any positive directions
for him in the future and ultimately his tragedy is that of the hybrid subject,
whose capacity for playing a multiplicity of roles remains unrecognized in a
society dominated by monocultural assumptions.

As counter-discourse, *Water with Berries* comes closer than most of the con-
texts considered in this study to adopting an overtly adversarial attitude

towards the English canon and with it the colonial metanarrative. From one point of view, Caliban is firmly instated as the protagonist, given the kind of centrality that Jean Rhys accords to Bertha/Antoinette in *Wide Sargasso Sea*. Moreover, the net effect of the text's various supplements to *The Tempest* is a thorough-going indictment of Prospero and all that he represents. Yet, the very use of such supplements suggests the need to tell a different story and, again like many of the other texts examined in this study, *Water with Berries* displaces the very ground of the colonizer–colonized encounter onto new terrain. The archetypal figures of *The Tempest* recur, but appear in a series of new incarnations that ultimately rejects the stereotyping practices of colonial discourse. Teeton, Roger and Derek all contain a number of overlapping personalities; their tragedy is that they are consigned to play the role of Caliban – or Othello.

Lamming includes a further overt reference to *The Tempest* in *Water with Berries*, when he has a character quote Trinculo's words on Caliban:

> 'Were I in England now, as once I was, and had but this fish painted, not a holiday fool there but would give a piece of silver. There would this monster make a man. Any strange beast there makes a man. ... When they will not give a doit to relieve a lame beggar, they will lay out ten to see a dead Indian'
>
> (*Water* 159–60; *Tempest* II, ii, 27–32).

The quotation is put in the mouth of a reporter who is trying to locate Teeton for an interview and the implications seem clear enough. In the eyes of the contemporary media, the Caribbean artist remains a freak, who has a commodity value because of his exotic animality, just as the 'salvage' of the Elizabethan and Jacobean fairs was a valuable source of income for his exhibitor. Trinculo seems to see this dubious English practice as mistakenly elevating Caliban's position on the chain of being. *Water with Berries* also suggests that the Caribbean artist is an extravagant stranger,[18] but never really allows him to assert his humanness in a manner that can be reconciled with Albion's needs. Habitually forced to 'offer the self which [white society is] looking for' (*Pleasures* 87), Caliban finally decides to opt out of the colonial pantomime and exact a terrible revenge, which has consequences that are as disastrous for him as they are for Prospero, but in the mood of the period enable certain ghosts to be exorcized.

III

Like *Water with Berries*, 'Caliban' by Lamming's fellow-Barbadian Edward Kamau Brathwaite, is set at the beginning of the post-imperial era, but the poem deals with changing Caribbean political hegemonies rather than the situation of the migrant writer in Britain. It offers variations on the lines from Act II, scene ii of *The Tempest*, where a drunken Caliban envisages liberation from Prospero and proclaims his allegiance to the comic figure of the drunken butler, Stephano: 'Ban' ban' Ca-caliban/Has a new master' (II, ii, 178–9). This is not, however, evident in the first of its three sections, a jeremiad which suggests that the poverty of ninety-five per cent of the Caribbean population has been perpetuated in the post-independence period.[19] Uncle Sam has replaced John Bull as the 'new master' who controls Caliban's fate and a new elite has stepped into the shoes of the plantocracy, while the majority of the islands' inhabitants remain consigned to persistent poverty. Brathwaite sees ordinary Caribbean people as continuing to suffer from economic exploitation, in the form of American economic neo-colonialism: 'the Chrysler stirs but does not produce cotton' (191).

However, as the poem continues, the attitude becomes more complex. Like Wilson Harris, Brathwaite repeatedly transforms archetypes to give them new significances and this practice is particularly prominent in the poems of *Islands*, the third part of the *Arrivants* trilogy, where 'Caliban' first appeared. Section II of the poem opens with words that closely echo those sung by Caliban to declare his allegiance to Stephano: 'And/Ban/Ban/Cal-/iban/like to play/pan/ at the Car-/nival' (192). In this incarnation Caliban is a Trinidadian masquerader enjoying the release offered by the island's annual Carnival. In Gordon Rohlehr's words, 'Carnival is depicted as an escape through descent into self, from daily encounter with the agencies of oppression: "down/down/ down/so the god won't drown/him" ' (224–5). Again, such a reading refracts back on the pre-text itself, opening up the possibility of staging this aspect of Caliban's behaviour not as that of a drunken savage in the comic sub-plot of the play, but as a liberating carnivalesque alternative to Prospero's rule.

Such an interpretation acquires added valency if one relates *The Tempest* back to its own masque origins. Clearly two different, but not necessarily opposed, concepts of Carnival are involved: the Jacobean court masquerade does not appear to have had the same degree of counter-discursive potential as Trinidad Carnival, an annual festival offering at least temporary liberation from 'the agencies of oppression'. The gap may not, however, be as great as one might initially expect: partly because Trinidad Carnival had dual origins, which came together to produce a distinctively Creole festival in the late nineteenth century, and partly because Carnival in the period since the Second World War has been an ambivalent site. According to Errol Hill, the earliest clearly recognizable antecedents of modern-day Trinidad Carnival are to be found in the pre-Lenten masquerades and festivals of the French plantocracy who settled in Trinidad after the upheavals in the Francophone Caribbean occasioned by the Haitian Revolution (*Trinidad Carnival* 7–11). The other side of the origins of Carnival lies, of course, in the folk culture of the island's Afro-Caribbean population, particularly the ritual of *canboulay*, which developed from the practice of extinguishing plantation fires (Hill, *Trinidad Carnival* 23–31) and, unlike the French fêtes, which can be related to European Catholic Carnival forms, this was celebrated not in the pre-Lenten period but on 1 August – Emancipation Day. So Trinidad Carnival has double origins, as a time of 'frivolous enjoyment' and as 'a symbol of freedom for the broad mass of the population' (Hill, *Trinidad Carnival* 21). Incompatible though these two genealogies may seem, they came together in the late nineteenth century to produce a range of cross-pollinated forms that provided the central discourses of twentieth-century Carnival. At the same time the tensions between the two sets of origins persisted and in the second half of the twentieth century debates have continued as to whether Carnival is simply a time of licensed escapism or whether it can offer a route to genuine revolutionary change.[20]

In Brathwaite's poem, the emphasis on Caliban's having a new master at least raises the possibility of emancipation from the cultural and economic legacy of Prospero. As in Shakespeare's original, the 'new master' is a lord of misrule figure and within *The Tempest* the comic trio of Trinculo, Stephano and Caliban, can be seen as offering a challenge to the solemnity of the dominant form of masquerade, the genre of romantic pastoral framed to appeal to the Stuart court. The more conventional view sees Trinculo and Stephano as 'the dregs and jesters of a debased colonizer culture' (Rohlehr 221),[21] but there is ample evidence to justify a performance that sees the trio as a parodic version of the trinity of Prospero, Miranda and Ariel, offering a bacchanalian rite that provides release from a stifling colonial situation. In addition to labelling Caliban a 'salvage', the dramatis personae of the Folio describes Stephano as 'a drunken butler' and Trinculo as 'a jester' (140), but this does nothing to negate the possibility of carnivalesque staging, which seems particularly appropriate for a con-text from the Caribbean, where 'nobility' has been an object of mimicry since the time when performances by newly emancipated slaves parodied the mores of the plantocracy by donning royal costumes. Where Caliban in particular is concerned, such carnivalization holds a mirror image up to Miranda, his 'innocent half' (Lamming, *Pleasures* 15), who shares with him the situation of having grown up outside the usual forms of socialization. Significantly, although he complains that Prospero's gift of language has only enabled him to curse, and when he contemplates murdering Prospero realizes a necessary first step will be to seize his books (III, ii, 89) and thereby destroy his logocentric power, Caliban is not denied the gift of poetry. It is Caliban who asserts 'The isle is full of noises' (III, ii, 126), and in so doing suggests the possibility of an alternative, local music that can rival the alchemy of Prospero's books.

The second section of Brathwaite's poem, then, raises the possibility of achieving release from colonial control through immersion within Carnival discourses, which, although their provenance may be partly European, offer a way out of the oppositional stance of *cursing* in Prospero's language. The body becomes paramount, as Caliban sheds the accretions of his social existence in a descent into self, which endeavours to respond to the call of 'black/gods' (193). Characteristically, however, even as he suggests the positive potential of Carnival, Brathwaite calls it into question, by likening the descent into self to a descent into the bowels of a slave ship and it becomes clear that no bacchanalian celebration of the body can eliminate the legacy of the Middle Passage. In Rohlehr's view Carnival music only offers 'a refuge and escape, rather than the sound of his liberation' and Caliban remains 'triply debased by his contact with Britain's Prospero, America's Trinculo and his new local masters' (Rohlehr 225, 224).

Obviously immersion in music is not an obstacle to self-fulfilment *per se* and, throughout *The Arrivants* trilogy, Brathwaite deploys a broad repertory of New World 'African' or 'African diaspora' musical forms, attaching very particular cultural values to each, while also suggesting their malleability in different performance contexts. In the third movement of 'Caliban' the steelband music of Carnival is replaced by the limbo, a dance sometimes believed to have evolved in the cramped conditions of the Atlantic slave ships. An earlier section of the trilogy (*Islands*, II) has been entitled 'Limbo' and the word carries connotations of the classical situation of an in-between purgatorial condition, which can again be related to the harrowing legacy of the Middle Passage crossing. In the third section of 'Caliban', limbo undergoes a metamorphosis that unleashes new creative possibilities. Although the dance takes its performer back to the memory of the slave ship – the limbo stick is associated with a whip – the movement backwards in time involves a return to the African heritage that preceded it and so the dance becomes a symbol of release, as the descent down into self culminates in a process of ascent. Here the limbo dancer is no night-club entertainer,[22] performing for tourists in the Caribbean, but a self-possessed Caliban who escapes definition by Prospero through listening to the call of a different drum. Throughout the trilogy, and particularly in its second part, *Masks*, where both poet and poem undertake a roots journey to Africa and the text engages with an extensive repertory of Ghanaian rites, the drum is the central symbol of African experience. Here, responding to its call allows the Caribbean subject to transcend a history of poverty, suffering and external definition, through a response that appears to afford more potential for genuine self-fulfilment than the temporary escape offered by Carnival. Fittingly, there is no mention of Prospero or Caliban at this point, for the escape route into a genuinely creative alternative possibility involves removing oneself from colonial (or postcolonial) definition. The drum revives the possibility of African memory and, as Jane Wilkinson has pointed out, postcolonial refashionings of *The Tempest* have not only engaged with 'Prospero and Miranda's language lessons and Caliban's subversive response. ... An alternative, perhaps equally fertile model of domination to respond to is found in Prospero's invitation to Miranda to look into the "dark backward and abysm of time" to see what she can retrieve' (11).[23] Brathwaite's poem displaces this injunction to retrieve the past from Miranda to her alter ego, Caliban, with the 'dark backward and abysm of time' relating to the slave ship's hold and the potential for a new beginning to be found further back in memory in neglected Afro-Caribbean cultural retentions. It moves beyond the oppositional encounter between Prospero and Caliban into a terrain where, in accordance with Dorsinville's model for postcolonial aesthetics, Caliban emancipates himself from Prospero by beginning to move outside his cultural agendas. How far such a position is finally sustainable remains, of course, a major subject for debate, not only because the poem, like most of Brathwaite's work uses the medium of English, but also because the possibility of separating oneself off from the impact of Western civilization is a utopian project for the postcolonial writer, in a world where globalization ensures that the West's tentacles have an even longer reach. Nevertheless, 'Caliban' demonstrates an idealistic commitment to a new terrain that is a far cry from Lamming's pessimism in his roughly contemporary *Water with Berries*.

IV

English-Canadian literature has also produced a number of notable responses to *The Tempest*, including novels by prominent Canadian writers such as Charles G. D. Roberts, Robertson Davies, Audrey Thomas and Margaret Laurence,[24] which as Diana Brydon notes focus primarily on Miranda rather than Caliban, though she sees Davies as identifying with Prospero (77). One might expect Davies's *Tempest-Tost*, the first part of his Salterton trilogy',[25] to engage especially closely with *The Tempest*, since it is about a Little Theatre production of the play. In fact, the Shakespearean references, while ubiquitous in such a plot, are fairly incidental;[26] and, although Davies is a professed believer in the way Jungian archetypes manifest themselves in theatrical characters,[27] the novel's use of *The Tempest* initially appears to demonstrate comparatively little concern with allegory and symbol, let alone culturally specific references to colonialism. *Tempest-Tost* is, first and foremost, an exposé of the foibles of small-town Canadian life[28] in the tradition of Stephen Leacock's *Sunshine Sketches of a Little Town* (1912).[29] As with Leacock, the characters demonstrate various shortcomings and, within the satirical mode, attract varying degrees of sympathy. Only the play's director, Valentine Rich, a professional woman of the theatre who has recently returned from New York and has been described by Davies as representative of 'the Canadian artist [who] has had to go abroad to do her work' (Davis, ed., *Conversations* 36), is exempt from the satire. Prospero is played by Professor Vambrace, a pedantic Classics Professor at Salterton's Waverley University; Miranda by his daughter Pearl, whose development has been stifled by her father, but who is seen by Valentine as possessing hitherto untapped potential; Ariel by Griselda Webster, daughter of the town's richest inhabitant; and Caliban by Geordie Shortreed, a practical joker and steward for the Ontario Liquor Control Board, who has a fairly minor role in the main action. However, the character on whom Davies lavishes most attention is the middle-aged mathematics teacher, Hector Mackilwraith, who plays the part of Gonzalo.

Hector is an obvious forerunner of Davies's most assured fictional creation, Dunstan Ramsey, the schoolmaster protagonist of *Fifth Business* (1970), and one attractive reading of the later novel suggests that Dunstan, whom Davies identifies as 'fifth business', the 'odd man out' from the main quartet of characters in an opera (the soprano heroine, her tenor lover, her contralto rival and the basso threat to the tenor) but a necessary catalyst for the plot (227),[30] represents Canada, a country that has usually played a minor role on the world stage. Such an interpretation offers an interesting parallel with *Tempest-Tost* where a Gonzalo, of questionable acting ability, is given a central role in the novel's narrative, while the converse is true of the Prospero and Caliban figures. Given that Salterton lends itself to interpretation as a Canadian microcosm, the suggestion seems to be that the relative importance of the roles has shifted in what Davies views as a provincial, and sometimes positively philistine, society. Diana Brydon suggests that there is often a doubling of roles within the novel and finds character parallels with *The Tempest* in the frame action that do not correspond to the parts the characters play in the production (80–2). Where Hector is concerned, she argues that he is less Gonzalo than Caliban, since his emotional immaturity, a product of Canadian puritanical repression, makes him the real monster of the text. The evidence for such doubling is, however, less compelling than it is in, say, *Water with Berries* and the suggestion that Hector is a monster overlooks the fact that his psychology is more fully and more sensitively explored than that of any other character in the novel. His repression is traced back to childhood influences, particularly that of his Presbyterian minister father, and his immaturity, manifest in a late-flowering quasi-adolescent crush on Griselda, is observed from the inside. Consequently, it seems more straightforward to see Davies's novel as moving its *Tempest* parallels from a focus on Prospero and Caliban, or Miranda and Ferdinand, into a skewed Canadian world where Gonzalo has become the leading protagonist − and, instead of acting as a wise old counsellor, is making a fool of himself by becoming infatuated with Ariel. Brydon's comment remains useful in directing attention to the difficulty of finding neat *Tempest* correspondences for Davies's repertory of characters and in fact one of the most telling scenes in the novel comes when parts for the play are being cast. As Hugo McPherson points out, 'In the jejune and complacent community of Salterton it is almost impossible to find people who might be appropriately cast in the various roles of *The Tempest*' (23). However, the central irony *is* that, in Davies's version of provincial Canada, Gonzalo has assumed centre-stage. Whether this legitimizes any kind of postcolonial reading remains debatable, but one obvious possibility that it opens up is that of seeing the satire of provincialism as satire of an essentially colonial mentality.

There is, however, another possible reading in which Prospero remains central. In this reading, the real Prospero of the novel is neither the person who plays the part, Professor Vambrace, nor the director, Valentine Rich, but the author himself. Responding to an article (McPherson), which linked the characters in *Tempest-Tost* with those of *The Tempest*, Davies said in a 1968 interview with Gordon Roper:

> It never occurred to me that the characters in that play [*sic*] had much association with the characters in *The Tempest*. I mean the fact that Professor Vambrace was a kind of two-bit magician and that he had a captive daughter never really quite struck me. I have known many people who have had captive daughters.
>
> (Davis, *Conversations* 34)

In the same interview, he said that he chose *The Tempest* for the Salterton Little Theatre's production, because it was 'probably [his] favourite play', mentioning that he had 'christened [his] first daughter Miranda'[31] and that it subsequently occurred to him 'that people might think I was casting myself as Prospero' (34). Such an identification proves more rewarding than attempts to discover precise *Tempest* correspondences for particular characters: if there are parallels to be found, they function mainly as mock-heroic analogies that diminish the pretensions of the Salterton cast, with their efforts to stage a pastoral being wryly mocked through a novelistic technique that operates through comedy of manners. The real Prospero is, then, the author, the invisible magician who orchestrates all the action and takes upon himself the right to pass judgement on all his fictional subjects. Such an interpretation accords with Shakespeare's emphasis on Prospero's *books*: his magical powers have an alchemical dimension and his hermetic knowledge is related to his monopoly of the written word. Davies's own life-long fascination with magic is well documented – and particularly manifest in his later Deptford trilogy, where the Presbyterian legacy of the small town that renders Dunstan Ramsey another case study of the Canadian 'unlived life' (*Fifth Business* 226) is contrasted with the myth, magic and alchemy of the world of wonders,[32] an alternative set of catholic values that fascinate both Dunstan and his creator and provide further support for viewing the Davies author as a Prospero figure, who assumes a hegemonic power, akin to that of a colonial ruler over his fictional subjects, as he pontificates on the shortcomings of their provincialism.

Davies's storytelling method is a world away from the postmodernist self-consciousness of Coetzee and Carey and there is no overt authorial figure in the text, as there is in both *Foe* and *Jack Maggs*, but the tone of the novel establishes the narrative voice as its most powerful presence. It is a voice that presides with satirical Tory aloofness, like Stephen Leacock's persona in *Sunshine Sketches*, observing small-town foibles through a technique that moves between kindliness and razor-sharp irony, but exhibiting more disdain than the chronicler of Mariposa, whom Davies views as a writer 'who tried very hard to keep his Sunshine Sketches sunny' (*Stephen Leacock* 21). Diana Brydon's discussion of *Tempest-Tost* concludes, 'Like most English Canadians, I suspect, Davies is still trying to meet Prospero's standards even as he recognizes that the *Tempest* paradigm must be re-written to accommodate a Canadian experience' (82). This was published in 1984 and it seems reasonable to argue that there has been considerable movement away from 'Prospero's standards' in the intervening years. At the same time, the extent to which *Tempest-Tost*, written nearly a quarter of a century earlier, 'recognizes' a need for reinscription is debatable. Davies talks about Leacock as an author who in his *Sunshine Sketches* adopts a 'godlike view, the assumption by the writer of a power to judge his characters' (*Stephen Leacock* 25) and, while he would move away from such omniscience in his later fiction where first-person confessional modes predominate, the authorial voice of *Tempest-Tost* assumes a similar Prospero-like authority. Thus, in a passage such as the following, where Geordie Shortreed is introduced, the satirical narrative voice assumes the 'godlike' right to judge the small-town Canadian 'niceness' of the great and the good of Salterton and remains equally aloof from its 'Caliban' and his peers among the town's 'gentle and simple':

George, or as he preferred to be called, Geordie Shortreed, was a steward in the government liquor store and in that capacity was acquainted with all the gentle and simple of Salterton. He knew who drank wine, who drank imported Scotch, who drank the cheaper liquors, and who bought good stuff for themselves and what he called belly-vengeance for their guests. He had a large bass voice and a monkey-like physique which had persuaded Valentine to cast him as Caliban. Because Caliban is a large and important part, and one which was coveted by several other actors in the Little Theatre, it was thought that in casting a man who was, in essence, a bartender for it the Little Theatre had behaved in a commendably democratic way. Canadians are, of course, naturally democratic, but when they give some signal evidence of this quality in the social life, they like to get full marks for it. Everybody had, therefore, been a little nicer to Geordie than was strictly required, nicer, that is to say, than they would have been to someone who was an unquestionable social equal. Geordie, however, refused to play this game according to the rules. Instead of being quietly grateful for the friendliness of professors and business men who always bought the best Scotch, he was rather noisily familiar with them, and revealed himself as a practical joker. (146–7)

No one escapes the implied author's scalpel here and the same patrician tone informs passages in the novel where this author is commenting on Salterton locations, again with the suggestion that they are metonyms of Canadianness:

As well as its two cathedrals it [Salterton] has a handsome Court House (with a deceptive appearance of a dome but not, perhaps, a true dome) and one of His Majesty's largest and most forbidding prisons (with an unmistakable dome). And it is the seat of Waverley University. To say that the architecture of Waverley revealed its spirit would be a gross libel upon a centre of learning which has dignity and, in its high moments, nobility. The university had the misfortune to do most of its building during that long Victorian period when architects strove like Titans to reverse all laws of seemliness and probability and when what had been done in England was repeated, clumsily and a quarter of a century later, in Canada. (10–11)

The Prospero-like author demonstrates intimate knowledge of Salterton life, but at the same time exhibits no compunction about adopting a judgemental tone towards its provincialism. Salterton can be measured by a European yardstick and found wanting and yet, in its immersion in the specifics of small-town Canadian life, *Tempest-Tost* remains, at least in one sense, unequivocally

Canadian. So, while on the one hand the novel is anything but a con-text – it makes no real attempt to refashion *The Tempest*, apart from making a foolish Gonzalo figure the centre of attention – it nevertheless relies for much of its effect on *placing* Salterton in terms of national and provincial specifics, stressing its cultural insularity. The irony, like Leacock's, may be directed against Canadian parochialism, but even the disparagement conveyed by the authorial voice is a recognizable Canadian discourse. When Alice Munro's *Who Do You Think You Are?* (1978) was first published outside Canada, the title was changed to *The Beggar Maid* on the grounds that the 'put-down' aspect of the phrase ('Who do you think *you* are?'), supposedly a particularly Canadian utterance directed against those with ideas above their station, would be lost on American and European readers. Irregardless of the soundness of this view (the original Canadian title has been reinstated in later non-Canadian editions), it nevertheless relates interestingly to Davies's view that Canada is fifth business. Adapting this, one might say it reflects the belief that Canada is a Gonzalo in the identity politics theorizing that has found *The Tempest* such a rewarding pre-text. Perhaps the very suggestion that reading Canada through the prism of *The Tempest* has to focus on Gonzalo points up the limitations of viewing first-world texts as national allegories, which would lend support to Fredric Jameson's contention that national allegory is a feature that distinguishes third-world cultural production from analogous modes in the first world (68). Nevertheless, *if* one wishes to pursue such an approach, then the most obvious representative of Canadian identity in the text is Hector, the emotionally underdeveloped son of a Presbyterian minister, who has refused the call to the ministry himself, but buried himself in the surrogate religion of schoolteaching. Quite apart from his infatuation with Griselda, his desire to play Gonzalo is itself an imaginative flight of fancy for him, but to most readers it will seem a modest enough rush of blood to the head, albeit one which is consonant with the Calvinist legacy that has stunted his development. Hector may be more sympathetic than most of the novel's characters, but he lacks the self-knowledge to be taken seriously as a Gonzalo; and, in any case, setting one's sights on playing Gonzalo is a world away from the attempts to contest or transcend oppositional binaries that characterize Lamming's and Brathwaite's responses to the colonial aspects of *The Tempest*. In *Tempest-Tost*, such a tension is never present in the first place.

V

The Tempest is a more incidental intertext in Margaret Laurence's *The Diviners* than in *Tempest-Tost*, but it bears a closer relationship to the other postcolonial con-texts discussed in this chapter than Davies's novel, particularly since Laurence identified with writers from postcolonial societies that had suffered from more direct forms of colonization. She had lived in Africa – in what were then Somaliland and the Gold Coast – from 1950 to 1957 and when she subsequently read Mannoni's *Prospero and Caliban* found it 'a revelation' (Laurence, *Dance* 155). Later, when she was resident in England in the 1960s, she met Wole Soyinka and Christopher Okigbo, wrote a book on Nigerian writing[33] and speaks of having 'found it exciting that African writers were producing what I thought I and many Canadians were producing: a truly non-colonial literature' (*Dance* 185). So, even though she and Davies shared a common ancestry – they were both Canadians of Scottish descent – their attitudes to Canadian identity differ considerably. Whereas Davies can be seen to be to be aligning himself with the filiative strain of Scots-Canadian identity that had played an important part in the process of nation-building after Confederation in 1867, Laurence sees her Scottishness in terms of a rather different, *affiliative* identification.

The Diviners is the last novel in Laurence's Manawaka sequence: a complex polyphonic text that moves beyond the primarily realistic mode of her earlier Manawaka fiction, employing a fragmentary, often metafictive technique to develop the feminist and Western Canadian concerns that dominate the sequence. *The Tempest* only figures as an intertext in brief references to the writer/protagonist Morag Gunn's second novel, *Prospero's Child*. Morag describes this novel as 'semi-allegorical' (329–30) and, since the title character is a Miranda figure who marries the text's Prospero and is infantilized by him, the main thrust of the allegory appears to be an attack on patriarchal repression. Diana Brydon (77ff.) and Chantal Zabus (119ff.) have both noted that Canadian responses to *The Tempest* mainly focus on Miranda, but in Laurence's case, instating Miranda/Morag as the protagonist not only makes for a contestation of paternal lines of influence, it also facilitates a re-examination of Canada's – and particularly Western Canada's – 'aspirations as a dutiful daughter of the empire' (Brydon 77). Laurence's Miranda is very clearly the other half of Caliban, an islanded woman who is the 'innocent' victim of double colonization.

Incidental though the *Tempest* references may be, *Prospero's Child* has a force that radiates outwards into *The Diviners* as a whole. Morag gives an account of what her novel is about in a letter:

> It's called *Prospero's Child*, she being the young woman who marries His Excellency, the Governor of some island in some ocean very far south, and who virtually worships him and then who has to go to the opposite extreme and reject nearly everything about him, at least for a time, in

order to become her own person. It's as much the story of H. E. I've always wondered if Prospero really would be able to give up his magical advantages once and for all, as he intends to do at the end of *The Tempest*. (330)

The only other information given about this novel has to be gleaned from reviews that are quoted in the text:

'A revealing study of the dependence complex and its final resolution.'
'Yet another updating of *The Tempest*. Boring and contrived.'
'The character of Mira shows an interesting development from a child-like state to that of a limited independence and the eventual possibility of spiritual maturity.' ...
'The character of H. E. is a perceptive study of authoritarianism, while at the same time retaining his individuality as a human being.'
'H. E. (a too-obvious play on "He") is cardboard through and through.' (332)

Just as the name 'H. E.' suggests both a colonial ruler and an archetypal male, 'Mira' obviously evokes Miranda, while the 'dependence complex' comment in the review, brings to mind Mannoni's interpretation of Caliban and by extension Mira's affinity with Shakespeare's other child of 'nature'. Laurence may well be indebted to Lamming as well as Mannoni. She knew the Barbadian novelist in Canada and, according to her biographer, James King, had an affair with him that led her to travel to England in search of him.[34] Certainly the use of the name Mira echoes that of Lamming's Miranda variant in *Water with Berries* and, while *The Diviners* may initially seem a far cry from Lamming's responses to *The Tempest*, when *Morag* travels to England, she lives in Hampstead in the same fictional time as Lamming's Teeton, Derek and Roger. Clearly *The Diviners* differs from *Water with Berries* in shifting its main emphasis from Caliban to Miranda, but in both cases the Caliban–Miranda *relationship* is central. In *The Diviners*, it is present not only in Morag's overlapping identities – her 'dependence complex' makes her both a Caliban and a Miranda – but also in her relationship with her Métis lover, Jules Tonnerre, whose construction as an ethnic other by Manawaka society renders him a more obvious candidate for the role of Caliban. And Morag's daughter by Jules, Pique, becomes the personification of a Canadian future, in which a hybrid society, born from a consensual union between Miranda and Caliban, may be viewed more positively.

Mira's marriage in *Prospero's Child* relates fairly obviously to Morag's own marriage to the Englishman, Brooke Skelton, whom she initially meets as one of her literature teachers while at college in Winnipeg, and *The Tempest* parallel offers a framework for reading the sections of the novel that describe this marriage. Brooke is Morag's mentor and, even after their marriage, infantilizes her until she reaches a point where she leaves him 'in order to become her own person'. Again, the main emphasis is clearly feminist. However, *Prospero's Child* has a colonial setting and Brooke has been brought up in the India of the British Raj, which has left him permanently traumatized. So, like Morag's novel, *The Diviners* suggests links between domestic and macro-colonial forms of authoritarian control. Morag's freeing herself from Brooke is, however, not simply a liberation from a repressive relationship. It is also a break with the literary world that he represents. Named after two English poets, he is a teacher of seventeenth-century literature and Morag's initial passion for him is as much a response to the discourse of Platonic love, in its original sense, as to his physical person. As a student in his classes on Donne, she is particularly drawn to the lines:

> Our eye-beams twisted, and did thread
> Our eyes, upon one double string.
> (Diviners 190; 'The Extasie', ll. 7–8)

and when they subsequently make love, temporarily believes that she is entering a world beyond language, in which their 'separate selves' become one (201). Such a belief is not sustained for long after they marry, but it suggests the extent to which she is Prospero's child in a broader sense than may immediately be obvious. She is the willing acolyte of a Prospero who exerts control through the magic of his books – one might say, a slave to the English canon. Seen in this light, the ending of her relationship with Brooke signals not only a feminist assertion of a need for physical independence, but also a break with the literary traditions that have made her the dependent partner in the marriage. Throughout, *The Diviners* contrasts different modes of writing, for example Wordsworth's 'Daffodils' with the poems of Ossian and the 'official' version of Canadian history with an oral Western Canadian counter-discourse, with the latter alternatives being preferred in both cases; and, after Morag leaves Brooke and all he represents, the remainder of her multi-faceted story is centred on her gradual emergence as a novelist who writes directly from her own experience. In so doing, she both changes her own past and also provides a revisionist perspective on Western Canadian history. She replaces a view that privileges the received narrative of the Canadian past with an account in which founding fathers such as the nation's first prime minister, the Scottish-born Sir John A. MacDonald, are supplanted by the Métis leader, Louis Riel, who led two rebellions against federal

Canadian authority in the late nineteenth century. At the same time, *The Diviners* employs a multiplicity of narrative modes and the effect of this polyphony is not simply to tell a revisionist history in a variety of ways, but to interrogate the historiographic process itself. In *The Tempest*, Caliban realizes that he will need to seize Prospero's books, if he is to divest his master of his power. Here it is Miranda who undertakes this task and, unlike Caliban in the pre-text, succeeds, by virtue of becoming a highly successful author. As Gayle Greene notes, Morag wonders towards the end of the novel whether she has created her own unreal island, before deciding, in what could be seen as a reversal of one of Donne's most famous utterances, that her present home is 'not an island' (Greene 195–6; *Diviners* 357). Morag contains elements of both Miranda and Caliban within her personality, but she has also appropriated the role of Prospero by virtue of becoming an author. However, she totally repudiates Prospero's isolation from 'human community and ... the past' (Greene 196). She is settled in a Canadian present and her 'quest for islands' (*Diviners* 357) is behind her.

So *The Diviners* redeploys *Tempest* archetypes, particularly the role of Miranda, to fashion a response that gives voice to the hitherto disempowered subjects of the colonial 'island'. While looking into the 'dark backward and abysm of time', it uses its retrospective viewpoint to suggest the possibility of a multi-cultural Canadian future; and finally, another Miranda figure, Morag's racially mixed, folk-singing daughter Pique, becomes the artist who will assume Prospero's mantle. The novel is altogether more optimistic than *Water with Berries* in its reworking of *The Tempest*, but Laurence shares both Lamming's and Brathwaite's concern with Ariel-like transformations of the roles assigned to Caliban and Miranda. So the expectation that Canadian and Caribbean con-texts will yield very different perspectives is not really borne out in these instances. However, Davies's *Tempest-Tost* offers a very different window on Shakespeare's last play, by placing its Gonzalo figure at the centre of the action. The attitude here is clearly less 'non-colonial', but nevertheless the vicissitudes that surround the Little Theatre's production of *The Tempest* still indicate that the play cannot be translated into a Canadian context, without all kinds of complications. Although there is no explicit questioning of the filiative relationship with the English canon, the difficulties that surround the casting of Salterton citizens in the roles of *The Tempest* and the problems that readers have in identifying neat correspondences between the main action of the novel and Shakespeare's play both suggest postcolonial disjuncture.

Notes

1.   See Vaughan and Vaughan, *Shakespeare's Caliban*, Hulme and Sherman (eds) and Dymskowski (ed.), for recent accounts of colonial interpretations.
2.   See Kermode xxvi-xxxiv.
3.   The play is said to be set on an 'uninhabited island', even though Prospero and Miranda have been on the island for twelve years and Caliban and Ariel predate them there.
4.   He is referred to as such in the 'Names of the Actors' in the Folio. Some editors emend 'salvage' to 'savage', e.g. Vaughan and Vaughan in the third Arden edition (140). Kermode justifies 'salvage' by linking Caliban with the 'salvage man of Europe', who was 'a familiar figure in painting, heraldry, pageant, and drama' (xxxix).
5.   It was originally published in Paris as *Psychologie de la colonisation* (1950).
6.   Fanon is mentioned in Lamming's Introduction to the 1984 edition ([6]).
7.   See Chapter 3 above.
8.   Sylvia Wynter points out the extent to which 'the *anatomical* model of sexual difference' is privileged over 'the *physiognomic* model of racial/*cultural* difference', arguing that 'the most significant absence of all' in *The Tempest* is 'that of Caliban's Woman, of Caliban's physiognomically complementary mate' (358, 360; italics in original). *The Pleasures of Exile* and *Water with Berries* replicate this exclusion of the black woman. See Djanet Sears's *Harlem Duet*, discussed in Chapter 7 below, for an example of a text that very obviously addresses this omission.
9.   It is central in *Season of Adventure* (1960) and also employed in *Water with Berries*.
10. See Chapter 7 for a fuller discussion of the casting of the title role of *Othello*.
11. E.g. the jacket blurb of the 1973 Longman edition.
12. Cf. *Tempest* I, ii, 41. Line references are to the 3rd Arden edn, ed. Vaughan and Vaughan. Just as *The Tempest* is said to be set on an 'uninhabited island', 'alone' is a relative term here too, since Myra's father has his own Caliban (148ff.). The exclusions involved obviously deny humanity to the 'salvage and deformed slave'.
13. Cf. Paquet: 'She is the white West Indian in exile first in San Cristobal, and later in the land of her parents as well' (85).
14. Lamming quotes the passage three times in *Pleasures* (101, 114, 117).
15. A parallel that can be traced back to Wilson Knight's *The Crown of Life* (Cartelli 98).
16. I am indebted to Suzanne Scafe for a comment that led me towards this formulation.
17. His fear of 'impurity' and his surname, Capildeo, also suggest V. S. Naipaul's similar comments on racial taint, particularly, as Pouquet notes (98–9), in *The Mimic Men*. Capildeo was Naipaul's mother's maiden name, see Chapter 1 above. This motif is particularly developed in a passage in section 2, 3 of *Water with Berries*, where Naipaulian imagery is prominent, e.g. 'It seemed that history had amputated his root from some other human soil, and deposited him, by chance, in a region of time which was called an island' (70). Ralph Singh, Naipaul's protagonist in *The Mimic Men*, repeatedly expresses a similar sense of having been uprooted and the theme of dislocation runs through Naipaul's entire œuvre. Drawing a parallel between Ralph Singh's fear of racial hybridity and

Prospero's has, of course, the effect of constructing another racially mixed identity: by relocating Prospero as a displaced Indo-Caribbean! The name Derek could just possibly allude to Derek Walcott, who in addition to sharing a first name with the character also had a Methodist upbringing.

18. The phrase is from *Othello,* where the protagonist is referred to as an 'extravagant and wheeling stranger' (Arden 3rd edn, I, i, 134). Cf. Caryl Phillips's use of it for the title of his anthology, *Extravagant Strangers: A Literature of Belonging* (1997).

19. Gordon Rohlehr sees this as 'the poet's reaction against the tiresome statistics of imperialist exploitation' (221), i.e. he views Brathwaite as distancing himself from it. See Rohlehr 220–1 and Paquet 98 for other Caribbean uses of the Prospero/Caliban paradigm. More recent treatments include Michelle Cliff's *No Telephone to Heaven* (1987), which also engages with *Jane Eyre* as mediated by *Wide Sargasso Sea,* and David Dabydeen's poems on the Caliban–Miranda relationship in *Coolie Odyssey* (1988).

20. This debate is central to literary texts such as Earl Lovelace's novel *The Dragon Can't Dance* (1979) and Derek Walcott's play *The Last Carnival* (in *Three Plays,* 1986).

21. Lamming simply views them as 'crooks' (*Pleasures* 108), whom Caliban is unable to recognize as such.

22. Cf. Trinculo's 'holiday fool' speech and Lamming's response to it in *Water with Berries* (159–60).

23. The phrase 'dark backward and abysm of time' alludes to *Tempest* I, ii, 50.

24. Brydon discusses these texts, along with Phyllis Gotlieb's *O Master Caliban!* (1976), which, she notes, is 'the only Canadian novel to deal explicitly with Caliban [and] also the only one that is set outside Canada (and outside traditional realism)' (88).

25. The other two parts are *Leaven of Malice* (1954) and *A Mixture of Frailties* (1958).

26. *Pace* John Moss: 'The play echoes through Davies' complicated plot on several levels. The dominant echo is the most superficial: who plays what, why, and how well' (53–4).

27. See, e.g., his comments in *One Half of Robertson Davies* 143–60.

28. Salterton is generally considered to be based on Kingston, Ontario, where Davies lived in his youth.

29. Davies wrote a short critical study of Leacock, *Stephen Leacock* (1970), and edited *Feast of Stephen: An Anthology of the Less Familiar Writings of Stephen Leacock* (1970). His comments on Leacock include the following, which has particularly interesting reverberations for his own comic technique: 'I think we do have something which more or less approaches a national humour, and it's something that Stephen Leacock evolved with great brilliance. The characteristic of it is a kind of patterned innocence which covers a very great bitterness. Never is it so sharply shown as in Leacock's *Sunshine Sketches.* You analyse what he says about the little town and it's a snake-pit. But he says it with such charm!' (Twigg 34).

30. Cf. the novel's epigraph, quoted from Tho. Overskou's *Den Danske Skueplads*: '*Fifth Business* ... Definition/Those roles which being neither those of Hero nor Heroine, Confidante nor Villain, but which were nonetheless essential to bring about the Recognition or the dénouement, were called the Fifth Business in

drama and opera companies organized according to the old style; the player who acted these parts was often referred to as Fifth Business' ([5]).

31.   Cf. Jane Urquhart's choice of the name Emily for her daughter.

32.   *World of Wonders* (1975) is the title of the third part of the Deptford trilogy, which *Fifth Business* initiates. The second part is *The Manticore* (1972).

33.   *Long Drums and Cannons: Nigerian Dramatists and Novelists, 1952–1966* (1968). Her other 'African' books were: *A Tree for Poverty* (1954), translations of Somali folk tales and poetry; *This Side Jordan* (1960), a novel; *The Prophet's Camel Bell* (1963), an account of her experiences in Somaliland; and *The Tomorrow-Tamer* (1963), a collection of short stories.

34.   As reported by John Levesque W4. King apparently draws on a diary that Laurence kept during the last months of her life and her correspondence with her friend, the novelist Adele Wiseman.

7

Removing the black-face: a different *'Othello* music'

How did Othello live in this astonishing city? Sixteenth-century Venetian society both enslaved the black and ridiculed the Jew. This black 'extravagant and wheeling stranger' must have lived on a knife-edge. Out of this tension Shakespeare spun great drama. But the true nature of Othello's psychological anguish is often missed in productions of the play. We have been subjected to a procession of sun-blotched Oliver Hardy lookalikes waddling across the English stage, causing worry both to themselves and their audiences as to whether or not the make-up will come off on the face of Desdemona.

(Caryl Phillips, *European Tribe* 45–6)

Othello had haunted me since I was first introduced to him. Sir Laurence Olivier in black-face. Othello is the first African portrayed in the annals of Western dramatic literature. In an effort to exorcise this ghost, I have written *Harlem Duet. Harlem Duet*, a rhapsodic blues tragedy, explores the effects of race and sex on people of African descent. It is a tale of love. A tale of Othello and his first wife, Billie. ... The exorcism begins.

(Djanet Sears 15–16)

I

Although they lack the overt colonial implications of *The Tempest*, *Othello* and *The Merchant of Venice* are, self-evidently, the two other Shakespeare plays that deal most overtly with 'race' and, as Caryl Phillips makes clear in both his travel-book *The European Tribe* (1987) and his novel *The Nature of Blood* (1997), they converge in the trading capital of Renaissance Europe, Venice. Shakespeare's Italy is usually even more of a fantasy land than Conrad's never-named Congo or for that matter Defoe's Caribbean. However, in his representation of Venice, far from creating an extra-social site in which distance apparently intervenes between the pastoral world of the play and the social realities of Renaissance England, Shakespeare clearly constructs a locus for investigating his own society's anxieties about alterity. On the evidence of *The Tempest*, where Milan is seen as a seaport, and *Two Gentlemen of Verona*, which has a journey from Verona to Milan being undertaken by sea,[1] it seems that he had comparatively little knowledge of, or interest in, the 'real' geography of Italy. However, in the *Merchant*, Venice is no never-never land, but rather a fulcrum for the exploration of social changes occasioned by the contemporary mercantile culture. To quote Phillips again, Venice 'was the New York of the Renaissance, controlling the whole of the Western world, dedicated to capitalism and an unthinking exploitative trade' (*European Tribe* 45). As such, it was a world away from Elizabethan and Jacobean England. Nevertheless, its colonial sphere of influence offered a model for the capitalist-imperialist ventures on which Britain was embarking, ventures that increasingly involved contacts with 'other' races and peoples. For this reason alone, *Othello* and the *Merchant*, plays that foreground *contemporary* inter-cultural encounters relating to colonialism, are precursors of *The Tempest* in a way that plays about southern England's conflicts with other parts of Britain and with France in the first tetralogy of history plays, or Rome's relationship with Egypt in *Antony and Cleopatra*, are not, though obviously these lent, and continue to lend, themselves to interpretation as political allegories.

This chapter is centred on two postcolonial writers' responses to *Othello*:[2] on the Phillips works mentioned above and on the British-born African Canadian dramatist Djanet Sears's play, *Harlem Duet* (1997), in which Desdemona is relegated to the sidelines with her place – and indeed, one might argue, that of Othello himself as the protagonist – being taken over by Othello's black first wife, 'Billie'. Both writers are concerned with the role of the 'extravagant and wheeling stranger' who has been co-opted into white society and finds himself 'a sad black man, first in a long line of so-called achievers who are too weak to yoke their past with their present' (Phillips, *Nature* 182) and both displace aspects of the action of Shakespeare's play into broader con-texts, making their 'achiever' figures part of a larger design. However, despite these commonalities, the two responses also exhibit considerable differences and ultimately inhabit different discursive universes.

II

In recent decades, the volume of critical commentary on *Othello* has reached a point where, in Thomas Cartelli's words, the play 'is well on the way to replacing *The Tempest* as a favored field of debate and contention for both scholars and critics of Shakespeare, and for the increasingly numerous workers in the field of postcolonial studies' (124).³ Part of this shift may have to do with the extent to which ' "First World" societies find themselves compelled to address the inequities of internal colonization' and the fact that, unlike Caliban who is 'locked into his island kingdom where he must sink or swim, Othello has functioned from his moment of production as the exotic outsider, licensed, from the early modern period to the present, to move freely about the metropolitan "First World" and to interact, on a privileged basis, with its movers and shakers' (Cartelli 124). Looking at this from the point of view of the 'outsider', who after all is the protagonist, Ania Loomba points out that 'the play is not just about race in general but about a black man isolated from other black people. His loneliness is an integral feature of the play's racial politics' (148).

Clearly there are differences between Caliban and Othello that have to do with both the geopolitical situations in which they find themselves and the ways in which their ethnicity is staged. Debates about Caliban have tended to centre on whether he should be regarded as an Amerindian or an Afro-Caribbean, transported to the New World as it were ahead of his time, though as Vaughan and Vaughan note, he has increasingly been used to represent 'any group that felt itself oppressed' (194).⁴ Similar arguments about Othello's racial identity have had to decide whether he should be played as a North African Moor or sub-Saharan black African.⁵ While the identification of him as a 'Moor' in the dramatis personae would seem to suggest that he belongs to a North African world that was frequently stereotyped, in terms of Orientalist codes, as exotic (which, of course, fits with the 'extravagant and wheeling stranger' description), the play also offers support for viewing him as a black 'Noble Savage', albeit before the later more widespread dissemination of this stereotype through the work of Rousseau and other eighteenth-century writers;⁶ and there is evidence for suggesting that Shakespeare's contemporaries made little distinction between North and sub-Saharan Africa.⁷ More importantly, he has frequently been represented as black and Derek's experience of being cast in the role in *Water with Berries* links him with such distinguished black Othellos as those created by Ira Aldridge (1833), Paul Robeson (1930) and John Kani (1987). Equally, the role has been all too readily available to the succession of 'sun-blotched Oliver Hardy look-alikes' that Phillips comments on in the passage quoted as the first epigraph to this chapter – and Sears's reference to Laurence Olivier's 1964 performance,⁸ quoted in the second epigraph, appears to express a similar discomfort. It is a cliché to say that Shakespeare's tragic heroes are re-created for each age – and indeed each performance in each age – and only slightly less so to point out that they take on different cultural baggage in each of the different social contexts in which they are performed. However, it is a cliché that takes on an added force in postcolonial con-texts. Thus, commenting on her 1987 production of *Othello* at Johannesburg's Market Theatre, Janet Suzman point outs that staging it with John Kani in the title role was a politically charged act, since 'the play addresses the notion of apartheid four hundred years before the epithet was coined'.[9] Equally, while such a production represented a radical statement in 1980s South Africa, it moved away from Shakespeare's text's location of Othello in Europe (see Loomba 148), as a licensed exotic who forms a minority of one. It also becomes interesting to note that Ira Aldridge and Paul Robeson both succeeded in the role on the London stage, when they had not found similar success in America. At the same time, lest this suggests a significantly greater degree of tolerance in Britain, casting Robeson against Peggy Ashcroft in 1930 elicited a Brabantio-like response from some commentators,[10] while a century before, Aldridge, who was almost certainly born in New York, found himself reinvented as a kind of real-life Othello: as an 'African Roscius' of royal parentage. Absorption into the canon could hardly go further!

There are, however, comparatively few situations in which the positioning of Othello as a racial outsider can be ignored. A modern production *might* attempt to suggest that Othello is a black man who is exempt from racial prejudice, but this exemption only operates in institutional contexts. As a military commander in the Venetian Republic, he moves in a world that may appear to be colour-blind, but his licence does not extend very far even in these professional contexts — and matters are very different in the private sphere. To be Othello is to be confined to a white stereotype of blackness. Lamming's Derek, in *Water with Berries*, clearly represents the convergence of the characters of Caliban and Othello and, when he resurrects himself to rape the actress who is standing over him, he is acting out the charge that has been levelled against Caliban by Prospero, although he has achieved success as Othello. Othello's violence is of a different kind, but it is arguably more disturbing to white liberals since it represents the failure of the assimilative project, while for black audiences it is, as Ben Okri sees it, troubling in 'more secret' ways (quoted by Cartelli 124). Moreover, the murder, which symbolizes the end of his precarious love affair with white society, is occasioned not simply by Iago's rhetoric, but also by the expiry of his licence, in the eyes of Brabantio and others, when he marries Desdemona. Venetian society needs Othello and allows him a degree of privilege, but Brabantio's response parallels Prospero's fear of Caliban consorting with *his* daughter as a classic instance of the failure of certain forms of liberalism when confronted with inter-racial conjunction that involves 'one's own'. These are among the concerns that Caryl Phillips explores in *The Nature of Blood*, but his primary emphasis is on his outsider's nervous restiveness.

III

In one sense, Othello does not appear at all in *The Nature of Blood*, apart from a brief reference in an encyclopaedia-like entry towards the end (166–7), which provides factual information about Shakespeare's play and its main source, Giraldo Cinthio's *Hecatommithi*, but has no direct connection with the fictional parts of the narrative. Obviously this mention confirms the novel's connection with *Othello*, if any such confirmation be needed, but the racial outsider of the novel is distanced from Shakespeare's 'original', because he tells his own story and, just as Rhys's version of Rochester is never referred to by *his* name in the pre-text, Phillips's character is never called Othello. Indeed, with the single exception of Cassio, none of the characters in the 'Othello' sections of *The Nature of Blood* inherits a name from the 'original', So, while the encyclopaedia-like entry and the naming of Cassio are sufficient to establish *Othello* as the point of departure for this section of the novel, this anonymity has the effect of releasing the action from the predeterminants of Shakespeare's play.

In fact, the 'Othello' story is not introduced until nearly half way through *The Nature of Blood* and it is one of a number of narrative components that gradually intersect across countries and centuries to provide a commentary on aspects of the way 'the European tribe' treats its ethnic others. Initially, the novel seems to tell a multiplicity of stories, employing a polyphonic range of voices to do so, but these gradually converge into three main narratives: the story of a Jewish family, who are victims of the Holocaust, mainly seen from the point of view of Eva Stern, a deeply traumatized Anne Frank-like character who lives to tell the tale, and her Uncle Stephan, a Zionist who continues to live in Israel in the present, when the novel ends; a story of Jewish persecution in the town of Portobufolle near Venice in the late fifteenth century; and the 'Othello' story. This is mainly concerned with the prehistory of the events in Shakespeare's play, with contextualizing Othello's situation in Venice and, although it does transport him to Cyprus, it does not follow the action of Shakespeare's play to its tragic climax and is consequently unlike the other two narratives in this crucial respect. In addition to the movement across centuries and between locations, there are numerous time shifts and changes in the angle of focalization *within* the particular stories, leaving readers frequently feeling dislocated, not only by the cross-cutting between the different actions, but also by the introduction of initially unidentified narrative voices whose identity only becomes clear as one reads on.

In *The European Tribe*, Phillips talks about his early indignation at the Holocaust and the Middle Passage and how:

As a child, in what seemed to me a hostile country, the Jews were the only minority group discussed with reference to exploitation and racialism, and for that reason, I naturally identified with them. ... The bloody excesses of colonialism, the pillage and rape of modern Africa, the transportation of 11 million black people to the Americas, and their subsequent bondage were not on the curriculum, and certainly not on the television screen. As a result I vicariously channelled a part of my hurt and frustration through the Jewish experience. (54)

He goes on to talk about finding Shylock a 'hero', who pointed up the hypocrisy of European mercantilist culture, particularly noting that in the trial scene of the *Merchant*, Shylock attacks Christian Venice's treatment of its slaves (55). In a later section of *The European Tribe* (66–71), he writes about his teenage fascination with Amsterdam and the Nazi rounding up of the Jews and this is followed by an account of a visit to Anne Frank's house, which again provokes comparisons between the persecution of Jews in Europe and racism directed against blacks. Given Phillips's comment on his 'vicarious' displacement of part of his 'hurt and frustration' onto an interest in the Jewish experience, one might, when one finds a similar set of analogies being implied in *The Nature of Blood* through the juxtaposition of narratives that reflect on Europe's treatment of its others, be excused for thinking that the Jewish experience is being used as a metaphor for the racism directed against blacks.

In fact, the novel devotes far more space to the Holocaust narrative, telling Eva's story in particular in minute detail and complementing it with the story of Jewish persecution in early Renaissance Venice, which subtly suggests links across the centuries. For example, the Jewish community of Portobuffole has migrated to the Venetian Republic from Germany in the previous century, at a time when an irrational fear of the plague has fomented racist violence against Jews, and the narrative voice dryly comments, 'Such is the way of the Germans with their Jews' (51). The Holocaust narrative involves numerous shifts in viewpoint. It begins in post-Second World War Cyprus (again suggesting a loose connection with *Othello*), with a focus on a doctor who has committed himself to the ideal represented by 'Israel', another motif that cuts across the centuries. Then it loops back in time to tell the story centred on his niece, whose chronicle of her growing unease in an unnamed wartime European city parallels Anne Frank's record of her movement from innocence to a dawning awareness of the atrocities being committed against her people.[11] Unlike Anne Frank, Eva never really keeps a diary: she begins one at one point, but gives it up within a week. Instead, Phillips's narrative becomes the vehicle for her personal testament, and her survival enables her to provide an account that encompasses the horrors of the concentration camp and her subsequent traumas, as well as the pre-internment phase of her life.

Eva's narrative, then, both parallels Anne Frank's diary and provides a sequel to it, giving a version of the rest of the Holocaust story that employs plural vantage points and narrative techniques ranging from personal testimony to coldly clinical, accounts of gassing (177) and Eva's 'emotional anaesthesia' (174) after the war, as a way of facing the historiographic challenge of articulating the unspeakable. In contrast, the 'Othello' story is more prequel than sequel. Though it does progress to the moment of his marriage to Desdemona and beyond this to his subsequent arrival in Cyprus, it stops well short of the play's tragedy and a particularly significant difference is the virtual omission of the Iago figure. Towards its end, Othello's 'Ancient' is mentioned, but unlike the pre-text, where his soliloquies allow him a degree of privileged access to the audience, this figure never actually appears. The effect is to locate the whole of this section of the narrative within Othello's mind. The cross-cutting with the Jewish narratives casts an ominous shadow over Othello's future, but tragedy lies ahead in his own story and the main emphasis is on his psychological condition, which is rife with doubts and anxieties generated from within – or at least through the role he has chosen to adopt in relation to the metropolis – rather than by the external machinations of a white Machiavel.

The 'Othello' sections of *The Nature of Blood* begin at the moment when he and the equally anonymous Desdemona have just consummated their marriage and Phillips's Othello's first thoughts are of the insecurity into which *she* has been plunged through choosing him. This mirrors his own anxieties and the first paragraph of his account continues with a passage that reflects his uncertainty with regard to the classic issue of whether he is the victim of a plot or paranoid, a problem he is unable to resolve because of his unfamiliarity with Venetian social codes: 'Has some plot been hatched about me? I am a foreigner. I do not know' (106). This strikes the note that dominates his subsequent narrative, in which he repeatedly expresses his 'fears and insecurities' (117). In *The European Tribe*, Phillips asks, 'How did Othello live in this astonishing city?' and speaks of his 'psychological anguish [which] is often missed in productions of the play' (45). *The Nature of Blood* addresses this issue, presenting its Othello as an isolate in a city, which becomes as much a protagonist as any of the people he encounters. At one point he says, 'I had once more fled to the only person I could rely upon in these circumstances: the city herself, which had remained ever faithful to her enchanted promises' (122) and this summarizes his response on several occasions, when he wanders alone through the streets of Venice, trying to calm his troubled nerves. He takes a delight in his adopted city, which parallels the ambivalent romantic vision of London to be found in novels by first-generation Caribbean migrants to

Britain, such as Sam Selvon's *The Lonely Londoners*, seeing it as an 'enchanted city' (121) that welcomes 'strangers from various exotic corners of the known world' (120). In another sense, though, the city remains inscrutable to the outsider, as 'strange' as it is 'wondrous' (121), and he realizes that its tolerance is only superficial and that his belief in the kind of 'conjunction of traditions' (120) that he enacts through his marriage to Desdemona is invalidated by the role he is forced to play in the city. Phillips goes to some length to document the 'Contract of Moses' (54–5), the means by which Jewish usurers were allowed to operate in the 'Most Serene Republic', and his Othello realizes that he occupies a similarly licensed role as a military leader: 'My own position in Venice could be explained by the fact that the republic preferred to employ the services of great foreign commanders in order that they might prevent the development of Venetian-born military dictatorships' (117).

His wanderings through the streets are not exempt from panic attacks and on one occasion when he finds the world 'muffled in mist',[12] he comes to the realization 'that this city was betraying me, and I was betraying myself' (118). In *The European Tribe*, Phillips identifies Othello's frame of mind as that of what Fanon has called the ' "abandonment neurotic" ' (50) and the character in the novel seems to suffer from a similar syndrome. Without Iago's intervention, he comes to see himself as an 'Uncle Tom ... Fighting the white man's war for him' (181). The novel retains Shakespeare's Othello's rhetorical gift for telling stories of his travels and exploits, but suggests that these simply make him an exhibit of the kind it is assumed Caliban might become, if he were brought to England to be exhibited at fairs. When Othello is first invited to Brabantio's house for a social evening, it does not take him long to realize that he is intended 'to be the chief amusement of this evening' (125) and, in the final paragraph of his narration, he refers to himself as 'A figment of a Venetian imagination' (183). In short, he concludes that, although his licence extends beyond the professional sphere – like Lamming's Teeton, he is tolerated as a 'holiday fool' – it is only valid while he plays the colonial power game according to Venetian rules. His transgression is, of course, to marry Desdemona, an act which, it appears, is taboo not only because of its inter-racial dimension, but because he has not gone through the complicated courtship rituals required by Venetian society. In a passage that may initially appear to provide little more than background detail, Phillips has him instructed in the society's 'rules of courtship' (113–14) by a courtesan whom he has been in the habit of entertaining. Later, this passage assumes greater significance when it becomes clear that he has flouted the required forms, again paying the price for being the extravagant stranger who is betrayed by the 'mist' of a city that enchants him, but only opens its doors to outsiders according to strict and limited conditions.

So the most important aspect of the 'Othello' sections of *The Nature of Blood* is the representation of the protagonist's psychic dislocation in an alien situation; and to convey this Phillips adopts an approach that renders the external action of *Othello* peripheral, as well as failing to follow the Shakespeare parallels through to the completion of the tragedy. At the same time, the strategy of making the 'Othello' story just part of a larger narrative pattern has the effect of creating a structure that enacts the ways in which supposedly different histories that cut across swathes of time – as well as place, gender and race – overlap and intertwine. There is no neat mapping of the stories of Eva Stern and the Jews of Portobuffole onto that of Othello, but as readers gradually discover links within and between the various strands, the authority of unitary narratives that implicitly present themselves as the *only* way of recording history collapses. As with con-texts such as *Foe* and *Jack Maggs*, Phillips's novel suggests that stories cannot be separated out and told as though historiography is exempt from partial narrative agency.

IV

Sylvia Wynter has drawn attention to the omission of an archetype of the black woman in *The Tempest*, pointing out that Caliban's corresponding gender opposite in the play is Miranda not a 'physiognomically complementary mate' (360). Much the same point can be made in relation to *Othello* and one of Phillips's Othello's anxieties in *The Nature of Blood* is that he has forsaken his first wife and a son in his native country, although he consoles himself with the semantic solecism that his 'native wife was not a *wife* in the manner that a Venetian might understand the term', while wondering if this is 'not simply a convenience of interpretation on my part' (146). Djanet Sears's *Harlem Duet* directly addresses the omission of a 'physiognomically complementary mate' for Othello by telling the story of his 'first wife', Billie, and leaving Desdemona as a voice waiting in the wings, as it were for an opportunity to attempt to stage her identity in a walk-on part. According primacy to the hitherto silenced and invisible figure of the black first wife is a more radical gesture than, say, allowing Bertha to emerge from the attic of Thornfield Hall, since whereas *Jane Eyre* deprives the female Other of humanity by immuring her in the margins of the text, and characterizing her as an animal, *The Tempest* and *Othello* omit such a figure altogether. Prospero, Miranda and Caliban form a triptych that creates a powerful dynamic for the exploration of inter-racial personal relationships, especially when Prospero charges Caliban with having tried to rape Miranda, and Brabantio parallels this in his reaction to his daughter's marriage to the 'extravagant stranger' he has welcomed into his household. In *Water with*

Berries, Lamming challenges the paternalism of Prospero (and, one might say by extension, Brabantio) and exacts a kind of revenge by having Caliban act out Prospero's fantasies, but still does not offer a complementary black female archetype.[13] Phillips nods in the direction of this absence in his passing references to his Othello's guilt over having discarded his first wife. Sears goes further and seemingly makes gender as important an element as race in her con-textual reclamation of alterity from the canonical margins. In fact, though *Harlem Duet* redresses the omission that Wynter identifies by restaging *Othello* three times, it does so with a cast of characters that lacks any white male – Othello has a colleague called Chris Yago who is mentioned by name but never seems likely to show up in Harlem – and by relegating the white female, now significantly renamed Mona,[14] to the role of pure voice: she is heard but not seen. So the play becomes an African American con-text,[15] in which race remains the most important component of identity, but the focus has been shifted to the experience of black *women*, albeit as problematized by black men's relationships with white women, the pivotal point of the dialogue between Othello and Billie that forms their Harlem duet.

Relocating her response to *Othello* in Harlem allows Sears to situate it in an all-black context, but the play provides its audiences with three Harlems. While the main story takes place in the 'present' of the 1990s, there are two other actions, set in 1860 and 1928, in which the main characters, Othello and Billie, play essentially the same roles, though they are called 'Him' and 'Her' in the nineteenth-century action, which takes place in the period of hope just before Emancipation, and 'He' and 'She' in the middle phase, which again holds out hope, this time as particularly epitomized by the promise of the Harlem Renaissance.[16] Contemporary Harlem remains a homeland to Billie, but much of the earlier optimism has evaporated amid 'the weeds growing in the Soweto of America' (25). Nevertheless 'Harlem' affords an ideal setting for a theatre aimed at 'people of African descent' (12). Like Derek in Lamming's *Water with Berries*, He is a putative actor who suffers from the lack of available black parts. Reminded by She that he has become a minstrel, he resolves not to 'die in black-face to pay the rent', expressing his desire to emulate Ira Aldridge by playing Hamlet and Macbeth, as well as Othello (97). The reality is his minstrel-like persona and his involvement with a white woman, confine him, like the male protagonists of the other two actions, to playing the role of Othello offstage, but *Sears* is clearly committed to extending the repertory. In her prefatory comments to the play, she talks of how, 'As a young actor, I soon realized that a majority of the roles that I would be offered did not portray me in the way I saw myself, my family, or my friends' (13) and *Harlem Duet* sets out to remedy this situation by making its own distinctive contribution to creating a theatre for her community and to writing strong parts for black women in particular.

It does so by exorcizing the ghost of Othello and admitting equivalent black female archetypes into its dialectic. Like Phillips, Sears reconfigures Shakespeare's protagonist as an assimilated black 'achiever', who is losing touch with his own people. Her contemporary Othello is an academic, whose former dreams of asserting the equality of black culture have given way not only to deserting Billie for Mona, but also to collusion in a challenge to affirmative action led by Chris Yago. At the same time, he tells Billie he will be taking charge of his department's summer courses in Cyprus, and the suggestion is that the groundwork has been laid for him to suffer the fate of his Shakespearean eponym. This, however, is an element that is left undeveloped in the play, just as Othello's tragedy lies ahead in Phillips's novel. Like *The Nature of Blood*, *Harlem Duet* is, then, more prequel than sequel; unlike Phillips's novel it does not put its primary focus on Othello's entanglement with the white world in the form of the Desdemona figure. Instead, like such texts as *Wide Sargasso Sea*, *Foe*, *Jack Maggs* and *Water with Berries*, it offers a supplement, supplying what are seen as missing elements in the pre-text.

Sears describes the play as a 'rhapsodic blues tragedy' (14) and it is first and foremost the tragedy of its heroine, who has the same first name as one of the most famous of all blues singers, Billie Holiday. At one point She sings Lady Day's 'Ain't Nobody's Business' (72);[17] more generally the whole mood of the play casts Billie in the role of a tragic blues singer. One of the most famous twentieth-century essays on *Othello*, Wilson Knight's chapter in *The Wheel of Fire* (1930), discusses 'The Othello Music', analysing the 'silver rhetoric' (103) through which Othello expresses his 'personal passion' (97) and perhaps the most distinctive achievement of *Harlem Duet* is to produce a different Othello music that is altogether more relevant to its protagonist. Each of the play's scenes is introduced by mood music, mainly blues, varying from Delta blues associated primarily but not exclusively with the nineteenth-century experience to the harsher sounds of urban blues, particularly associated with the more contemporary Harlem experience. The music functions as a kind of counterpoint to the main action, taking on a more discordant tone in the later scenes, where a 'distorted sound loop' (94, 99) contributes to the 'rising tempo' (99). At the same time, music is used, extremely subtly, to suggest the ambivalence of Billie's situation in Harlem. In a flashback scene set seven years earlier, in which she and Othello pay their first visit to the apartment they will subsequently occupy and in which Billie is living in the present, she responds to the positive side of Harlem as a black oasis, rhapsodizing about 'Black streets teeming with loud Black people listening to loud Jazz and reggae and Aretha' (106) and starting to sing Aretha Franklin's 'Spanish Harlem'. There is dramatic irony as she does so, since the song has been heard earlier in a scene set in the period after her desertion by Othello; and Franklin's 'funky rendition' (79) of it seems to encapsulate Billie's bitter-sweet predicament.

Along with the obvious 'music' of the text, the action is also played out against a litany of speeches that brings together some of the most influential African American political figures and discourses of the twentieth century. Set at the corner of 'Martin Luther King and Malcolm X boulevards (125th and Lennox)' (17), it returns on several occasions to these two complementary if opposed leaders, locating them at the centre of a web of intertexts that includes Booker T. Washington, Marcus Garvey, Jesse Jackson and Louis Farrakhan. Meanwhile references to the O. J. Simpson trial (75, 92)[18] offer an obvious parallel with Othello's murder of Desdemona[19] and even an interview with Michael Jackson and Lisa Marie Presley (the most extraordinary unconsummated black-white erotic encounter of all?[20]) finds its way onto Billie's television screen at one point (79). Ubiquitous though the music, speeches and other media parallels are, they are finally only the tip of an iceberg. Sears's very different Othello music is integral to her play's own dialogue: to be seen in the all-American 'prospecting' first phase of her love story:

> HER: Oh-oh. You're prospecting again.
> HIM: I'm exploring the heightening Alleghenies of Pennsylvania.
> > (HIM kisses HER.)
> > The curvaceous slopes of California.
> > (HIM kisses HER.)
> > The red hills of Georgia, the mighty mountains of New York.
> > (HIM kisses HER again.)
> > I'm staking my claim.
> HER: I don't come cheap you know. (36)

In the poetry of Billie's grief:

> I have nothing to say to him. What could I say? Othello, how is the fairer sexed one you love to dangle from your arm the one you love for herself and preferred to the deeper sexed one is she softer does she smell of tea roses and baby powder does she sweat white musk from between her toes do her thighs touch I am not curious I just want to know do her breasts fill the cup of your hand the lips of your tongue not too dark you like a little milk with your nipple don't you no I'm not curious I just want to know. (43)

And in the streetwise urban argot of Billie's landlady, Magi, perhaps the play's finest creation:

I'm telling you, girl. Macho Mack, spot him at any locale selling six-packs. Easily recognizable, everything about him is permanently flexed. (64)

Harlumbia — those 10 square blocks of Whitedom, owned by Columbia University, set smack dab in the middle of Harlem. (67)

Phillips's 'sad' black man's psychic dislocation comes from being completely isolated in the metropolis, but at the very end of his 'Othello' narrative, there is a hint of another discourse on which he could draw, as he reflects 'the Yoruba have a saying: the river that does not know its own source will dry up. You will do well to remember this (*Nature* 182). Billie becomes equally disturbed and by the end of the play is receiving psychiatric treatment from a white establishment that does not admit the racially induced aspects of mental disorders, preferring to operate simply in terms of a pragmatic policy of trying to rehabiliate the socially dysfunctional. The play is open-ended, but there is a strong sense that Billie has the resources to climb back to health, not only because unlike the various reconstructions of Othello she is not predetermined by the 'original', but also because she has a community and an alternative body of discourse on which she can draw. Sears associates this not only with Harlem, but also with the Nova Scotian community of freed blacks that has it origins in the pre-Emancipation period, before the underground railroad was established. Her father, named 'Canada', comes to visit her and a flight to this alternative homeland north of the border is a possibility for her in the closing stages, but unlike, say, Margaret Atwood's *Handmaid's Tale* (1985), where escape to Canada offers a possible refuge from the horrors of a fundamentalist American dystopia, *Harlem Duet* stays true to its Harlem setting, while allowing Billie the comforting presence of her African Canadian father.

    In short, *Harlem Duet* employs a range of alternative discourses to exorcize Othello. In one respect, however, it directly addresses an element that has been a particular focus for postcolonial, as well as other, critics of *Othello*.[21] The play's epigraph quotes the passage from *Othello* III, iv (57–74; *Harlem Duet* [19]), in which Othello explains the Egyptian provenance and magical powers of the handkerchief to Desdemona and this becomes a central motif in *Harlem Duet*. In an interesting reversal on the charge that Othello has used sorcery to win Desdemona, *Billie* is represented as a potential sorceress in the play. Her 'real' name is Sybil (cf. *Othello* III, iv, 72) and she has been sending away for various books and chemicals, from which in the latter stages it seems she may concoct a potion that will poison Othello through the medium of the handkerchief. The practical Magi (who herself, of course, has a name that *could* be associated with 'black arts') has no doubt that this magic has no efficacy, but nevertheless it represents a counter-discourse to the rationalism of Othello's work and, without decisively indicating whether such alchemy does have power, Sears interestingly makes its practitioner, not Othello, or Prospero, but Caliban's 'physiognomically complementary mate'. Ultimately, though, the protagonist is *Billie*, the suffering blues heroine, not Sibyl, and Sears's process of 'exorcism' substitutes a very different Othello music as a means of ensuring that both Billie and the play elude definition in relation to the canon.

Notes

1. See *Tempest*, I, ii, 144 and Kermode's note to this line in the second Arden edition.
2. Other notable recent responses include Salman Rushdie's *The Moor's Last Sigh* (1995) and a 1996 Kathakali dance-theatre adaptation of the play. Both are discussed by Loomba.
3. See Cartelli 204, Note 2 and his bibliography for details of some of the responses to the play that appeared between 1987 and 1994.
4. See Dymkowski, ed. 65–71 for a summary of post–1980 treatments of Caliban as a representative of various groups that see themselves as underdogs.
5. See E. A. J. Honigmann's Introduction to the third Arden edition for a discussion of this issue (14–17).
6. Additionally, recent work in the field of postcolonial Shakespeares has directed attention towards the multiple locations in which the plays dealing with 'colonial' or 'racial' issues can be situated. See, e.g. Jerry Brotton's emphasis on *The Tempest's* Mediterranean contexts and Ania Loomba's discussion of Indian contexts for *Othello* (Loomba and Orkin, eds 23–42 and 143–63).
7. Honigmann disputes this view, popularized by Bradley and Dover Wilson, pointing out that London had a Moorish ambassador in 1600 and 1601 (Introduction to third Arden edn 16) and listing four plays about Moors that had been performed in London theatres in the years immediately before *Othello* was first staged (30, Note 2). Shakespeare had himself, of course, earlier represented a Moor in the figure of Aaron in *Titus Andronicus*, but this provides little evidence to support either interpretation.
8. The film of this production, at London's National Theatre, was released in 1965.
9. 'Othello in Johannesburg', Channel 4 televison, 1988.
10. See Honigmann, Introduction to third Arden edn 31.
11. Eva's survival distances her from Anne Frank, but the other members of her family, apart from her Uncle Stephan, die in the concentration camps. The most precise link with the real-life Anne's family is the name of her sister, Margot (cf. Phillips, *European Tribe* 69), whom she believes has escaped to America, but whom, it transpires, *has* perished in the Holocaust.
12. Cf. the openings of Selvon's *The Lonely Londoners* (7) and Lamming's *Water with Berries* (11), in both of which mist seems to be a correlative of the migrant's mental situation as well as an indication of the meteorological conditions in which he finds himself.
13. He does focus on such a figure elsewhere, most notably in the character of Fola, in *Season of Adventure* (1960), who is mentioned incidentally on one occasion in *Water with Berries* (47).

14. The named is linked in the play with a classic icon of white beauty, Mona Lisa (100), but obviously also suggests 'Moaner'. Cf. Lamming's use of the name for the London pub in *Water with Berries*, where in addition to the Desdemona suggestion, there is just possibly an allusion to the name of the Mona campus of the University of the West Indies in Kingston, Jamaica.

15. Strictly speaking one should perhaps say North American, since Sears sites Nova Scotia as a potential black homeland and Billie's father is 'Canada'. See below.

16. One of its leading figures, Langston Hughes, is quoted in Sears's prefatory Notes (15) and again in the final scene (114).

17. Holiday recorded the song, by Peter Grainger and Everett Robbins, during what many regard as her finest period, with the Decca label between 1944 and 1949.

18. There is also a possible pun on Simpson's name in a reference to Orange Juice as 'O. J.' (46).

19. See Cartelli 123 and 204, Note 1 for references to this comparison.

20. Lisa Marie Presley's official website issued a statement on 4 January 2001, saying she 'has never met Michael Jackson as an adult', www.i-lisa-marie.com.

21. See, e.g., Orkin.

8

Conclusion and postscript: narrative agency in Pauline Melville's *The Ventriloquists's Tale*

Ventriloquism n. Act or art of speaking or uttering sounds in such a manner that the voice appears to come from some other source than the speaker.

(Concise Oxford Dictionary)

I

The counter-discursive strategies employed by the texts considered in this book are, then, so numerous and varied, that generalizations about their practice are hard to sustain. Certainly there are comparatively few instances where their approach is straightforwardly adversarial and Terdiman's view that, although dominant discourses may be challenged by counter-discourse, it is a mode that cannot ultimately offer 'genuine revolution' (15–16), is supported by the evidence afforded by the postcolonial con-texts discussed here. The engagement with the canon inevitably locks them into a relationship with their pre-texts and one might argue that a genuinely revolutionary project would necessitate a cleaner break with English culture, though whether such emancipation is a utopian ideal rather than an attainable goal remains a moot point, especially when one takes into account the renewed dominance of English as a global language. From another point of view it could be argued that, given the 'peculiar authority' of the literature that comes with the English language (Naipaul, *Overcrowded Barracoon* 23), an encounter with English cultural baggage is unavoidable, not only for the postcolonial subject, but also for the ever-growing number of 'global' citizens who become members of the Western-dominated communications web, though here accompanying *American* luggage becomes more central.

Writing back to the canon is, then, a vital act of exorcism that dispels the Gothic dust of English literature, and with the West constantly reinventing itself and subsuming other regions into its projects, dialogue with its discursive hegemonies remains as necessary as ever and counter-discourse continues to function as a metonym for the ongoing struggle to find alternative definitions of identity. To attempt to avoid this struggle, by suggesting that there are pure national or communal spaces untouched by the West's discursive networks is to argue for the myth of 'pure', 'authentic' cultures that have in effect remained frozen in time, like mammoths in a glacier, seemingly isolated from the evolutionary changes going on around them. Remarkable work has, of course, been done to locate non-Western traditions, particularly in the field of historiography where, for example, the Subaltern Studies scholars have contended that in India:

> parallel to the domain of elite politics there existed throughout the colonial period another domain of Indian politics in which the principal actors were not the dominant groups of the indigenous society or the colonial authorities but the subaltern classes and groups constituting the mass of the labouring population and the intermediate strata in town and country – that is, the people. This was an *autonomous* domain.
>
> (Guha 4; italics in original)

However, despite the fascinating case-studies that the Subaltern Studies project has yielded, even strategic essentialism becomes hard to sustain in the face of ubiquitous evidence of cultural interaction between different groups, not to mention the participants' own use of English to mediate their alternative historiographies and the institutional and geopolitical locales from which they write. Moreover, a belief in such autonomy *could* (though this is, of course, the opposite of what the project intends) lead to the kind of thinking that has characterized the communal separatism advocated by various fundamentalist factions. Apartheid as practised by subalterns may be very different from the forms employed by 'dominant groups', but it remains a discourse of exclusivity that is hard to support either as an ideal or as an account of an existing social reality.

So postcolonial cultures are inevitably caught in the dilemma of needing to make a decisive break with old and new forms of imperialism, but finding themselves enmeshed in a network of hybrid cultural formations, which exist at different points on a continuum between the notional poles (these are never actually achieved) of complete complicity with and total independence from Western hegemonies. Like Caribbean speakers who may appear to speak with a single voice but frequently shift registers in mid-sentence, postcolonial writers invariably occupy creolized, multivocal positions. Thus a novel such as Carey's

Jack Maggs presents very few problems of interpretation to its international readership, but phrases that have particular resonances in Australian cultural contexts ('magsman', 'for the term of his natural life', 'such is life') arguably add a dimension that, despite its 'classic' English setting, distances the work from Dickens's idiolect and, for that matter, contemporary British English. Needless to say, texts such as Selvon's *Moses Ascending* and Brathwaite's 'Caliban' do this rather more obviously.

I will conclude with a postscript on a novel that responds to English literature in a manner that is, if anything, even more remote than Achebe's brief encounter with Conrad in *Arrow of God*. Pauline Melville's *The Ventriloquist's Tale* (1997) invokes an episode in the life of Evelyn Waugh, along with passing reference to Waugh's writing, so briefly that it almost bypasses him completely. As such it affords an instance of a text that nods in the direction of English representations of the South American terrain in which it is located, but effectively relegates such representations to its margins; and it becomes interesting to consider whether it succeeds in liberating itself from 'Europe' to a greater extent than the majority of the con-texts discussed here.

Before embarking on this account, it may, however, be useful to summarize and assess the main counter-discursive responses that can be found in the works discussed. They include con-texts that tell the other side of the story (*Wide Sargasso Sea, Jack Maggs*) and narratives that suggest the fluidity of colonial archetypes (*Pantomime, Moses Ascending*, 'Caliban' and *Water with Berries*) as a way of opening up possibilities for transforming identities. Several of the texts provide supplements to their 'originals': prequels, sequels or simply developments of elements that are omitted or suggested but left undeveloped in the pre-texts (*Harlem Duet, Water with Berries, The Nature of Blood, Wide Sargasso Sea*). Sometimes the con-texts offer full-blown reworkings of their supposed precursors; sometimes they simply employ incidental allusions, though these can usually be seen to have ramifications for the work as a whole (*Arrow of God, Lady Oracle, Guerrillas, Tempest-Tost, The Diviners*). Several of the texts concerned overtly foreground issues of authorship (*Foe, Jack Maggs, Miss Peabody's Inheritance*) or include writer or artist figures, who raise questions concerning the appropriateness of particular local, regional or national aesthetic practices (*Changing Heaven, The Diviners, Water with Berries,* Walcott's 'Crusoe' poems). Issues of literary genealogy are frequently thematized through characters with problematic parentages (*Jack Maggs, Water with Berries, The Diviners*), while inheritance is also a major trope for the right to claim, or reject, the filial legacy offered by the canon (*Jack Maggs, Miss Peabody's Inheritance*).

What arguably links all these approaches is a consensus about the need to change the ground of the 'original': to bring the supposed margins to the centre; to tell a plurality of stories; to break down stereotypes; to interrogate the very notion of individual source-texts. Ultimately, counter-discourse functions less as a mode that opposes the English canon than as a mode that subverts its practice of telling singular stories. The authority of literary modes that speak *ex cathedra* through a unitary narrative voice, as it were to suggest that this is *the* only way the story can be told, is unsettled by a range of strategies that imply there are always multiple optics on any situation, multiple voices for telling any story. The polyphonic method of novels such as *The Nature of Blood, The Diviners, Badlands* and *Wide Sargasso Sea* particularly exemplifies this, but elsewhere, in texts where shifts of register are less obvious, multiple focalizers are frequently used (*Changing Heaven, A Grain of Wheat, Tempest-Tost*), while in *Palace of the Peacock* the identities of characters overlap to a point where they dissolve into one another.

There are, of course, major differences in the cultural politics of the con-texts examined. Racial and other stereotypical constructions of identity predictably loom large in most of the texts considered and an emphasis on role reversals and exchanges is central to the challenge offered to essentialist constructions by perspectives that demonstrate that identities are made and not born. This is at its most obvious in the revisionist perspectives on the figures of Caliban and Prospero and Friday and Crusoe. However, Miranda tends to displace Caliban in Canadian versions of *The Tempest* and responses to the Brontës, but Margaret Laurence seems at least in part to take her inspiration from Lamming, while Robertson Davies put his main emphasis on Gonzalo. So it becomes facile to try to argue overarching national theses about the way con-texts operate, when there are so many determinants shaping the constructions involved. One needs to return to the specifics of each text to see how it positions itself, but again an emphasis on manifold ancestries and plural aesthetics seems to provide a link between writing from many different parts of the globe.

Again and again, con-texts generate re-readings of pre-texts, with children begetting parents, as postcolonial orphans and bastards, literal and metaphorical, join Rushdie's Saleem Sinai in claiming multiple genealogies. Such a practice is foregrounded in *Foe* and *Jack Maggs*, where several pre-texts by the canonical author who provides the main point of departure overlap with one another to a point where any attempt to trace a 'pure' genealogy crumbles. The process also occurs in texts that are slightly less obviously metaliterary: *Othello* finds its way into the *Tempest*-based relationships of *Water with Berries*; Tintoretto parallels Emily Brontë in *Changing Heaven*; Naipaul's more incidental allusions to the Brontë novels rub shoulders with references to *The Woodlanders*. Elsewhere, despite the canonical departure point, the con-text shifts the ground to incorporate non-European pre-texts ('Caliban', *Harlem*

Duet, brief references in *The Nature of Blood*). In short, the emphasis in virtually every case is on multiple intertexts with varied provenances and the overall effect is to dismantle binary paradigms, to interrogate the very notion of alterity that consigns postcolonial subjects and texts to the margins. So, without wishing to obscure the extent to which particular con-texts articulate cultural difference, for which one has to return to the individual texts themselves, the question of whether they are adversarial or complicitous finally becomes less urgent than the *way* in which they bring new identities into play by locating the counter-discursive encounter on freshly ploughed ground.

One might ask whether such a model of literary influence is unique to the postcolonial relationship with the canon; arguably all texts bring something new into being by assembling a patchwork of traces to form a totality that never existed before. Models of literary transmission tend to be historio-graphic, but if one concedes that geography, understood in its broadest cultural sense, is as important as history in all instances, then clearly the model of influence suggested here cannot be seen as the peculiar property of postcolonial con-texts. They may, however, collectively claim particular importance in their redirection of emphasis away from cultural paradigms that have privileged time over place. In this respect, at least, the model of influence implied by postcolonial con-texts *does* initiate a different focus — albeit one that has validity for all cultural production. The canon is, of course, constantly reshaping itself and new historicism, for example, has increasingly admitted the importance of the range of geographical determinants suggested here. Nevertheless, the process of refraction generated by re-reading pre-texts through the prism of alternative con-texts is part of counter-discourse's distinctive contribution to remapping the fields of literary and cultural studies more generally; and, in this sense, they do fulfil Tiffin's claim that they are writing back to 'the whole of the discursive field' (23) within which canonical texts operate.

II

In the Prologue to Pauline Melville's novel *The Ventriloquist's Tale*, readers are introduced to an elusive 'South American Indian' (1) narrator, with shape-shifting characteristics that suggest affinities with both 'magic realist' fictional modes and with the shamanistic transformation of both matter and identities that are prominent in several of the stories in Melville's earlier short-story collection, *Shape-Shifter* (1990).[1] This narrator, who presents himself as a ventriloquist capable of mimicking both the animal life of the Guyanese interior and metropolitan discursive modes ('I could reproduce the flickering hiss of the labaria snake and sing the Lilliburero signature tune of the BBC's World Service within seconds of hearing them' (8), moves teasingly between allusions to apparently traditional Amerindian cultural practices and representing himself as a citizen of the contemporary world. Thus, on the one hand, he introduces himself as a repository of the ancestral oral tradition:

> As for my ancestry, it is impeccable. I will have you know that I am descended from a group of stones in Ecuador. Where I come from people have long memories. Any one of us can recite our ancestry back for several hundred generations. I can listen to a speech for an hour and then repeat it for you verbatim or backwards without notes. Writing things down has made you forget everything.
> My grandmother distrusts writing. She says all writing is fiction. ...
> Grandmother swears by the story of the stones in Ecuador, although sometimes she might say Mexico or Venezuela for variety's sake — variety being so much more important than truth in her opinion. More reliable, she says. Truth changes. Variety remains constant. (2–3)

However, in parallel with this, he is equally at pains to locate himself as a cross-cultural traveller in the world of international global capitalism:

> Rumbustious, irrepressible, adorable me. I have black hair, bronze skin and I would look wonderful in a cream suit with a silk handkerchief. Cigars? Yes. Dark glasses? Yes — except that I do not wish to be mistaken for a gangster. ... A black felt fedora hat worn tipped forward? Possibly. A fast-driving BMW when I am in London? A Porsche for New York? A Range Rover to drive or a helicopter when I am flying over the endless savannah and bush of my own region? Yes. Yes. Yes. (1–2)

In short, the narrator defies easy categorization and consequently, among other things, clearly represents a challenge to discursive practices which attempt essentialist or authentic constructions of the indigene. On one level, his elusiveness is presented as characteristic of Amerindian culture: 'Where I come from it's not done to give your real name too easily' (1); 'Where I come from, disguise is the only truth' (7). On another, it relates to his willingness to offer scribal witness, to 'write the stories down' (8), an activity which moves away from the traditional oral culture and which angers his grandmother who believes 'we Indians should keep ourselves to ourselves, retreating from the modern world like the contracting stars' (9). It can also be connected with the multi-cultural polyphony of voices he is able to mimic:

> I can do any voice: jaguar, London hoodlum, bell-bird, nineteenth-
> century novelist, ant-eater, epic poet, a chorus of howler monkeys, urban
> brutalist, a tapir. The list is infinite. (8)

The list is also extremely impressive and, in her three published works to date,[2]
Melville has demonstrated *her* ventriloquial virtuosity in handling a not-
dissimilar range of modes. However, despite this and despite her acknow-
ledgement of the influence of Wilson Harris,[3] *The Ventriloquist's Tale* as a whole
does *not* employ the same kind of polyphonic, 'magic realist' mode as the
narrator of the Prologue. This narrator explicitly dismisses himself at its end
('That's all for now, folks. The narrator must appear to vanish. I gone' [9]) and
only returns in the final pages of the novel to narrate a short epilogue. The
shamanistic attributes of this character[4] and the transformational narrative
practice associated with him give way, in the main body of the narrative, to a
more unitary narrative mode,[5] and before he bows out at the end of the
Prologue he foregrounds the fact that the ensuing narrative will be written
within the Puritan-derived conventions of the realist novel:

> Sad though it is, in order to tell these tales of love and disaster, I must put
> away everything fantastical that my nature and the South American
> continent prescribe and become a realist. No more men with members the
> size of zeppelins and women flapping off into the skies — a frequent
> occurrence on the other side of the continent. Why realism, you ask.
> Because hard-nosed, tough-minded realism is what is required these days.
> Facts are King. Fancy is in the dog-house. Perhaps it has something to do
> with protestants or puritans and the tedious desire to bear witness that
> makes people prefer testimony these days. (9)

While it would be wrong to suggest that *The Ventriloquist's Tale* is a latter-day
Robinson Crusoe, it would be even more mistaken to align it with the fabulist
'South American' fictional modes of, say, a Wilson Harris or a Gabriel García
Márquez. Melville tells a story, which, despite the use of two time sequences,
is basically linear and couched within the conventions of action and character
that one associates with the realist novel. This raises a set of questions about
narrative agency within the text. Ventriloquism may suggest a way out of the
complicitous situation in which postcolonial texts that write back to the canon
find themselves, but assuming that it is interpreted as involving more than the
practice that all writers engage in when they throw their voice by creating
first- and third-person narrators, one needs to examine the kind of
ventriloquism that is being employed in the novel. Is the use of polyphony
confined to the frame narrator, who flouts realist conventions, and

consequently little more than a perfunctory gesture in a text which subsequently largely deserts it? Or should we regard this vanishing narrator as the agent of everything that follows, a ventriloquist who chooses to adopt just one of the wide repertory of voices he claims to be able to render, that of 'nineteenth-century novelist', for the telling of this particular story? If so, what are the implications of this particular form of throwing one's voice? Since this set of questions relates to the cultural stance adopted by *The Ventriloquist's Tale* and it is a text which represents a number of cross-cultural encounters, I should like to consider this aspect of the novel before returning to the issue of narrative agency at the end of the discussion.

Towards the end of the novel, an explosive device planted by two Americans, who are surveying the Guyanese savannahs as part of their company's oil-prospecting activities, kills Bla-Bla, a child of the Wapisiana Indian family, the McKinnons, who are the text's main protagonists. This act may not be intentional, but it remains the most overt of several instances in the text of Western disruption of the seemingly homogeneous world of the local Amerindian cultures. *The Ventriloquist's Tale* also depicts the interventions of a Jesuit missionary, Father Napier, who sets out 'to evangelise the most remote regions of the empire' (107); a Czech anthropologist, M. J. Wormoal, whose specialism is comparative mythology and whose work on incest motifs in Amerindian cultures bears a marked resemblance to that of Claude Lévi-Strauss; and a Jewish Englishwoman, Rosa Mendelson, who has come to Guyana to do research on Evelyn Waugh's visit to British Guiana in the 1930s, a visit which yielded source material for his novel *A Handful of Dust* (1934). Father Napier's mission very obviously sets out to change the lives of the Macusi and Wapisiana Indians he encounters, but the two researchers also run the risk of 'contaminating the Indians' (79) by their very presence among them. As Wormoal puts it, 'We try just to observe but our very presence alters things' (79); and in his view the ethnographical eye of the researcher is itself 'a new form of colonial power' (80).

From a 'literary' point of view Rosa Mendelson's intrusion is perhaps the most interesting of these interventions, particularly since it supports the possibility of reading *The Ventriloquist's Tale* as a counter-discursive con-text. The Waugh intertexts in *The Ventriloquist's Tale*, which have been examined by Sarah Lawson Welsh,[6] are precise and yet far from central to the narrative. They include allusions to entries from the diaries Waugh kept during his visit to South America in late 1932 and early 1933[7] and a short story, 'The Man Who Loved Dickens', as well as the Guianese[8] sections of *A Handful of Dust*. Yet the reader – and particularly the Western reader – who comes to the novel with the assumption that the links with Waugh will provide some kind of key to the text's meaning is almost certain to be disappointed. Once again the centre of the narrative has been relocated elsewhere. Rosa Mendelson's attempt to find material relating to her research topic, Evelyn Waugh's attitude to the colonies, is not entirely unsuccessful, and this motif is certainly not a red herring in a text which so obviously concerns itself with cross-cultural contacts and the potentially deleterious effects of the ethnographical eye, but it is finally a comparatively minor strand in a novel which, superficially at least, chooses to tell an Amerindian tale rather than develop its counter-discursive relationship with an English text.

Before Rosa leaves England she makes contact with a Guyanese woman, Nancy Freeman, who was acting as a tutor to some of the McKinnon family's children during the period of Evelyn Waugh's visit. Nancy relates how she cut Waugh's hair during his short visit, but remembers little else of him; she refers to another story, concerning Danny McKinnon and his sister Beatrice, which would have provided him with useful source material but which he has 'missed' (49). This story is the narrative that lies at the centre of *The Ventriloquist's Tale*. So, as with texts such as *Foe*, *Jack Maggs* and *Harlem Duet*, it begins to look as though the novel is trying to dismantle the hegemonic assumptions of much European discourse by insisting that the *real* story exists elsewhere. Nancy Freeman tells Rosa that perhaps the novelist overlooked the McKinnon story, because 'it was not Evelyn Waugh's sort of story' (49) and the main detail of his visit that is given relates to his having read *Dombey and Son* to Danny McKinnon. The suggestion is that, like Father Napier's playing Mozart to the Amerindian peoples he encounters (119), reading Dickens is a European irrelevance in the Guianese interior.

At the same time it is an activity that bears an interesting relationship to Waugh's *A Handful of Dust*, where the hero, Tony Last, escapes death in the bush thanks to the intervention of the racially mixed Mr Todd, an illiterate with a manic passion for Dickens. Tony is persuaded to minister to Mr Todd's craving, by reading him first *Bleak House* and then a succession of other Dickens novels, including *Dombey and Son*. Although the Waugh episode in *The Ventriloquist's Tale* may initially seem to mirror this, it is significantly different in that in this case it is the visitor who inflicts Dickens on the local listener, while in Waugh's novel Tony finds himself a slave to Mr Todd's obsession with Dickens, kept 'chez Todd' (*Handful* 204) against his will and with no apparent means of escape from a life sentence of reading Dickens. Tony's fate seems sealed when Mr Todd gives three English visitors who might have rescued him the impression that he is dead and the final chapter, set in England, describes a memorial service and the unveiling of a plaque to his memory. On one level the South American narrative can be read as a wry account of a European being defeated by the Tropics, though it obviously lacks the portentousness of, say, Conrad's treatment of this trope in *Heart of*

Darkness or even Rochester's discomfort in *Wide Sargasso Sea*, where Romantic texts such as Byron and De Quincey are as out of place as Dickens is here.[9] However, it is also a fitting ending to a text which has generated a series of ironies concerning relationships between civilization and savagery and in which Tony has been represented as the largely innocent victim of the savagery of the English upper middle classes. Waugh's engagement with Amerindian culture is at best superficial, a detour from the main concerns of his novel, and the main players in the South American section of the novel are still either European or Europeanized. So it is highly appropriate that Tony's final persecution should take the form of imprisonment to an aspect of the English canon.

A Handful of Dust, like much of Waugh's fiction, is primarily a Condition of England novel; *The Ventriloquist's Tale* sets out to 'bear witness' to another culture and from this point of view it is equally appropriate, albeit for a different reason, that Melville represents *her* Evelyn Waugh reading Dickens, since this after all is the central referent for the Guianese sections of *A Handful of Dust*. Waugh is, however, only a bit player in Melville's larger Guianese story. The main action of *The Ventriloquist's Tale* spans a period of a century and revolves around two generations of the McKinnon family, with a central focus on the incestuous relationship of the brother and sister, Danny and Beatrice McKinnon, which fairly obviously re-enacts a myth noted by Lévi-Strauss and referred to in one of the novel's three epigraphs:

There is a myth which is known throughout the whole of the Americas from southern Brazil to the Bering Strait via Amazonia and Guiana which establishes a direct equivalence between eclipses and incest. ([ix])

So it would *seem* that an Amerindian story has been instated as the central narrative, while Evelyn Waugh is a very minor presence in the novel and the research projects of Rosa Mendelson and Wormoal occupy the margins of the contemporary story that frames this narrative. In this frame story Rosa, who has an affair with Chofy McKinnon, seems to come closer than Wormoal to an empathetic understanding of Amerindian culture. A self-proclaimed 'internationalist', she tells Wormoal that she believes in 'a mixture of the races', a viewpoint which he argues bucks the modern trend towards exclusiveness to be seen in groups such as Serbs, Muslims and his own people, the Czechs (78). In contrast, Wormoal's research is predicated on a belief in the purity and authenticity of cultures and, if at first this suggests an essentialism which could have fascist leanings, it is worth noting that it represents a viewpoint on which the received view of indigenous peoples' cultures, engrained in Lévi-Strauss's reading of Native American mythologies and classic structural anthropology more generally, appears to rest. Since there is no suggestion that the Lévi-Strauss epigraph quoted above has an ironic function in the novel, this seems to generate a tension in the text: Rosa's belief in racial intermixture is presented more sympathetically than Wormoal's belief that cultures are discrete, but the use of the Lévi-Straussian paradigm suggests a binarism in which 'the savage mind' is the foil to European rationalism, represented by the eye of the observing agent, whether he or she is an anthropologist, a literary researcher, a novelist or a missionary. And lurking below the tip of this iceberg is a deeper debate about the interaction of cultures, which challenges aspects of postcolonial thinking on the subject of hybridity. At the end of the novel Wormoal leaves congratulating himself on the success of his trip, secure in the belief that he has found out 'as much as it's possible to know about the eclipse mythology in these parts', while Rosa, her relationship with Chofy over, feels desolate in 'the hermetically sealed' world of the plane in which they both depart (351). The action of the novel seems in this and various other ways to imply that sustained cultural dialogue is finally impossible. Rosa's relationship with Chofy breaks down; Father Napier is driven mad by a preparation advocated by a local *piaiwoman*, suggesting the superior power of Amerindian medicine; the death of Bla-Bla is partly the result of a linguistic misunderstanding on the part of the American oil prospectors.[10] So in one sense at least cultures, like the plane in which Rosa is returning to England, appear to be hermetically sealed and attempts at interaction futile.

The treatment of this issue in the novel is, however, a good deal more complicated than this. While the frame story is ambivalent about cross-cultural contacts, the main narrative, the account of the incestuous affair of Danny and Beatrice, is apparently contextualized as an 'authentic' Native story: a fictional retelling of the Wapisiana version of Lévi-Strauss's pan-American incest myth. There are numerous codifying passages that ensure readers do not miss this significance. Most obviously, Melville uses the anthropologist Wormoal, who admits that his ' "knowledge of the Indians is a way of owning them" ' (80), as a vehicle for locating the story in this context. The novel includes the text of a Lévi-Straussian paper he has written on 'The Structural Elements of Myth'. This provides a coda to many of the novel's recurrent patterns of imagery, including those connected with a flood, the tapir and eclipses; and it contains passages such as the following:

The Wapisiana myth I am using also concerns the eclipse. They believed that man was at one with nature — incest I should add is the symbol of nature as opposed to society — until an eclipse separated humankind from the animals and plants. They believed that a brother came secretly to his sister at nights. She enjoyed this but, not knowing who he was,

blackened his face with the magical genipap plant to identify him. In his
shame he rose to the sky and became the moon. That is why the moon
has dark patches on its face. (82)

In other words, Wormoal, a self-confessed outsider who believes in notions of
racial purity, takes the view that ' "Indian culture is disintegrating [rapidly]
these days" ' (78) and readily admits that observation generates alteration,
becomes the spokesman for the bedrock of mythic information on which the
text seems to be constructed. When he first meets Rosa Mendelson, he
jokingly draws a parallel between their respective areas of research by saying
' "well, many of us anthropologists are just writing bad fiction these days. It
seems to be the fashion. Analysis by metaphor" ' (77); and this raises the issue
of the relationship between his colonizing anthropological eye and the stance
adopted by the novel itself.

The Ventriloquist's Tale appears to be wanting to tell the *other* story, to offer
a narrative of a group who have been doubly colonized, '[f]irst by the
Europeans and then by the coastlanders' (54). However, it does so by using a
classic Western anthropological model as its mediating lens. This is so not
simply because the central story is based on a supposedly originary narrative,
but also because *The Ventriloquist's Tale* appears to be promoting classic
structural binaries such as the opposition between culture and nature ('incest I
should add is the symbol of nature as opposed to society'), which are not so
very different from those that Achebe finds in *Heart of Darkness*. Hence the
need to ask questions about narrative agency and the angle of focalization
from which the story is being written.

   While biographical information about a writer may finally be irrelevant to
the authorial stances adopted within texts, a digression into Melville's own
background is interesting, since it helps to pinpoint the tension between
'insider' and 'outsider' perspectives that one finds within *The Ventriloquist's
Tale*. The family situation into which Danny and Beatrice are born – their
father, Alexander McKinnon, is a Scotsman who has married two Amerindian
women – directly parallels that of the equivalent generation of the Melville
family and its patriarch.[11] In an account of his 1955 visit to the Rupununi
region of what was then still British Guiana, Michael Swan writes:

All the ranches except two are owned by members of the half-
Amerindian Melville family. The first Melville was a Scotsman and a
man of some education who came to British Guiana in the nineties to
prospect for gold and diamonds. On one trip up the Essequibo river he
was attacked by malaria and his men left him for dead on a sand-reef.
Indians found him and nursed him back to health. He wandered with

them over the mountains to the Rupununi. He fell in love with the
savannas and the Indian way of life, took two wives and settled with
them, producing ten children. He was the first serious cattle-rancher in
the savannas. (201–2)

From one point of view, then, Melville appears to write about experiences that
are based on her own family background and so she has intimate 'insider'
knowledge, but the mixed ancestry of both the fictional McKinnons and the
actual Melvilles *could* lead to the charge that neither is really representative of
'authentic' Amerindian culture. Melville's own situation is further problematized by her having spent most of her life in England. In an interview with
Caryl Phillips, she provided information about her background, saying that her
father who married an Englishwoman was 'from a mulatto family' and that
while it would be 'ridiculous' for her to speak of herself as 'black', she has
'always been connected with that community'.[12] Asked to clarify details of her
movement between Guyana and England, she explained that she was born in
England and was sent to Guyana, where her grandmother raised her, at the age
of nine months, because her mother was ill. She returned to England, where she
attended school, at the age of five and went back to Guyana 'for a period'
when she was fourteen. Subsequently, she said, she has 'been back fairly
regularly'.[13] Can Melville, then, one might ask, be seen as an 'authentic'
spokeswoman for 'indigenous' peoples?

It is, however, more rewarding to consider the *kind* of representation of
indigenous people's experience provided by the text, particularly in relation to
the issue of whether it leaves them disempowered, than to engage in a
discussion of whether the racially mixed, British-based Melville should be
disqualified from writing about the Guyanese elements in her ancestry. At the
very least she foregrounds representational issues: the references to the
damage done by the anthropological eye make this abundantly clear and, as
Sarah Lawson Welsh has noted, these even extend to a 'fairly transparent
portrait of Anita Roddick, Body Shop Tycoon as the "Cosmetics Queen"'.[14]
On one level, then, *The Ventriloquist's Tale* is very knowingly *about* the dangers
inherent in Western representational practice; it is a self-referential investigation of the politics of speaking or writing for or about the Other. However,
this still leaves the question of whether its use of the Lévi-Straussian paradigm
leaves such binaries as 'civilized' and 'savage' in place unresolved.

Arguably the novel disturbs such binarism in a number of ways: the mixed-
race McKinnons are transgressive figures who challenge the crudeness of
binarisms based on the category of 'race'; and the suggestion that incest can
simply be equated with nature rather than culture is problematized by the fact
that Danny and Beatrice embark on their affair after receiving a European-

orientated education in the coastal world of Guyana's capital, Georgetown. After the Prologue, Melville eschews a magic realist technique in favour of a primarily realistic mode, which, for Western (and for that matter Guyanese coastlander) readers, familarizes material that could easily have been located within the realms of another type of alterity, the exotic. The Prologue has the effect of establishing a relativistic ambience, with the narrator not only occupying a double or multiple identity and laying claim to a capacity to speak a babel-like polyphony of voices, but also blurring the boundaries between myth and realism and, as happens in several of Wilson Harris's novels,[15] dismantling the social fiction of unitary identity. Subsequently, however, having established its capacity for ventriloquism – and thereby in one sense undermined the possibility of privileging any single fictional voice, canonical or otherwise – the text *is* almost entirely narrated though the mode of social realism. It employs a flat narrative manner which has the effect of domesticating its potentially sensational material. The reader is gradually drawn into a circumstantially realized picture of Amerindian society, as Melville employs a technique which makes it easy to tell her tale without resorting to the fabulist pyrotechnics employed (for quite other purposes) by such writers as Wilson Harris and Gabriel García Márquez. Contemporary South American fiction runs the risk of being stereotyped as 'magic realist' and Melville, despite her very obvious talent for writing in such a mode, prefers, here at least, to throw her voice into the more restrained, Protestant conventions on which the novel was founded. In this instance it proves a very effective choice, but it still leaves this reader slightly uneasy over her decision to rework a central Native American 'myth', as identified and mediated by a European structuralist intellectual, rather than attempt the extremely difficult project of trying to engage with an unmediated – or at least a non-European mediated – version of Amerindian discourse. My response may itself involve a failure to make adequate allowance for the major difficulties in representing the 'interior' cultures of Guyanese Amerindians; and perhaps it is possible to see the novel as supplanting colonial forms of hybridity with forms containing more positive 'local' potential. Nevertheless, I am left feeling that the comparatively understated use of the incest motif in *The Ventriloquist's Tale* has not sufficiently overcome the problem of slipping into a subtle form of sensationalism, since it still promotes a degree of intellectualized exoticism through its use of the Lévi-Strauss archetype; and my unease is compounded by the fact that Lévi-Strauss's approach is founded on a form of binary thinking that bears a marked similarity to the stereotyping that Achebe finds in Conrad. In short, *The Ventriloquist's Tale*, despite its immersion in cultural specifics, still relies on European mediation to tell its South American story. The Waugh intertexts are marginal to the point of being little more than a joke, but the influence of Lévi-Strauss permeates the text and is an index of the extent to which this compelling narrative has been conjured from a theoretical alchemy that originates outside the region.

This can only be a postscript. One swallow does not make a summer and one case-study does not make a thesis. However, if one agrees that Melville, while bringing a new mixed form of fiction into being, still writes under the influence of a Eurocentric mode of thinking, this may be a metonym for the difficulties facing progressive, postcolonial writers in liberating themselves from Western discursive hegemonies. As the colonialism of the European empires recedes into the past, it is increasingly being replaced by the new metanarratives. Melville's South American Indian narrator is represented as a cross-cultural traveller in the world of international global capitalism (Rosa, of course, extricates herself from complications as she leaves Guyana on a plane) and increasingly this becomes the pre-text which 'postcolonial' writers must contest. Along with it comes the cultural baggage of various forms of European theorizing, including postcolonial theory itself.

Notes

1. E.g. stories such as 'The Truth is in the Clothes' and 'The Girl with the Celestial Limb', Melville, *Shape-Shifter* 99–112 and 135–47. Cf. the second of the collection's two epigraphs, which refers to shamanistic transformation ([ix]).

2. The third is the short-story collection, *The Migration of Ghosts* (1998).

3. Pauline Melville with Caryl Phillips, Guardian Conversations, ICA Video, n.d. [1990?].

4. He can be identified as the legendary figure of Macunaima, who, in a Macusi aetiological tale, along with his brother Chico, chopped down 'a wonderful tree ... that had all the fruits of the earth on it' (114). At the outset he says, 'You can call me Chico. It's my brother's name but so what' (1); in the final paragraph he writes, 'Now that I'm leaving I will let you into the secret of my name. It is Macun ... No, I've changed my mind' (357). Within the non-mythic action of the narrative, he appears to be Sonny, the child of the incestuous union of Danny and Beatrice, see particularly 292. This, of course, opens up the possibility of a reading which sees Sonny as a contemporary version of Macunaima.

5. There are only occasional departures from this mode in the main body of the novel, e.g. the first part of the section 'Under the Eaves' (60–3), written in the form of a dramatic dialogue in which the identities of the two individual speakers and the order in which their remarks have been made are obscured.

6. 'Imposing Narratives: European Incursions and Intertexts in Pauline Melville's *The Ventriloquist's Tale* (1997)', paper read at the EACLALS/ASNEL 'Colonies, Missions, Cultures' Conference, Tübingen, 1999. I am grateful to Sarah Lawson Welsh for allowing me to read this paper in manuscript.

7. Lawson Welsh notes that he met members of the Melville family.

8. I have used 'Guianese' rather than 'Guyanese' in this section, when referring to the general region of the Guianas rather than (pre-independence) British Guiana or (post-independence) Guyana.

9. See Chapter 4 above.

10. They have been told that Chofoye, Bla-Bla's father's name, is 'the Amerindian word for explosion' (309) and so when they try to warn Bla-Bla, who speaks fluent English anyway, that he is running into danger, he thinks they are telling him his father has returned.

11. Cf. the beginning of the section of the novel entitled 'Blue Eyes Mean Ignorance' (96–8).

12. Pauline Melville with Caryl Phillips, Guardian Conversations, ICA Video, n.d. [1990?].

13. *Ibid.*

14. Lawson Welsh, *op. cit.*

15. Beginning with the doubling of the figures of Donne and the 'I' narrator and the overlapping identities of the various members of the crew in *Palace of the Peacock*. See above, Chapter 2.

Bibliography

Achebe, Chinua, *Things Fall Apart* (London: Heinemann, 1958).

Achebe, Chinua, *Arrow of God* (1964. 2nd edn, London: Heinemann, 1974).

Achebe, Chinua, *Hopes and Impediments: Selected Essays, 1965–87* (Oxford: Heinemann, 1988).

Ackroyd, Peter, *Dickens* (London: Sinclair-Stevenson, 1990).

Addison, Joseph, Richard Steele *et al.*, *The Spectator*, 1711–14, 8 vols (London: Dent, 1907).

Ahmad, Aijaz, *In Theory: Classes, Nations, Literatures* (London: Verso, 1992).

Allfrey, Phyllis Shand, *The Orchid House* (1953. Intro. Elaine Campbell, London: Virago, 1982).

Angier, Carole, *Jean Rhys* (London: André Deutsch, 1990).

Ashcroft, Bill, Gareth Griffiths and Helen Tiffin, *The Empire Writes Back: Theory and Practice in Post-colonial Literatures* (London: Routledge, 1989).

Atwood, Margaret, *Surfacing* (1972. London: Virago, 1979).

Atwood, Margaret, *Lady Oracle* (1976. London: Virago, 1982).

Atwood, Margaret, 'The Age of Lead', *Wilderness Tips* (Toronto: McClelland-Bantam, 1992), pp. 151–69.

Atwood, Margaret, *Strange Things: The Malevolent North in Canadian Literature* (Oxford: Clarendon Press, 1995).

Austen, Jane, *Pride and Prejudice* (1813. London: Dent, 1924).

Austen, Jane, *Mansfield Park* (1814. London: Dent, 1924).

Barthes, Roland, *The Pleasure of the Text*, trans. Richard Miller (New York: Hill & Wang, 1975).

Bassnett, Susan and Harish Trivedi (eds), *Post-colonial Translation: Theory and Practice* (London: Routledge, 1999).

Baugh, Edward, 'Friday in Crusoe's City: The Question of Language in Two West Indian Novels of Exile', *ACLALS Bulletin*, 5 (3) (1980), pp. 1–12.

Belsey, Catherine, *Critical Practice* (London: Routledge, 1980).

Bennett, Bruce and Jennifer Strauss (eds), *The Oxford Literary History of Australia* (Melbourne: Oxford University Press, 1998).

Bennett, Louise, *Jamaica Labrish* (Kingston: Sangster's Book Stores, 1966).

Bhabha, Homi, *The Location of Culture* (London: Routledge, 1994).

Birney, Earle, *The Collected Poems of Earle Birney*, 2 vols (Toronto: McClelland & Stewart, 1975).

Bliss, Carolyn, *Patrick White's Fiction: The Paradox of Fortunate Failure* (Basingstoke: Macmillan, 1986).

Boehmer, Elleke, *Colonial and Postcolonial Literature: Migrant Metaphors* (Oxford: Oxford University Press, 1995).

Bolt, Christine, *Victorian Attitudes to Race* (London: Routledge, 1971).

Boxill, Anthony, 'Mr Biswas, Mr Polly and the Problem of V. S. Naipaul's Sources', *ARIEL*, 8 (3) (1977), pp. 129–41.

Brathwaite, (Edward) Kamau, *The Arrivants* (Oxford: Oxford University Press, 1973).

Brontë, Charlotte, *Jane Eyre* (1847. Harmondsworth: Penguin, 1966).

Brontë, Emily, *Wuthering Heights* (1847. Intro. David Daiches, Harmondsworth: Penguin, 1965).

Brontë, Emily, *The Poems of Emily Brontë*, ed. Derek Roper with Edward Chisholm (Oxford: Clarendon Press, 1995).

Brotton, Jerry, ' "This Tunis, sir, was Carthage": Contesting Colonialism in *The Tempest*', in Loomba and Orkin (eds), pp. 23–42.

Brydon, Diana, 'Re-writing *The Tempest*', *WLWE* 23 (1) (1984), pp. 75–88.

Campbell, Joseph, *The Hero with a Thousand Faces* (1949. Cleveland, OH: Meridian, 1956).

Carey, Peter, *Illywhacker* (London: Faber, 1985).

Carey, Peter, *Oscar and Lucinda* (London: Faber, 1988).

Carey, Peter, *Jack Maggs* (London: Faber, 1997).

Carr, Helen, *Jean Rhys* (Plymouth: Northcote House/British Council, 1996).

Cartelli, Thomas, *Repositioning Shakespeare: National Formations, Postcolonial Appropriations* (London: Routledge, 1999).

Carthew, John, 'Adapting to Trinidad: Mr Biswas and Mr Polly Revisited', *Journal of Commonwealth Literature*, 13 (1) (1978), pp. 58–64.

Césaire, Aimé, *A Tempest* (1969. Trans. by Richard Miller, New York: G. Borchardt, 1986).

Chaudhuri, Nirad C., *The Autobiography of an Unknown Indian* (London: Macmillan, 1951).

Cliff, Michelle, *No Telephone to Heaven* (1987. New York: Vintage, 1989).

Coetzee, J. M., *Foe* (1986. Harmondsworth: Penguin, 1987).

Connor, Steven, 'Rewriting Wrong: On the Ethics of Literary Reversion', in D'haen and Bertens, pp. 79–97.

Conrad, Joseph, *Heart of Darkness* (1902. Harmondsworth: Penguin, 1994).

Conrad, Joseph, *Congo Diary and Other Uncollected Pieces*, ed. Zdzislaw Najder (Garden City, NY: Doubleday, 1978).

Cowper, William, *The Poetical Works of William Cowper* (London: Ward Lock, n.d. [1889?]).

Dabydeen, David, *Coolie Odyssey* (Århus: Dangaroo Press, 1988).

Daniels, Helen, *Liars: Australian New Novelists* (Ringwood, Victoria: Penguin, 1988).

David, Jack and Robert Lecker (eds), *Canadian Poetry*, 2 vols (Toronto: General; Downsville, ON: ECW Press, 1982).

Davidson, Arnold and Cathy, 'The Anatomy of *Surfacing*', *ARIEL* 10 (3) (1979), pp. 38–54.

Davies, Robertson, *Tempest-Tost* (1951. Harmondsworth: Penguin, 1980).

Davies, Robertson, *Fifth Business* (1970. Harmondsworth: Penguin, 1977).

Davies, Robertson, *Stephen Leacock* (Toronto: McClelland & Stewart, 1970).

Davies, Robertson, *One Half of Robertson Davies* (New York: Viking, 1978).

Davis, J. Madison (ed.), *Conversations with Robertson Davies* (Toronto: General, 1990).

Defoe, Daniel, *Robinson Crusoe* (1719. Intro. Angus Ross, Harmondsworth: Penguin, 1965).

Defoe, Daniel, *Roxana: The Fortunate Mistress* (1724. Oxford: Oxford University Press, 1964).

D'haen, Theo and Hans Bertens (eds), *Liminal Postmodernisms: The Postmodern, the (Post-) Colonial and the (Post-)Feminist* (Amsterdam: Rodopi, 1994).

Dickens, Charles, *Oliver Twist* (1837–39. Harmondsworth: Penguin, 1994).

Dickens, Charles, *Great Expectations* (1860–61. Harmondsworth: Penguin, 1965).

Dixon, Robert, ' "Travelling in the West": The Writing of Amitav Ghosh', *Journal of Commonwealth Literature* 31 (1) (1996), pp. 3–24.

Docker, John, *In a Critical Condition* (Ringwood, Victoria: Penguin, 1984).

Duerden, Dennis and Cosmo Pieterse (eds), *African Writers Talking* (London: Heinemann, 1972).

Dymkowski, Christine (ed.), *Shakespeare in Production: The Tempest* (Cambridge: Cambridge University Press, 2000).

Evans, Robert O., 'Conrad's Underworld', *Modern Fiction Studies*, 2 (2) (1956), pp. 56–62.

Fanon, Frantz, *Black Skin, White Masks* (1952. Trans. Charles Lam Markmann, London: Pluto, 1986).

Feder, Lillian, 'Marlow's Descent into Hell', *Nineteenth-Century Fiction*, 9 (4) (1955), pp. 280–92.

Fido, Martin, 'Mr Biswas and Mr Polly', *ARIEL* 5 (4) (1974), pp. 30–7.

Forster, John, *The Life of Charles Dickens* (1872–74, 2 vols, London: Dent, 1969).

Frye, Northrop, *Anatomy of Criticism: Four Essays* (1957. Princeton: Princeton University Press, 1971).

Gardam, Jane, *Crusoe's Daughter* (London: Hamish Hamilton, 1985).

Gérin, Winifred, *Charlotte Brontë: The Evolution of Genius* (Oxford: Oxford University Press, 1967).

Gérin, Winifred, *Emily Brontë: A Biography* (1971. Oxford: Oxford University Press, 1978).

Ghosh, Amitav, *The Shadow Lines* (London: Bloomsbury, 1988).

Ghosh, Amitav, *The Calcutta Chromosome* (London: Picador, 1996).

Gibson, Ross, *The Diminishing Paradise: Changing Literary Perceptions of Australia* (Sydney: Angus & Robertson, 1984).

Gilbert, Sandra M. and Susan Gubar, *The Madwoman in the Attic* (1979. New Haven: Yale University Press, 1984).

Gilkes, Michael, *Wilson Harris and the Caribbean Novel* (London: Longman; Trinidad and Jamaica: Longman Caribbean, 1975).

Green, Martin, *The Robinson Crusoe Story* (University Park: Pennsylvania State University Press, 1990).

Greene, Gayle, 'Margaret Laurence's *The Diviners*: The Uses of the Past', in *Critical Approaches to the Fiction of Margaret Laurence*, ed. Colin Nicholson (Basingstoke: Macmillan 1990), pp. 177–207.

Griffiths, Trevor R., ' "This Island's Mine": Caliban and Colonialism', *The Yearbook of English Studies*, 13 (1983), pp. 159–80.

Guha, Ranajit, Introduction, *Subaltern Studies I: Writings on South Asian History and Society* (1982. Delhi: Oxford University Press, 1994).

Hamner, Robert D. (ed.), *Joseph Conrad: Third World Perspectives* (Washington, DC: Three Continents Press, 1990).

Hamner, Robert D. (ed.), *Critical Perspectives on Derek Walcott* (Washington, DC: Three Continents Press, 1993).

Harris, Wilson, *Palace of the Peacock* (1960. London: Faber, 1968).

Harris, Wilson, *Heartland* (London: Faber, 1964).

Harris, Wilson, *Tradition, the Writer and Society: Critical Essays* (London: New Beacon, 1967).

Harris, Wilson, 'A Comment on *A Passage to India*', *Literary Half-Yearly*, 10 (2) (1969), pp. 35–40.

Harris, Wilson, *History, Fable and Myth in the Caribbean and Guianas* (Georgetown, Guyana: National History and Arts Council, 1970).

Harris, Wilson, *Explorations: A Selection of Talks and Articles 1966–1981*, ed. Hena Maes-Jelinek (Mundelstrup, Denmark: Dangaroo Press, 1981).

Harris, Wilson, *Selected Essays of Wilson Harris*, ed. Andrew Bundy (London: Routledge, 1999).

Hasluck, Nicholas, *Quarantine* (1978. Ringwood, Victoria: Penguin, 1986).

Hawes, Donald, *Who's Who in Dickens* (London: Routledge, 1998).

Hayward, Arthur L., *The Dickens Encyclopaedia* (London: George Routledge and Sons, 1924).

Hearne, John, 'The Wide Sargasso Sea: A West Indian Reflection', *Cornhill Magazine*, Summer 1974, pp. 323–33.

Hergenhan, Laurie, *Unnatural Lives: Studies in Australian Fiction about the Convicts, from James Tucker to Patrick White* (St Lucia, Queensland: University of Queensland Press, 1983).

Hill, Errol, *The Trinidad Carnival: Mandate for a National Theatre* (Austin: University of Texas Press, 1972).

Hill, Errol, *Plays for Today* (Harlow: Longman, 1985).

Hope, A. D., *Selected Poems* (Sydney: Angus & Robertson, 1973).

Hughes, Robert, *The Fatal Shore: A History of the Transportation of Convicts to Australia, 1787–1868* (London: Collins Harvill, 1987).

Hulme, Peter and William H. Sherman, *'The Tempest' and Its Travels* (London: Reaktion, 2000).

Humphry, Derek and David Tindall, *False Messiah: The Story of Michael X* (London: Hart-Davis, MacGibbbon, 1977).

Huxley, Aldous, *Collected Essays* (New York: Harper & Row, 1959).

Jackson, Rosemary, *Fantasy: The Literature of Subversion* (London: Routledge, 1981).

James, C. L. R., *The Black Jacobins: Toussaint L'Ouverture and the San Domingo Revolution* (London: Secker & Warburg, 1938).

James, Louis, *Jean Rhys* (London: Longman, 1978).

James, Selma, *The Ladies and the Mammies: Jane Austen and Jean Rhys* (Bristol: Falling Wall Press, 1983).

Jameson, Fredric, 'Third World Literature in the Era of Multinational Capitalism', *Social Text*, 15 (1986), pp. 65–88.

JanMohamed, Abdul R., 'The Economy of Manichean Allegory', *Critical Inquiry*, 12 (1) (1985), pp. 59–87.

Johnson, Samuel, *A Dictionary of the English Language* (1755. London: Times, 1983).

Jolley, Elizabeth, *Miss Peabody's Inheritance* (St Lucia, Queensland: University of Queensland Press, 1983).

Jose, Nicholas, 'Carey's Labyrinth', *Australian Book Review*, August 1997, p. 15.

Jung, Carl G., M.-L. von Franz, Joseph L. Henderson, Jolande Jacobi and Aniela Jaffé, *Man and His Symbols* (1964. New York: Dell, 1968).

Kermode, Frank, Introduction, *The Tempest* by William Shakespeare (Arden Shakespeare, 2nd edn, 1954. London: Methuen, 1964).

Kettle, Arnold, *The English Novel*, 2 vols (London: Hutchinson, 1951–53).

King, Bruce, 'Margaret Atwood's *Surfacing*', *Journal of Commonwealth Literature* 12 (1) (1977), pp. 23–32.

King, Bruce, *Derek Walcott: A Caribbean Life* (Oxford: Oxford University Press, 2000).

King, Bruce (ed.), *West Indian Literature* (London: Macmillan, 1979).

King, James, *The Life of Margaret Laurence* (Toronto: Knopf Canada, 1997).

Knight, G. Wilson, *The Wheel of Fire: Interpretations of Shakespearean Tragedy* (1930. London: Methuen, 1960).

Knowles, Owen and Gene M. Moore, *Oxford Reader's Companion to Conrad* (Oxford: Oxford University Press, 2000).

Knox, Robert, *An Historical Relation of Ceylon* (1681. Dehiwala, Sri Lanka: Tisara Press, 1958).

Kroetsch, Robert, *Alberta* (Toronto: Macmillan Canada, 1968).

Kroetsch, Robert, *The Studhorse Man* (Toronto: Macmillan Canada, 1969).

Kroetsch, Robert, *Gone Indian* (Toronto: New Press, 1973).

Kroetsch, Robert, *Badlands* (Toronto: New Press, 1975).

Kroetsch, Robert, *Completed Field Notes: The Long Poems of Robert Kroetsch* (Toronto: McClelland & Stewart, 1989).

Kroetsch, Robert, *The Lovely Treachery of Words* (Toronto: Oxford University Press, 1989).

Kroetsch, Robert, *The Man from the Creeks* (Toronto: Random House, 1998).

Kroetsch, Robert and Diane Bessai, 'Death is a Happy Ending: A Dialogue in Thirteen Parts', in *Figures in a Ground: Canadian Essays on Modern Literature Collected in Honour of Sheila Watson*, eds Diane Bessai and David Jackel (Saskatoon: Western Producer Prairie Books, 1978), pp. 206–15.

Lamming, George, *In the Castle of My Skin* (London: Michael Joseph, 1953).

Lamming, George, *Of Age and Innocence* (1958. London: Allison & Busby, 1981).

Lamming, George, *Season of Adventure* (1960. London: Allison & Busby, 1979).

Lamming, George, *The Pleasures of Exile* (1960. London: Allison & Busby, 1984).

Lamming, George, *Water with Berries* (1971. London: Longman Caribbean, 1973).

Lansbury, Coral, *Arcady in Australia: The Evocation of Australia in Nineteenth-Century English Literature* (Carlton, Victoria: Melbourne University Press, 1970).

Laurence, Margaret, *The Diviners* (1974. Toronto: McClelland & Stewart, 1978).

Laurence, Margaret, *Dance on the Earth: A Memoir* (Toronto: McClelland & Stewart, 1989).

Leacock, Stephen, *Sunshine Sketches of a Little Town* (1912. Toronto: McClelland Stewart, 1970).

Leavis, F. R., *The Great Tradition* (1948. Harmondsworth: Penguin, 1962).

Levesque, John, 'Charting the Life of a Diviner', *Hamilton Spectator*, 30 August 1997, pp. W1, W4.

Lodge, David, *Language of Fiction: Essays in Criticism and Verbal Analysis of the English Novel* (London: Routledge & Kegan Paul, 1966).

Lofting, Hilary, Introduction, *For the Term of His Natural Life* by Marcus Clarke (1929. Sydney: Angus & Robertson: 1979).

Loomba, Ania, ' "Local-manufacture made-in-India Othello fellows": Issues of Race, Hybridity and Location in Post-Colonial Shakespeares', in Loomba and Orkin (eds), pp. 143–63.

Loomba, Ania and Martin Orkin (eds), *Post-Colonial Shakespeares* (London: Routledge, 1998).

Lovelace, Earl, *The Dragon Can't Dance* (London: André Deutsch, 1979).

MacEwen, Gwendolyn, *Afterworlds* (Toronto: McClelland & Stewart, 1987).

McPherson, Hugo, 'The Mask of Satire: Character and Symbolic Pattern in Robertson Davies' Fiction', *Canadian Literature*, 4 (1960), pp. 18–30.

Maes-Jelinek, Hena, 'The True Substance of Life: Wilson Harris's *Palace of the Peacock*', in Rutherford (ed.), pp. 151–9.

Maes-Jelinek, Hena, *The Naked Design: A Reading of 'Palace of the Peacock'* (Århus: Dangaroo Press, 1976).

Maes-Jelinek, Hena, 'Fictional Breakthrough and the Unveiling of "Unspeakable Rites" in Patrick White's *A Fringe of Leaves* and Wilson Harris's *Yurokon*', *Kunapipi*, 2 (2) (1980), pp. 33–43.

Maes-Jelinek, Hena, *Wilson Harris* (Boston: Twayne, 1982).

Malik, Abdul, *From Michael De Freitas to Michael X* (London: André Deutsch, 1968).

Mannoni, Octave, *Prospero and Caliban: The Psychology of Colonization*, trans. P. Powesland (1950. London: Methuen, 1956).

Marr, David, *Patrick White: A Life* (London: Jonathan Cape, 1991).

Melville, Pauline, *Shape-Shifter* (1990. London: Picador, 1991).

Melville, Pauline, *The Ventriloquist's Tale* (1997. London: Bloomsbury, 1998).

Moody, Philippa, *A Critical Commentary on William Golding's 'Lord of the Flies'* (London: Macmillan, 1966).

Moss, John, *A Reader's Guide to the Canadian Novel* (Toronto: McClelland & Stewart, 1981).

Mukherjee, Sujit, *Translation as Discovery* (1981. 2nd edn, London: Sangam, 1994).

Murfin, Ross C. (ed.), *'Heart of Darkness': Case Studies in Contemporary Criticism* (2nd edn, Boston: Bedford Books; Basingstoke: Macmillan, 1996).

Murray-Smith, Stephen, Introduction, *His Natural Life* by Marcus Clarke (Harmondsworth: Penguin, 1970).

Naipaul, Seepersad, *The Adventures of Gurudeva and Other Stories*, Preface by V. S. Naipaul (London: André Deutsch, 1976).

Naipaul, V. S., *A House for Mr Biswas* (London: André Deutsch, 1961).

Naipaul, V. S., *A Flag on the Island* (London: André Deutsch, 1967).

Naipaul, V. S., *The Mimic Men* (London: André Deutsch, 1967).

Naipaul, V. S., *In a Free State* (London: André Deutsch, 1971).

Naipaul, V. S., *The Overcrowded Barracoon* (London: André Deutsch, 1972).

Naipaul, V. S., 'Portrait of an Artist: What Makes Naipaul Run', *Caribbean Contact*, 1 (6) (1972), pp. 16, 18–19.

Naipaul, V. S., 'Without a Dog's Chance', *New York Review of Books*, 18 May 1972, pp. 29–31.

Naipaul, V. S., *Guerrillas* (London: André Deutsch, 1975).

Naipaul, V. S., *India: A Wounded Civilization* (London: André Deutsch, 1977).

Naipaul, V. S., *A Bend in the River* (London: André Deutsch, 1979).

Naipaul, V. S., *The Return of Eva Perón with the Killings in Trinidad* (London: André Deutsch, 1980).

Narayan, R. K., *My Days: A Memoir* (New York: Viking, 1974).

Nasta, Susheila, 'The Moses Trilogy', *Wasafiri*, 1 (2) (1985), pp. 5–9.

Nazareth, Peter, '*The Mimic Men* as a Study of Corruption', in Hamner (ed.), *Critical Perspectives on V. S. Naipaul*, pp. 137–52.

Neuman, Shirley and Robert Wilson, *Conversations with Robert Kroetsch* (Edmonton, AB: NeWest Press, 1982).

Newman, Judie, *The Ballistic Bard* (London: Arnold, 1995). .

Ngugi wa Thiong'o, *A Grain of Wheat* (1967. Rev. edn, London: Heinemann, 1986).

Ngugi wa Thiong'o, *Homecoming: Essays on African and Caribbean Literature, Culture and Politics* (London: Heinemann, 1972).

Ngugi wa Thiong'o, *Decolonizing the Mind: The Politics of Language in African Literature* (London: Heinemann, 1986).

Obumselu, E., '*A Grain of Wheat*: Ngugi's Debt to Conrad', *Benin Review*, 1 (1974), pp. 80–91.

Ogude, James, *Ngugi's Novels and African History: Narrating the Nation* (London: Pluto, 1999).

Orkin, Martin, 'Whose *Muti* in the Web of It?: Seeking "Post"-Colonial Shakespeare', *Journal of Commonwealth Literature*, 33 (2) (1998), pp. 15–37.

Paquet, Sandra Pouchet, *The Novels of George Lamming* (London: Heinemann, 1982).

Phillips, Caryl, *The European Tribe* (1987. London: Picador, 1993).

Phillips, Caryl, *The Nature of Blood* (1997. London: Faber, 1998).

Phillips, Caryl (ed.), *Extravagant Strangers: A Literature of Belonging* (London: Faber 1997).

Pons, Xavier, *Out of Eden: Henry Lawson's Life and Works: A Psychoanalytic View* (Sydney: Angus & Robertson, 1984).

Porter, Dennis, 'Of Heroines and Victims', *The Massachusetts Review*, 17 (3) (1976), pp. 540–52.

Radford, Jean (ed.), *The Progress of Romance: The Politics of Popular Fiction* (London: Routledge & Kegan Paul, 1986).

Radway, Janice A., *Reading the Romance: Women, Patriarchy and Popular Literature* (1984. London: Verso, 1987).

Ramchand, Kenneth, *The West Indian Novel and Its Background* (London: Faber, 1970).

Ramraj, Victor, 'The All-Embracing Christlike Vision: Tone and Attitude in *The Mimic Men*', in Rutherford (ed.), pp. 125–34.

Rhys, Jean, *Wide Sargasso Sea* (1966. Harmondsworth: Penguin, 1968).

Rhys, Jean, 'Fated to Be Sad', interview with Marcelle Bernstein, *The Guardian*, 8 August 1968, pp. 40–2, 49–50.

Rhys, Jean, 'The Inscrutable Miss Jean Rhys', interview with Hannah Carter, *Observer Magazine*, 1 June 1969, p. 5.

Rhys, Jean, *Smile Please: An Unfinished Autobiography* (London: André Deutsch, 1979).

Richler, Mordecai, *Solomon Gursky Was Here* (Markham, ON: Viking, 1989).

Ricou, Laurence, 'Field Notes and Notes in a Field: Forms of the West in Robert Kroetsch and Tom Robbins', *Journal of Canadian Studies*, 17 (3) (1982), pp. 117–23.

Robson, C. B., *Ngugi wa Thiong'o* (London: Macmillan, 1979).

Rogers, Pat (ed.), *Defoe: The Critical Heritage* (London: Routledge & Kegan Paul, 1972).

Rohlehr, Gordon, *Pathfinder: Black Awakening in 'The Arrivants' of Edward Kamau Brathwaite* (Tunapuna, Trinidad: privately published, 1981).

Rowell, Charles H., 'An Interview with Olive Senior', *Callaloo*, 11 (3) (1988), pp. 480–90.

Rushdie, Salman, *Midnight's Children* (1981. London: Picador, 1982).

Rushdie, Salman, 'The Empire Writes Back with a Vengeance', *The Times*, 3 July 1982, p. 8 (Rptd as 'The New Empire within Britain' in Rushdie 1991, pp. 129–38).

Rushdie, Salman, *Imaginary Homelands* (London: Granta; New York: Viking, 1991).

Rutherford, Anna (ed.), *Common Wealth* (Århus: Akademisk Boghandel, 1972).

Said, Edward, *Orientalism: Western Conceptions of the Orient* (1978. Harmondsworth: Penguin, 1985).

Said, Edward, *The World, the Text and the Critic*, (London: Faber, 1984).

Said, Edward, *Culture and Imperialism* (1993. London: Vintage, 1994).

Sandison, Alan, *The Wheel of Empire: A Study of the Imperial Idea in Some Late Nineteenth and Early Twentieth-Century Fiction* (London: Macmillan; New York: St Martin's Press, 1967).

Sarvan, C. Ponnuthurai, 'Under African Eyes', *Conradiana*, 8 (3) (1976), pp. 233–40.

Schaffer, Kay, 'Australian Mythologies: The Eliza Fraser Story and Constructions of the Feminine in Patrick White's *A Fringe of Leaves* and Sidney Nolan's "Eliza Fraser" Paintings', *Kunapipi*, 11 (2) (1989), pp. 1–15.

Sears, Djanet, *Harlem Duet* (Toronto: Scirocco Drama, 1997).

Selvon, Sam, *The Lonely Londoners* (1956. London: Longman Caribbean, 1972).

Selvon, Sam, *Ways of Sunlight* (London: MacGibbon and Kee, 1957).

Selvon, Sam, *Moses Ascending* (1975. Intro. Mervyn Morris, London: Heinemann, 1984).

Selvon, Sam, '"Old Talk"', interview with John Thieme, *Caribana*, 1 (1990), pp. 71–6.

Senior, Olive, *Summer Lightning and Other Stories* (London: Longman, 1986).

Shakespeare, William, *Othello*, ed. E. A. J. Honigmann (Arden Shakespeare, 3rd edn, Walton-on-Thames: Nelson, 1997).

Shakespeare, William, *The Tempest*, ed. Virginia Mason Vaughan and Alden T. Vaughan (Arden Shakespeare 3rd edn, Walton-on-Thames: Nelson, 1999).

Shenfield, Margaret, 'Mr Biswas and Mr Polly', *English*, 23 (1974), pp. 95–100.

Spass, Lieve and Brian Stimpson (eds), *Robinson Crusoe: Myths and Metamorphoses* (Basingstoke: Macmillan, 1996).

Starr, G. A., *Defoe and Spiritual Biography* (Princeton: Princeton University Press, 1965).

Stoneman, Patsy, *Brontë Transformations: The Cultural Dissemination of 'Jane Eyre' and 'Wuthering Heights'* (Hemel Hempstead: Harvester Wheatsheaf, 1996).

Suárez, María Luz, *Robinson Crusoe Revisited: Contemporary Versions of the Crusoe Myth* (Braunton, Devon: Merlin Books, 1996).

Swan, Michael, *British Guiana: The Land of Six Peoples* (London: HMSO, 1957).

Terdiman, Richard, *Discourse/Counter-Discourse: The Theory and Practice of Symbolic Resistance in Nineteenth-Century France* (Ithaca: Cornell University Press, 1985).

Thieme, John, 'Beyond History: Margaret Atwood's *Surfacing* and Robert Kroetsch's *Badlands*', in *Re-visions of Canadian Literature*, ed. Shirley Chew (Leeds: Institute for Bibliography and Textual Criticism, University of Leeds, 1985), pp. 71–87.

Thieme, John, *The Web of Tradition: Uses of Allusion in V. S. Naipaul's Fiction* (Mundelstrup, Denmark: Dangaroo; London: Hansib, 1987).

Thieme, John, 'Passages to England', in D'haen and Bertens (eds), pp. 55–78.

Thieme, John, *Derek Walcott* (Manchester: Manchester University Press, 1999).

Thieme, John, 'The Discoverer Discovered: Amitav Ghosh's *The Calcutta Chromosome*', in *The Literature of the Indian Diaspora: Essays in Criticism*, ed. A. L. McLeod (New Delhi: Sterling, 2000), pp. 274–90.

Thomas, Peter, *Robert Kroetsch* (Vancouver: Douglas & McIntyre, 1980.)

Thorpe, Michael. '"The Other Side": *Wide Sargasso Sea* and *Jane Eyre*', *ARIEL*, 8 (3) (1977), pp. 99–110.

Tiffin, Helen, 'Post-Colonial Literatures and Counter-Discourse', *Kunapipi*, 9 (3) (1987), pp. 17–34.

Tillotson, Kathleen, *Novelists of the 1840s* (Oxford: Clarendon Press, 1954).

Twigg, Alan, *For Openers: Conversations with 24 Canadian Writers* (Madeira Park, BC, 1981).

Urquhart, Jane, *Changing Heaven* (1990. London: Sceptre, 1990).

van Herk, Aritha, *The Tent Peg* (Toronto: McClelland & Stewart, 1981).

van Herk, Aritha, *Places far from Ellesmere* (Red Deer, AB: Red Deer Press, 1990).

Vaughan, Alden T. and Virginia Mason Vaughan, *Shakespeare's Caliban: A Cultural History* (Cambridge: Cambridge University Press, 1991).

Walcott, Derek, *The Castaway* (London: Jonathan Cape, 1965).

Walcott, Derek, *Pantomime and Remembrance* (New York: Farrar, Straus & Giroux, 1980).

Walcott, Derek, *Three Plays* (*The Last Carnival, Beef, No Chicken* and *A Branch of the Blue Nile*) (New York: Farrar, Straus & Giroux, 1986).

Walmsley, Anne, *The Caribbean Artists' Movement, 1966–1972: A Literary and Cultural History* (London: New Beacon, 1992).

Watt, Ian, *The Rise of the Novel* (1957. Harmondsworth: Penguin, 1963).

Waugh, Evelyn, *A Handful of Dust* (1934. Harmondsworth: Penguin, 1951).

White, Patrick, *Voss* (London: Eyre & Spottiswoode, 1957).

White, Richard, *Inventing Australia* (Sydney: Allen & Unwin, 1981).

Wiebe, Rudy, *Playing Dead: A Contemplation concerning the Arctic* (Edmonton, AB: NeWest, 1989).

Wiebe, Rudy, *A Discovery of Strangers* (1994. Toronto: Vintage, 1995).

Wilde, William H., Joy Hooton and Barry Andrews, *The Oxford Companion to Australian Literature* (Melbourne: Oxford University Press, 1985).

Wilkes, G. A., *A Dictionary of Australian Colloquialisms* (London: Routledge & Kegan Paul, 1978).

Wilkinson, Jane, *Remembering 'The Tempest'* (Rome: Bulzoni, 1999).

Williams, Patrick, *Ngugi wa Thiong'o* (Manchester: Manchester University Press, 1999).

Williamson, Karina, *Voyages in the Dark: Jean Rhys and Phyllis Shand Allfrey* (Coventry: University of Warwick, Occasional Papers in Caribbean Studies no. 4, n.d).

Wynter, Sylvia, 'Afterword: "Beyond Miranda's Meanings: Un/silencing the 'Demonic Ground' of Caliban's 'Woman'"', in *Out of the Kumbla: Caribbean Women and Literature*, eds Carole Boyce Davies and Elaine Savory Fido (1990. Trenton, NJ: Africa World Press, 1994), pp. 355–70.

Zabus, Chantal, 'Prospero's Progeny Curses Back: Postcolonial, Postmodern and Postpatriarchal Rewritings of *The Tempest*', in D'haen and Bertens (eds), pp. 115–38.

Index